Microsoft® Office 2003
Standard Edition

Step by Step

Word Processing with Word

Presentations with PowerPoint

Spreadsheets with Excel

Computer
Literacy
Press

Cincinnati, Ohio

Bonita Sebastian

Design / InfoTech / Paul Quin
Cover / Carolyn Ayres
Production coordination / Zipporah Collins
Copyediting / Jessie Wood
Technical checking / Jessie Wood
Page layout / Computer Literacy Press, LLC
Imagesetting / Data Reproductions Corporation
Printing and binding / Data Reproductions Corporation

ISBN 1-57426-161-4

Copyright © 2004 by CLP Holding, LLC. All rights reserved.
No part of this book may be reproduced in any form or by any electronic or mechanical means, including information storage and retrieval systems, without prior written permission from the publisher.

Microsoft® and Windows® are registered trademarks of Microsoft Corporation.

This entire book has been user tested on computers with Microsoft Office 2003 Standard Edition and using Windows 2000 and Windows XP. All figures in the book were created from that software. Users of other versions of Microsoft Office may expect to see differences.

This book is a guide to learning and using Microsoft Office 2003 Standard Edition, not a formal specification of the software as delivered to the buyer now or in future software revisions. Microsoft Corporation makes no warranties with respect to this book or to its accuracy in describing any current or future version of Microsoft Office.

Computer Literacy Press, LLC
15 Triangle Park
Cincinnati, OH 45246

(800) 225-5413

http://www.compLitpress.com

Printed in the United States of America
10 9 8 7 6 5 4 3 2 1   0987654

Contents

Microsoft Office 2003 Basics

Start computer 2
Use mouse 3
Explore windows 4
Start & exit Word 5
Explore menus 6
Explore dialog boxes 7
Prepare floppy disk 8

Microsoft Word 2003 Word Processing

Set view options 10
Set user options 11
Explore task pane 13
Create new document 14
Save document 16
Save with new name 17
Open saved document 18
Print document 19
Explore views 21
Select text 23
Use clipboard editing 25
Use drag & drop editing 27
Undo changes 28
Find text 29
Replace text 30
Check spelling 31
Change fonts & sizes 33
Apply font styles 34
Use Font dialog box 35
Open many documents 36
Align text 37
Apply indents 39
Apply line spacing 40
Use Paragraph dialog box 41
Use tab stops 42
Use tab leaders 44
Define paragraph styles 45
Add graphic object 47
Use AutoText entries 48
Insert page breaks 50
Preview document 51
Change page margins 52
Add columns & breaks 53
Add headers & footers 54
Create sections 56
Insert table 57
Set up mail merge 60
Do mail merge 63
Insert hyperlink 64
Save as Web page 65

Microsoft PowerPoint 2003 Presentations

Start Microsoft PowerPoint 68
Set up new document 69
Draw graphic objects 70
Move, resize & delete object 71
Use drawing aids 72
Draw more objects 74
Select objects 75
Use line tools 76
Use Basic Shapes tools 77
Modify objects 78
Duplicate objects 79
Change stacking order 80
Align objects 81
Attach text to object 82
Change object fill 84
Change outline & shadow 86
Create presentation 88
Add text to slide 90
Add new slide 91
Use outline 92
View slides 94
Add dynamic effects 95
Check spelling 97
Edit & rearrange text 98
Rearrange slides 100
Delete slide 101
Change text formats 102
Use slide master 103
Add slide with chart 104
Format chart 106
Add clip art 108
Insert WordArt 110
Add objects to master 111
Change color scheme 113
Apply design template 114
Create speaker notes 115
Create audience handouts 117
Print overheads 118
Print notes & handouts 119
Use AutoContent wizard 120

Microsoft Excel 2003 Spreadsheets

Start Microsoft Excel 122
Explore cells 123
Enter text 124
Enter numbers & save 126
Select cells 127
Enter simple formulas 128
Use function to add 130
Copy formula (relative) 132
Create data series 133
Copy formula (absolute) 134
Insert function 136
Paste special 138
Format text 139
Change fonts & sizes 140
Change text alignment 141
Set column width, row height 142
Insert & delete cells 143
Format cell borders 144
Add cell shading 146
Format numbers 147
Enter & format dates 149
Sort data 151
Divide window into panes 153
Lock cells, protect worksheet 154
Create pie chart 156
Create column chart 159
Format chart text 161
Format chart objects 162
Reorganize sheets 164

Preface

Microsoft Office 2003 Step by Step is based on an old Chinese proverb: "I hear, and I forget. I see, and I remember. I do, and I understand." Each page of the book is a simple list of steps for you to do at the computer. With just a little reading and a whole lot of doing, you'll quickly see how to use each of the many Office 2003 tools for writing, editing, checking spelling, formatting text, printing form letters, using graphics tools to create appealing presentations, doing complex calculations, creating charts, and working with collections of data.

You need not go through the whole book from beginning to end. Everyone should do pages 1–24. After that, either continue in order or jump to topics you're especially interested in. To help you navigate from topic to topic, icons in the upper-left corner of some pages warn you when some previous topic or activity should have been done first. Here's a list of icons and what they mean:

- Be sure you have completed the previous topic before beginning this one.
- Before beginning this page, be sure the named document was previously created and saved.
- Read important information here before doing the first step on this page.

A word of advice. Read each step carefully, do exactly what it says, watch the screen to see what happens, and go on to the next step. Sometimes you'll be tempted to go off and check out a few ideas on your own. *Don't give in to the temptation!* The result can change things in ways that make later steps in the book produce surprising results.

This is not to say exploring on your own is bad. Just the reverse—you should feel free to try anything out. Just make sure you complete a set of topics in the book, save your document if necessary, and then do all the exploration you want. When you finish, discard the document you used for experimentation.

Microsoft Office 2003
Basics

/ 1

2 Start computer
3 Use mouse
4 Explore windows
5 Start & exit Word
6 Explore menus
7 Explore dialog boxes
8 Prepare floppy disk

> Experienced Windows users should skip to page 5.

Start computer

Every session begins with switching on the computer (which launches Windows software) and ends with shutting it down.

1 Start Windows

Remove any floppy disk from drive.

Switch on computer and display.

> *It takes some time for Windows to be launched. You may be asked for user name (and possibly password).*

If asked, enter (or choose from list) your name and password.

2 View Windows desktop

> *Display should have most items in figure below (or variations) and possibly others. Some icons shown may be missing or have different shapes.*

By the way

The figures in this book show what users of Windows XP see. With Windows 2000 and Windows 98, the normal appearance is quite different. All steps given in this book work the same way in all versions of Windows, or the difference is noted.

IMPORTANT

If labels under icons are underlined, Windows has "Web style" settings. This book assumes "classic style." To change settings in versions earlier than Windows XP, hold down CTRL *and tap* ESC. *Release both keys. Carefully tap this series of keys:* S F C ENTER.

All Windows activities begin and end at desktop.

If taskbar is thin gray line at any edge of display, use mouse to move pointer to very edge of desktop and see taskbar pop up.

> *Taskbar may be different size and may be on any edge of desktop. You'll soon use* Start *button to start Microsoft Word program.*

3 End session and shut down computer

Click **Start** button on taskbar. Click **Turn Off Computer** (in Windows 98 or 2000, click **Shut down**).

In dialog box that appears, click **Turn Off** (in Windows 98 or 2000, click arrow to right of text box; click **Shut down**; click **OK**).

> *Computer automatically turns off. You may have to switch off display.*

← *Complete previous activity before going on.*

Use mouse

To use Windows, you need to use the mouse. Don't worry about getting it right the first time. You'll get lots of practice.

BAS / 3

1 Start computer

2 Move pointer

Hold mouse on smooth surface, end with buttons away from you.

Watch pointer on display as you slide mouse toward and away from you.

Watch pointer as you move mouse left and right.

Move mouse in circle.

By the way
Unless told differently, use the left mouse button to click, drag, or double-click an object. (If your mouse is set up for left-handed use, use the right button.)

---

3 Click object (to select it)

Move pointer tip inside **Recycle Bin** icon (usually near top of desktop).

Watch display as you tap *left* button on mouse.

Selected icon darkens.

Click another icon at left of desktop.

Click in clear area of window to deselect icon.

4 Shift-click object (to extend selection)

Click **Recycle Bin** icon to select it.

Hold [SHIFT] down. Click another icon at left of desktop. Release [SHIFT].

All icons from Recycle Bin *to icon you clicked are selected.*

Click in clear area of desktop to deselect all icons.

5 Drag object (to move it)

Move pointer to **Recycle Bin** icon.

Press and hold left mouse button down. Move mouse right.

Release mouse button.

Icon stays where you dragged it (or jumps to line up with invisible desktop grid).

Drag **Recycle Bin** icon back to original location.

6 Double-click object (for special action)

With pointer tip inside **Recycle Bin** icon, quickly tap left mouse button twice.

Action is called "double-clicking." Double-clicking icon is shortcut for opening it. Recycle Bin *window appears. Button appears on taskbar.*

At upper-right corner of **Recycle Bin** window, click ☒ (close).

Window closes. Button disappears from taskbar.

Close any other open windows.

By the way
Double-clicking means different things in different situations. When you work with text, for example, you'll see that double-clicking a word usually selects all the letters in the word.

← *Complete previous activity before going on.*

Explore windows

Information is always displayed in windows. You control the position and size of windows.

---

1 Explore window control buttons

On desktop, double-click **Recycle Bin** icon to open window.

Look at small button in title bar just left of ☒ (close). If shape is ☐ (maximize), click it.

Window expands to fill desktop. Button changes to this: ⧉.

Click ⧉ (restore down).

Window returns to previous size. Button changes back to this: ☐.

At left in group of buttons, click ▬ (minimize).

Window collapses into its button on taskbar.

On taskbar, click **Recycle Bin** button to see window at previous size.

2 Move window

Move pointer inside dark area of title bar of **Recycle Bin** window.

Title bar ⎯⎯
Menu bar ⎯⎯

> **By the way**
> Settings made by the previous user may cause toolbars and other features to appear below the menu bar. Commands on the View menu show or hide these features. You won't use these features in this book, so settings are unimportant.

With left mouse button held down, drag window around desktop.

Try dragging window completely off top of desktop.

You can't do that. Part of title bar always remains in view.

Drag window near upper-left corner.

3 Resize window

Carefully move pointer to lower-right corner of **Recycle Bin** window.

When pointer has ⤡ shape, hold left mouse button down and drag diagonally down and to right to make window larger.

Release mouse button.

Drag up and to left to make window smaller.

Put pointer on right or left edge of window. Notice shape: ↔.

Drag pointer to right or left to change window width. Release mouse button.

You can also drag top or bottom of window up or down to change height.

4 Close window

Click ☒.

← *Complete previous activity before going on.*

Start & exit Word

The first step in using Microsoft Word is to start the application program running. To end, exit the program.

BAS / 5

1 Use Start menu to see list of programs

Click **Start** button on taskbar. On **Start** menu, move pointer to **All Programs**. (In Windows 98 or 2000, choose **Programs**.)

Submenu appears at right of main menu and shows contents of folder.

2 Locate Microsoft Word

Carefully move pointer horizontally to right, into submenu. Move pointer up or down to **Microsoft Office**, then to **Microsoft Office Word 2003** on next submenu.

If you're using earlier version of Windows and don't see Microsoft Word, *move pointer to tiny triangle at bottom of submenu to see more items.*

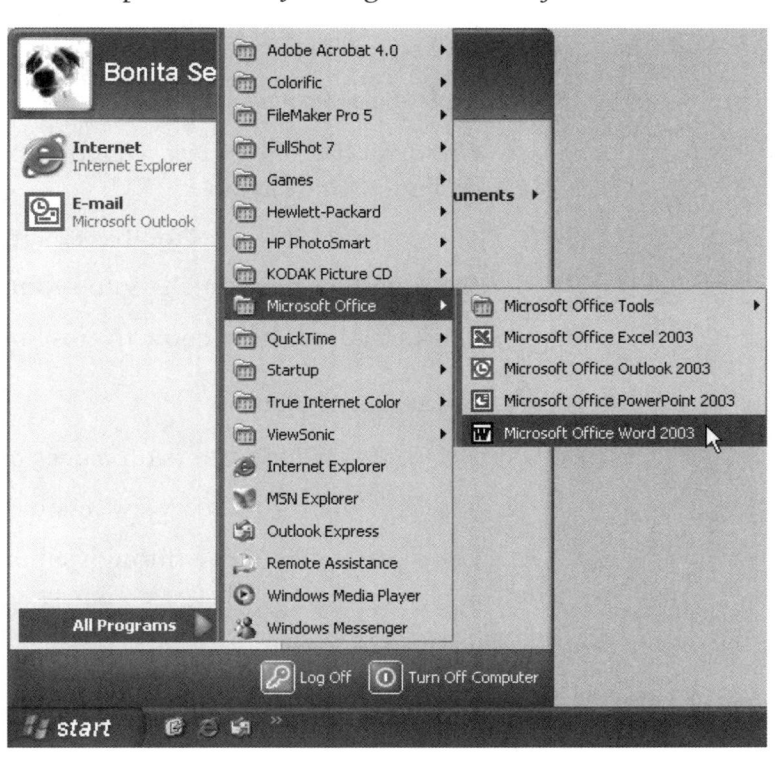

By the way

Your All Programs *submenu probably contains many other items not shown in the figure, and it may have more than one column.*

Tip

If the program you want is listed at the far left, just click it. Icons for recently used programs appear here, ready for a quick start

---

Tip

If Office Assistant (paper clip with eyes) appears, click it. Click the Options *button. Click the* Use the Office Assistant *check box to remove the mark. Click OK.*

3 Start program running

With pointer on program you want (**Word**), tap left mouse button.

Window titled Document1 – Microsoft Word *appears and may fill display.* Document 1 *button appears on taskbar.*

4 Hide and display Word window

At upper-right corner of window, click ▬ (minimize) to hide window.

On taskbar, click **Document1 – Microsoft Word** button to redisplay.

5 Exit program

On title bar, click ✕ to close program window.

Explore menus

Most commands you'll be learning to use appear on menus that drop down from the menu bar at the top of the window.

1 **Start Microsoft Word (see page 5)**

2 **Explore menu bar**

Locate menu bar just under title bar of window.

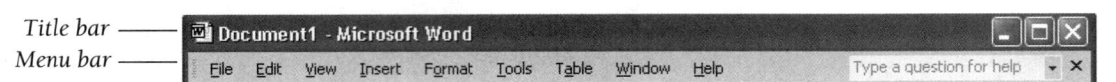

Title bar — [Document1 - Microsoft Word]
Menu bar — [File Edit View Insert Format Tools Table Window Help   Type a question for help]

Put pointer on **File**, and click to see menu. Wait five seconds or click tiny double arrows at bottom of menu to see all commands.

Less-used commands may be hidden at first.

Move pointer horizontally across names on menu bar to see more menus.

Click clear area of window to close menu without giving command.

3 **Explore menu commands**

On menu bar, click **View**. Watch command names as you move pointer down to **Print Layout**.

Move pointer down to **Toolbars**. Notice submenu appear to right.

Move pointer horizontally into submenu, then down and up.

Click clear area of window to close menu and submenu.

4 **Use keyboard shortcuts**

Notice underlined letters on names on menu bar.

Tap [ALT], then [V] to see **View** menu. Tap [T] to see **Toolbars** submenu.

Use [↓] and [↑] to move through submenus.

Tap [←] to close submenu.

Tap [ESC] to close **View** menu without giving command. Tap [ESC] again.

You would tap [ENTER] to give command you reached with arrow keys.

5 **Give menu command**

On menu bar, click **View**. Click **Task Pane** to hide (or show) pane.

Tap [ALT], then [V], then [K] to give same command and show (or hide) pane.

In future, we'll write "On View *menu, choose* Task Pane*" for either step.*

6 **Give submenu command**

On **View** menu, choose **Toolbars**; on submenu, choose **Drawing** (use mouse or keyboard).

Drawing toolbar appears, normally at bottom of window.

Repeat previous step to hide drawing toolbar.

By the way

A boxed check mark or icon to the left of a command means the command is now in effect. Choosing such a command cancels the effect and removes the box. Choosing it again restores the effect and the box.

← *Complete previous activity before going on.*

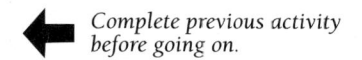

Explore dialog boxes

Many commands open a dialog box where you can choose among options, select an item on a list, or enter information.

BAS / 7

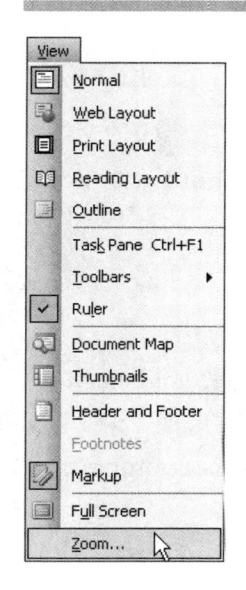

1 Give command that has dialog box

   On **View** menu, notice three dots (ellipsis) after **Zoom**.

   Dots mean command has dialog box.

   Choose **Zoom** to see dialog box.

   Dialog box named Zoom appears. Main features are labeled in figure.

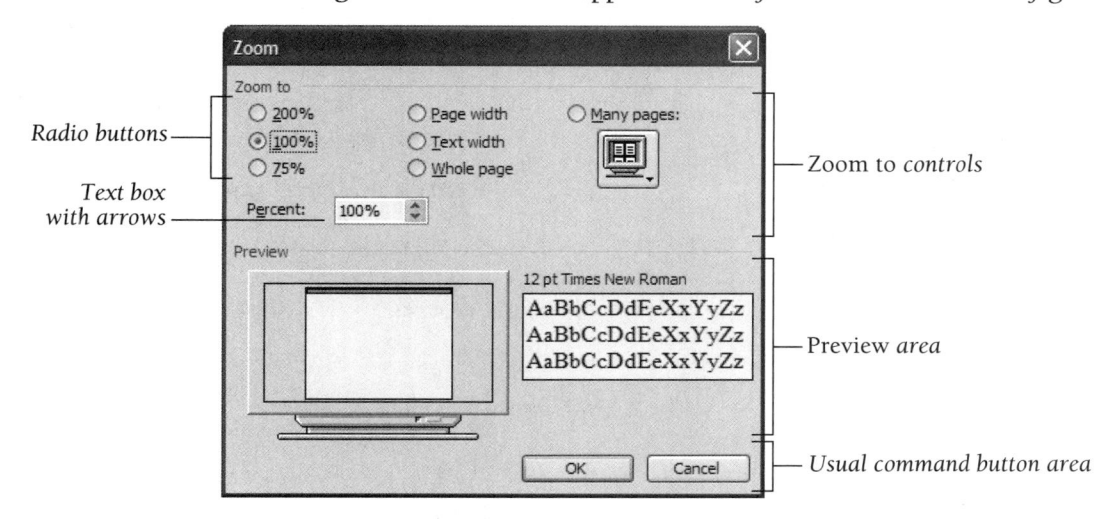

2 Explore radio buttons

   Click **200%**. Notice preview magnifies. Click **75%**. Notice preview shrinks.

   Click **100%** to return to standard view percentage.

3 Use text box arrows

   Arrows allow you to increase or reduce number now in box.

   Click up arrow to increase magnification; click down arrow to reduce.

4 Enter text in box

   You can enter exact percentage you want.

   Double-click number in **Percent** box, type   **120**   and tap TAB.

5 Explore command buttons

   Every dialog box has command buttons, usually at lower right.

   Click **OK** to accept changed view percentage.

   You'd use Cancel *button if you'd given* Zoom *command by mistake. All commands with dialog boxes have* Cancel *buttons.*

6 Exit Microsoft Word application

   On **File** menu, click **Exit**. If message to save appears, click **No**.

Tip

It's always safe to explore a menu command with three dots after its name. If you don't want to proceed after that, just click Cancel *in the dialog box that appears.*

Prepare floppy disk

You'll be saving your work on a floppy disk throughout this book. You'll need a new or recycled disk now.

IMPORTANT
You'll be saving your work often throughout this book. If your computer has no floppy drive, you'll have to save work on the hard drive (My Documents is a good place) or on a network drive. You'll have to return to the same computer or network drive to find what you've saved and continue working on it.

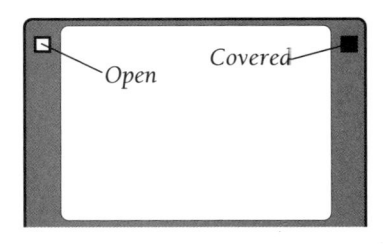

1 Start computer and Windows (see page 2, step 1)

2 Check disk and insert in drive

Hold disk up with large label side at top, metal or plastic slider at bottom.

Make sure small rectangular hole at top right is covered.

To cover hole, turn disk over and use ballpoint pen to move slider.

Make sure disk has second (open) hole at top left.

1.44 Mb disk has both holes; one-hole disks (720 Kb) won't hold much of your work and may not work on your computer.

Insert disk, slider end first, label side up, fully inside slot on computer.

3 Open My Computer window

If **My Computer** icon is on desktop, click it. Skip to step 4.

Otherwise, click **Start** button on taskbar

Click **My Computer** on list at upper right.

4 Format disk

In **My Computer** window, click icon labeled 3½ **Floppy** to select it.

Letter in parentheses after Floppy *identifies drive, usually A.*

On menu bar, click **File**, then **Format** (notice dots after command name).

Format dialog box appears.

If **Capacity** box does not contain **1.44 Mb**, click ▼ (drop-down list arrow), then **1.44 Mb** (or variation containing **1.44 Mb**).

Click **Start** button in **Format** dialog box (*not* on taskbar).

If warned that formatting will erase all data on disk, click **OK** to proceed.

Bar at bottom of dialog box shows formatting progress.

5 Close dialog boxes and eject disk

When formatting is complete, click **OK** button in results window.

Click **Close** button in **Format** dialog box.

Push eject button near slot on computer; remove and save floppy disk.

IMPORTANT
Make sure your floppy disk is not in the drive when you start your computer. If it is, you'll get a message about removing the disk. Just eject it and tap any key.

6 End session and shut down computer

Close **My Computer** window.

Shut down computer (see page 2, step 3).

Microsoft Word 2003
Word Processing

/ 9

- 10 Set view options
- 11 Set user options
- 13 Explore task pane
- 14 Create new document
- 16 Save document
- 17 Save with new name
- 18 Open saved document
- 19 Print document
- 21 Explore views
- 23 Select text
- 25 Use clipboard editing
- 27 Use drag & drop editing
- 28 Undo changes
- 29 Find text
- 30 Replace text
- 31 Check spelling
- 33 Change fonts & sizes
- 34 Apply font styles
- 35 Use Font dialog box
- 36 Open many documents
- 37 Align text
- 39 Apply indents
- 40 Apply line spacing
- 41 Use Paragraph dialog box
- 42 Use tab stops
- 44 Use tab leaders
- 45 Define paragraph styles
- 47 Add graphic object
- 48 Use AutoText entries
- 50 Insert page breaks
- 51 Preview document
- 52 Change page margins
- 53 Add columns & breaks
- 54 Add headers & footers
- 56 Create sections
- 57 Insert table
- 60 Set up mail merge
- 63 Do mail merge
- 64 Insert hyperlink
- 65 Save as Web page

10 / Word Processing with Microsoft Word

Set view options

You are now ready to explore the Microsoft Word application window and set view options used in this section of the book.

1 **Start Microsoft Word (see page 5)**

In title bar, notice document name **Document1** and application name.

If window does not fill display, click ▢ (maximize) in title bar.

Your window may not match figure below. You'll fix that next.

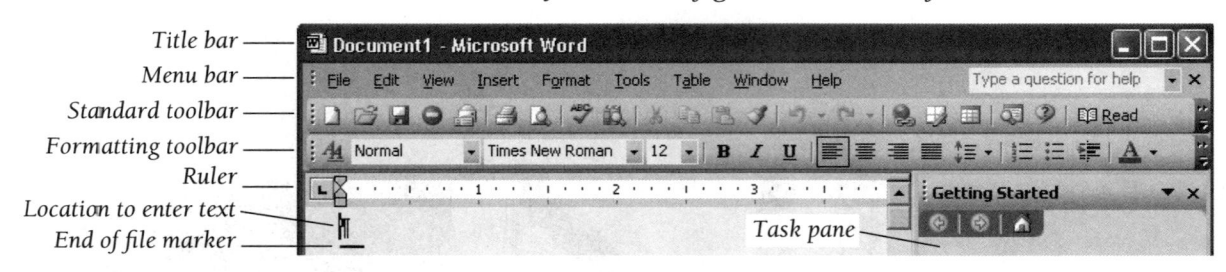

Title bar
Menu bar
Standard toolbar
Formatting toolbar
Ruler
Location to enter text
End of file marker
Task pane

Notice status bar at bottom of window.

Status bar has information about document, such as page you're working on.

2 **Set view to Normal and make ruler visible**

On **View** menu, choose **Normal**.

Click **View** to see menu. Wait five seconds or click tiny arrow at bottom.

Less-used commands may be hidden at first.

If **Ruler** has boxed check mark to left, close menu. Otherwise, click **Ruler**.

Ruler should appear as in figure above.

3 **View toolbars**

On **View** menu, move pointer to **Toolbars** to see submenu.

Figure at left shows setup you'll need for this section. Checked items are for toolbars that should be present.

If your submenu already matches figure at left, click clear area of window to close submenu. Skip to step 4.

If any item is different from figure, click it. Repeat above steps until submenu matches figure.

4 **Display standard and formatting toolbars on two rows**

On **Tools** menu, choose **Customize**. Click **Options** tab.

Click check boxes as necessary to match figure below.

Click **Close**.

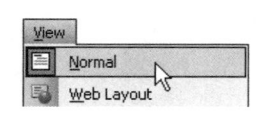

Tip

After making the settings beginning at step 2, your window should look like the figure above. If as you work through the book your window looks different, return to this page and redo the settings.

← *Complete previous activity before going on.*

Set user options

User settings affect the way a program works. Here, you'll set standard options for use with Microsoft Word in this book.

DOC / 11

1 Set default font format for new documents

On **Format** menu, choose **Font**. Make any changes to match figure.

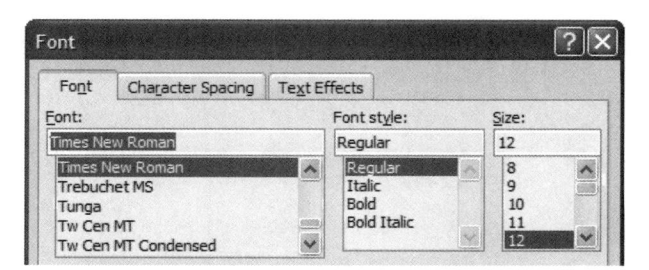

Click **Default** button at bottom. When asked, click **Yes** to approve change.

2 Check document zoom scale

If zoom scale (number at right of standard toolbar) is not **100%**, click tiny arrow to right.

On drop-down list, choose **100%**.

3 Open Options dialog box

On **Tools** menu, choose **Options**. Notice many tabs at top of dialog box.

Click each tab and look at many options you can set. End at **View** tab.

Click any check boxes necessary to make marks exactly match figure.

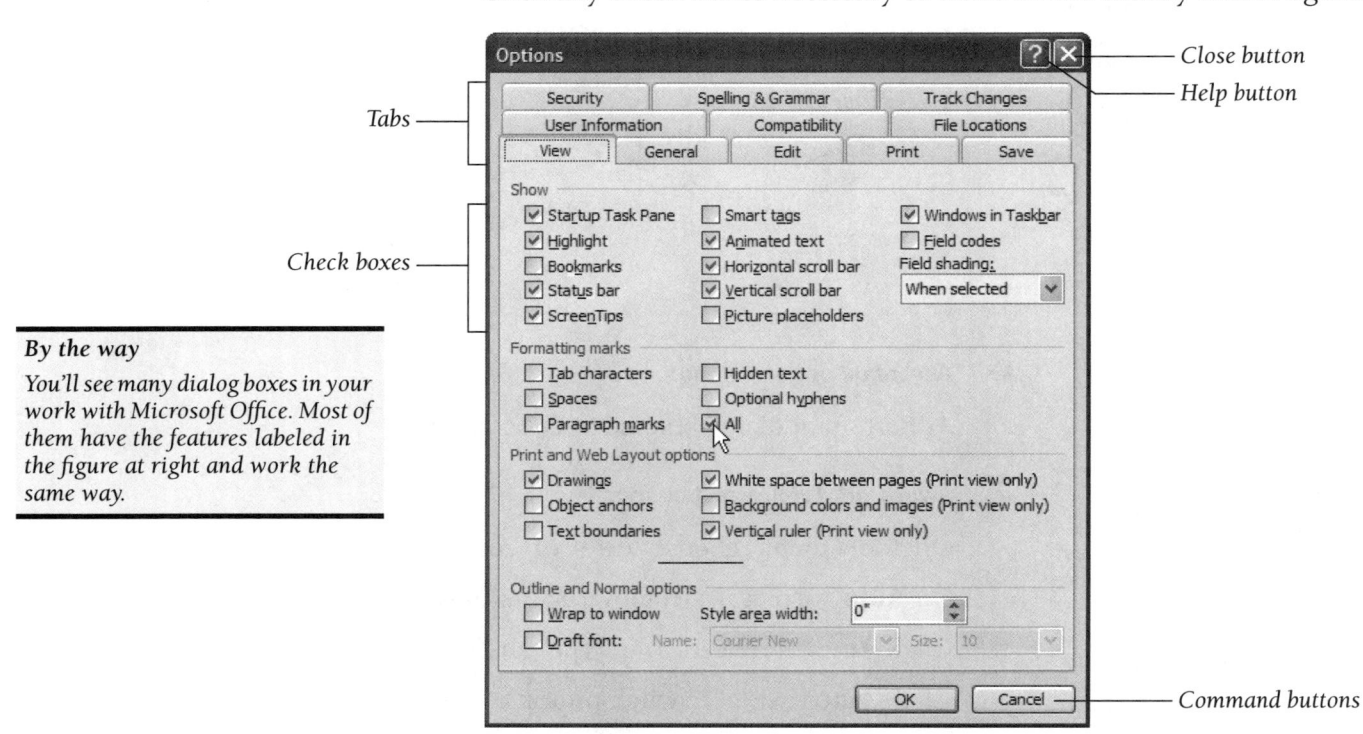

Tabs — *Close button* / *Help button*
Check boxes —
Command buttons

By the way

You'll see many dialog boxes in your work with Microsoft Office. Most of them have the features labeled in the figure at right and work the same way.

Click 🛈 to open help window; in dialog box, click **View** tab. Review any options you have questions about.

Close help window.

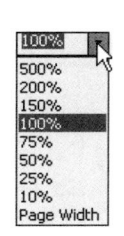

Set user options *continued*

4 Set spelling options

Click **Spelling & Grammar** tab. Make all options match figure below.

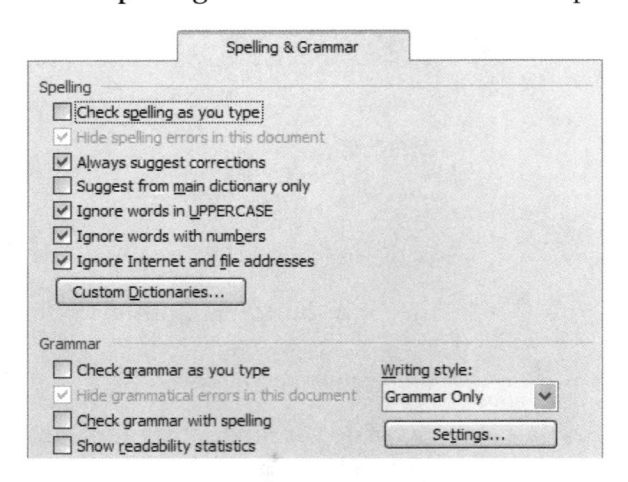

[Spelling & Grammar dialog tab shown]

5 Set editing options

Click **Edit** tab. Make all options match figure below.

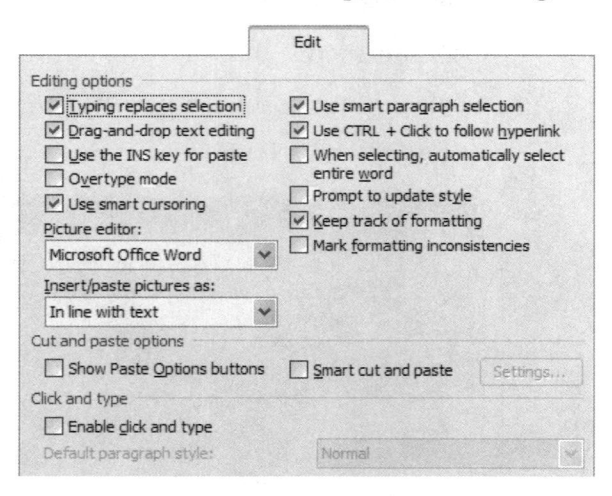

[Edit dialog tab shown]

Tip

If in the future your program seems to be behaving strangely, check the Options and AutoCorrect dialog boxes. Some other user may have changed an option.

6 Accept all option settings

At bottom of dialog box, click **OK** button.

By the way

With AutoCorrect options switched off, what you see on the screen is what you type. As you gain experience, you may want to switch some options back on and see whether they are helpful in your work. See page 48 for more information about this feature.

7 Switch off AutoCorrect options

On **Tools** menu, choose **AutoCorrect Options**.

On **AutoCorrect** tab, remove marks in all check boxes.

Click **AutoFormat As You Type** tab. Switch off all five options in middle.

Click **AutoText** tab. Switch off top option. At bottom of dialog box, click **OK**.

8 Exit Word (see page 5, step 5); if asked, don't save changes

Next time you start Word, all options you set will still be in effect.

Explore task pane

The task pane appears at the right of the document window. It contains many useful tools and options.

By the way

If you do not see the task pane at the right of the window, choose Task Pane *on the* View *menu to display it.*

If you do not see Getting Started at the top of the task pane, choose it from the drop-down Task Pane *menu.*

1 **Start Microsoft Word (see page 5)**

2 **View options in Getting Started task pane at right of Word window**

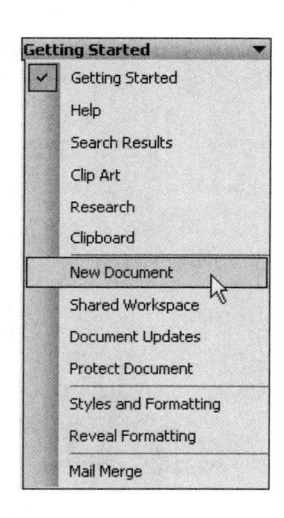

3 **Explore Task Pane menu**

Click title bar of pane to see list of other task panes.

On list, choose **New Document**.

Title bar and items in task pane change to reflect your choice.

4 **View options for starting new document**

Starting Word automatically creates new blank document. Task bar shows other options.

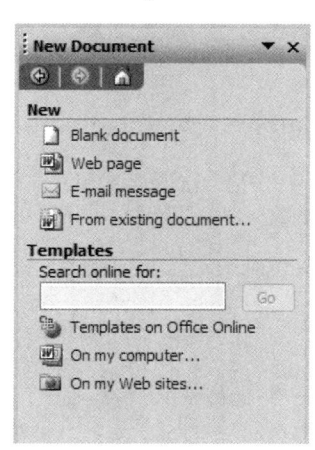

By the Way

All Word documents are based on templates, which contain basic settings for the way the document looks. Unless you change it, a document is based on the default template, Normal.

5 **Close task pane**

Click ☒ at right end of pane's title bar (or choose **Task Pane** on **View** menu).

Task pane appears automatically when you start Word and from time to time as you choose commands in Word.

Complete previous activity before going on.

Create new document

Entering text into a new document is usually the first step in using a word processor program.

Tip
If you need to open a new document later, choose New *on the* File *menu. When the task pane reappears, click* Blank document. *(A shortcut is to click ▢ on the standard toolbar.)*

1 Locate insertion point

Look for small blinking vertical line to left of paragraph mark.

Insertion point is where characters appear when you type.

2 Locate end of file marker

Look for short, horizontal line just below paragraph mark.

End of file marker moves as you enter text. You can't enter anything below marker.

3 Enter text

Type following text without tapping (ENTER) at ends of lines. (Don't worry about errors now.)

Spaces you type appear as centered dots between words.

```
Today many people use very fast and powerful
computers in business, at school, and at
home. The computer revolution is the fastest-
growing technology in recorded history.
```

Insertion point moves as you enter text. Notice that words in paragraph automatically "wrap" (continue on next line when end of line is reached).

Tap (ENTER) now.

(ENTER) is at right of main group of keys and may look like this: ⏎.

Look at insertion point and new paragraph mark.

Tapping (ENTER) marks end of paragraph ¶ and moves insertion point to next line.

Tip
Type just one space between your sentences. Typing two spaces is a habit left over from the days of using a typewriter with fixed-width characters. The period was in the middle of a wide space, so extra space after it helped show that a new sentence was beginning.

4 Enter more text

Tap (ENTER) again to create blank line.

Another end-of-paragraph mark is visible on blank line.

Type following text.

Don't worry about typing errors now. You'll fix them later.

```
It is easy to assume that computers are a
recent addition to our lives. However, the
start of the modern science that we call
"computer science" can be traced back to the
dust abacus, which was probably invented in
Babylonia almost 5,000 years ago.
```

Tap (ENTER) twice.

By the way
If you see a red zigzag line under a misspelled word you type, the option to check spelling as you type has been switched on. Either ignore the mark or switch the option off (see page 12, step 4).

5 *Enter another paragraph*

Type following text. Ignore typing errors for now.

> `Throughout the centuries, there have been many inventions and innovations that aided in the evolution of computer science. In the 1950s, two inventions dramatically changed the computer industry and caused the beginning of the "computer revolution."`

Tap ENTER twice.

6 *Add your name to end of document*

Type your name.

7 *Correct any error*

Move I-beam pointer just right of error, and click.

Insertion point appears where you clicked.

Tap BACKSPACE one or more times to remove characters.

Backspace key is at upper-right corner of main group of keys. It may look like this on your keyboard: ←.

Enter correct characters.

Finished document should look like this.

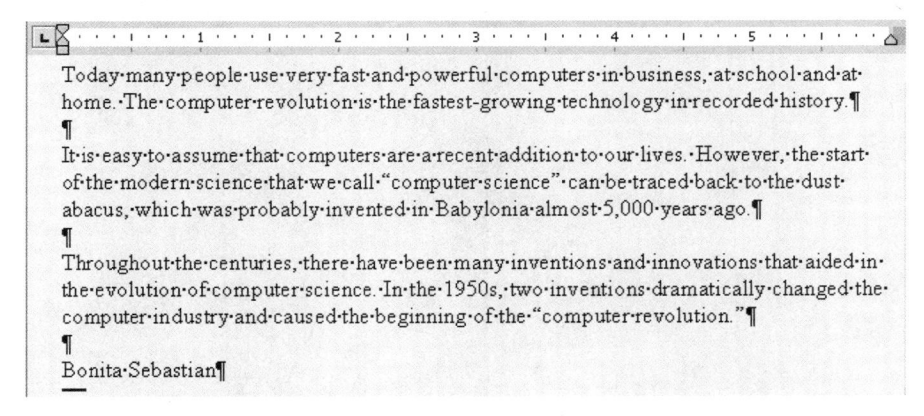

> Today many people use very fast and powerful computers in business, at school and at home. The computer revolution is the fastest-growing technology in recorded history.¶
> ¶
> It is easy to assume that computers are a recent addition to our lives. However, the start of the modern science that we call "computer science" can be traced back to the dust abacus, which was probably invented in Babylonia almost 5,000 years ago.¶
> ¶
> Throughout the centuries, there have been many inventions and innovations that aided in the evolution of computer science. In the 1950s, two inventions dramatically changed the computer industry and caused the beginning of the "computer revolution."¶
> ¶
> Bonita Sebastian¶

If you don't see paragraph marks, click ¶ on standard toolbar.

Tip

You can also move the insertion point through a document by using the four arrow keys to the right of the main group of keys.

← *Complete previous activity before going on.*

Save document

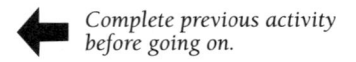

After creating and editing a new document, you should save it on a disk. You'll need a blank, formatted floppy disk.

IMPORTANT
If your computer doesn't have a floppy drive, you'll need separate instructions for saving files. If you save a file on the hard drive (in My Documents, for example), you'll have to return to this computer to continue work on the file.

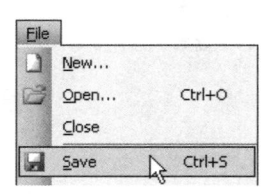

By the way
Ctrl+S at the right of the Save command means you can give the command from your keyboard. Just hold down CTRL *and tap* S. *In the future, we'll write such keyboard shortcuts as* CTRL S.

By the way
When saving is finished, Computers, the new document name, appears in the title bar.

1 Insert floppy disk

Insert disk, slider end first, label side up, into floppy drive.

2 Give Save command

On **File** menu, choose **Save** (or click 🖫 toward left on standard toolbar).

Save As dialog box appears on first use of Save command. You must name document and say where to save it.

3 Name document

Notice suggested file name is highlighted in **File name** text box at bottom.

Type **Computers** in text box. Use BACKSPACE to erase errors.

Typed characters replace highlighted text.

4 Say where to save document

Locate **Save in** box at top of dialog box.

Click ▼ at right of box to see drop-down list of locations. On list, choose **3½ Floppy** (or other location if you're not using floppy).

Save As dialog box should look like figure below.

Location where you want document saved

Name of document

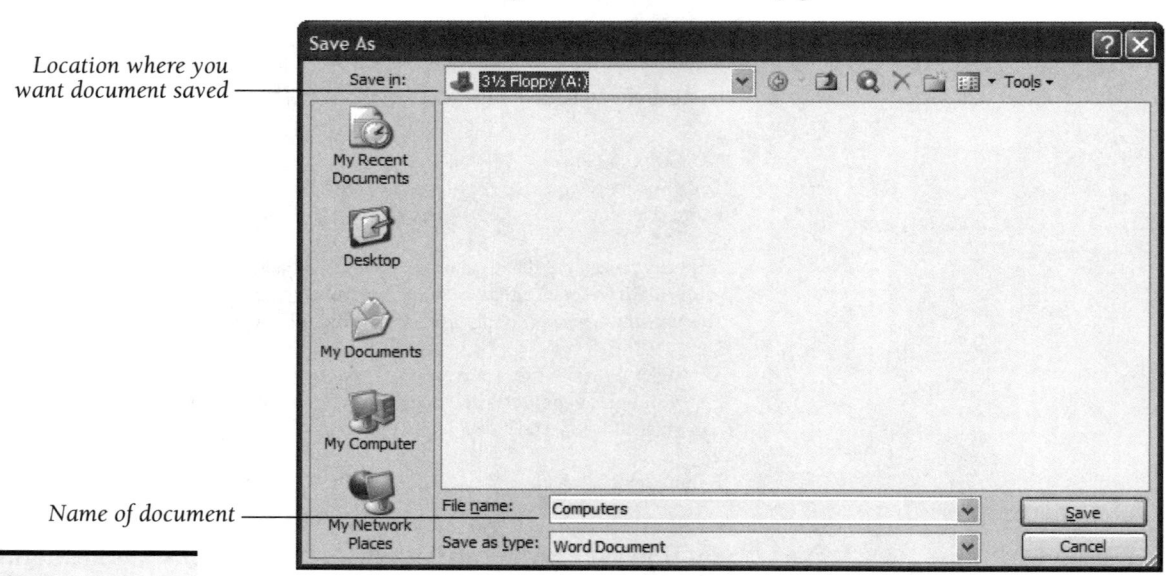

Click **Save** to save document with name **Computers** on disk.

5 Add to document and save again

Click after "**revolution.**" in last body paragraph. Tap SPACEBAR.

Type **The first was the transistor; the second was the integrated circuit or chip.**

On **File** menu, choose **Save** (or click 🖫 on toolbar, or tap CTRL S).

No dialog box appears this time. Changed file takes place of original.

Complete previous activity before going on.

Save with new name

Often you need to save a changed document with a new name or in a new location so it won't erase the original.

1 *Add more text to document*

Click at end of your name.

Tap ENTER twice.

Type following addition:

```
What do you think the future will bring to
this exciting and fast-moving industry?
```

2 *Save changed document without erasing original*

On **File** menu, choose **Save As** (*not* Save).

Save As dialog box shows current name and location of document. You can change either or both.

Type **Revision** as file name for changed document.

Leave location unchanged in **Save in** box.

Word remembers location from previous save.

Click **Save** button.

You now have two documents on disk. Computers *has original text.* Revision *has original plus addition.*

Look at title bar in document window.

Title bar now shows new document name. If you use Save *command now, only new document is affected.*

3 *Close Revision document*

On **File** menu, choose **Close**.

Look at title bar.

Missing document name means no Microsoft Word document is open now.

Look at toolbars.

Most tools are grayed out. This means there's nothing to use tools on.

Look below toolbars.

Missing insertion point means there's nothing to enter text into.

4 *Exit Microsoft Word*

On **File** menu, choose **Exit**.

Now your files exist only on disk.

Eject floppy disk. Take it with you if you're not going on to next activity.

Whenever you leave computer, remember to take disk from drive.

By the way

If you close a document with changes you haven't yet saved, a dialog box asks whether you want to save the changes and offers three command buttons: Yes is the same as giving the Save command before closing; No ignores changes and closes the document; Cancel stops the Close command and returns to the document. You have to choose Cancel if you want to save the document with a new name.

> ⛔ Computers *as completed on page 16 must be saved on disk.*

Open saved document

After saving a document on a disk and exiting the program, you must open the document from the disk to continue work.

1 Start Microsoft Word

See page 5 (or, in Windows XP, click **Word** icon in left column of **Start** menu).

2 Prepare to open document on disk

In this exercise, you'll open Computers *document.*

If you're using floppy disk, insert it in drive.

On **File** menu, choose **Open** (or click 📂 on standard toolbar).

3 Say where to look for document

Locate **Look in** box at top of dialog box.

Open dialog box is similar to Save As *dialog box.*

Click ▼ at right of box to see drop-down list of locations.

On list, choose **3½ Floppy** (or other location if you're not using floppy).

Open dialog box should look like figure below. File name text box at bottom of dialog box should be blank. In Files of type *text box,* All Word Documents *should appear.*

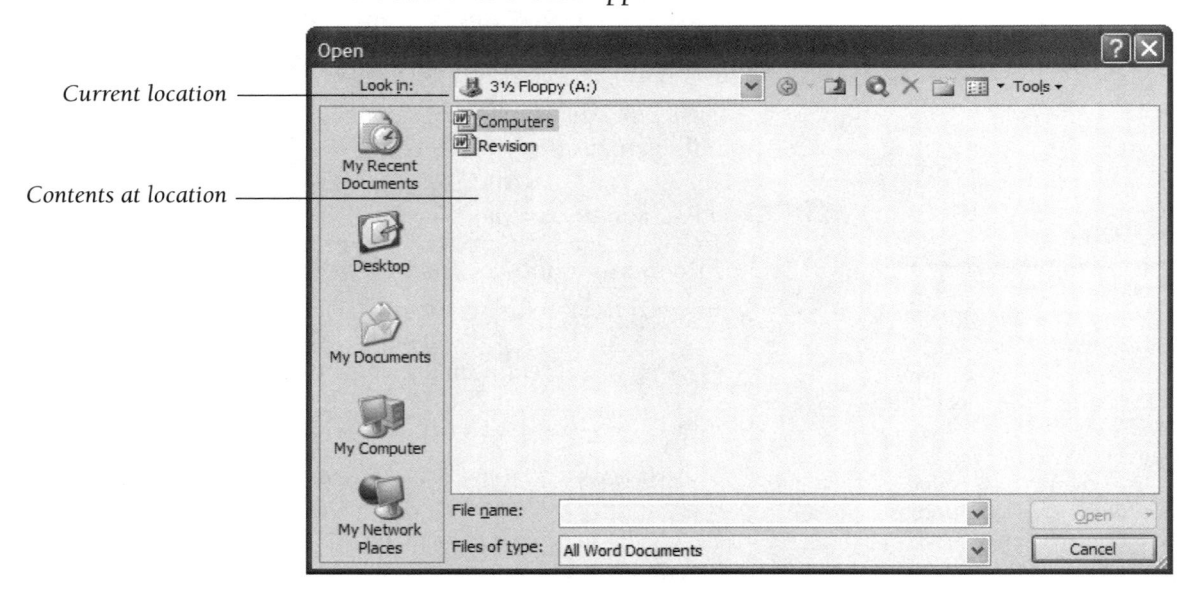

Current location
Contents at location

4 Open file you want

Click **Computers** to select it as document to open. Then click **Open**.

OR

Double-click **Computers**.

Document Computers *opens.*

Tip

Names and locations of recently saved files appear at the bottom of the File *menu and at the top of the task pane. You can open one of them just by clicking its name.*

> A word processor document must be open.

Print document

After you work on a word processor document, you often need to print a copy to take away, read, and correct.

DOC / 19

1 Check paper size

On **File** menu, choose **Page Setup**. Click **Paper** tab at top of dialog box.

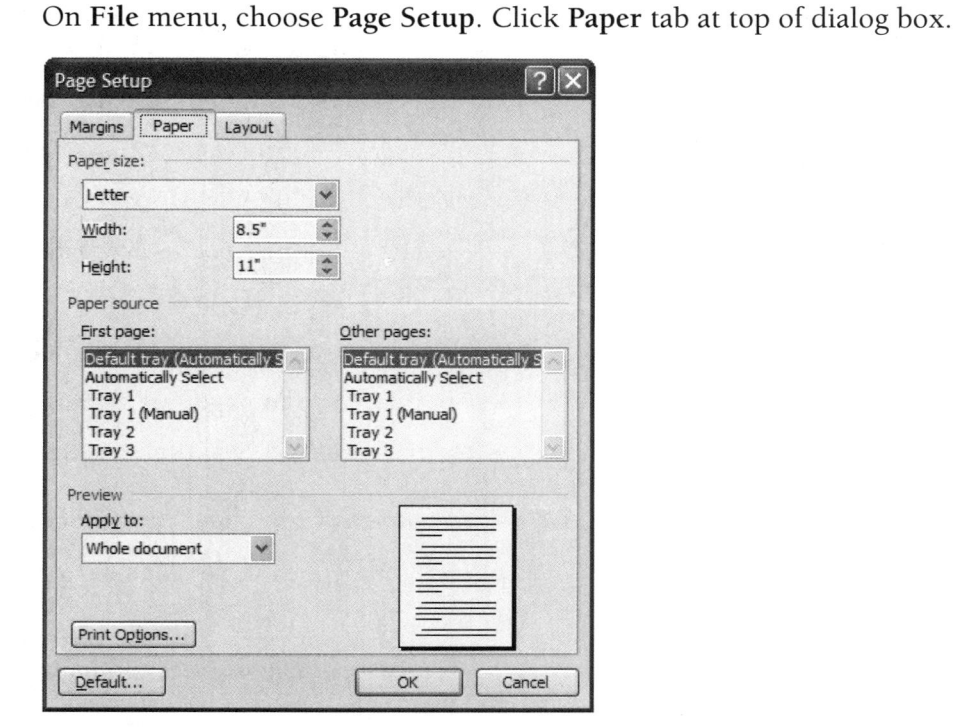

Click ▾ to see **Paper size** list; click size of paper used in your printer.

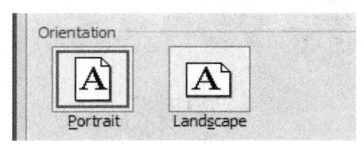

> *By the way*
> Options in this dialog box may vary depending on your printer.

2 Choose orientation of printed image on page

Click **Margins** tab. If necessary, in Orientation area, click **Portrait**.

Click **OK** to accept options.

3 Check printer to make sure it is on and has paper

4 Open Print dialog box

On **File** menu, choose **Print** (or click 🖨 on standard toolbar).

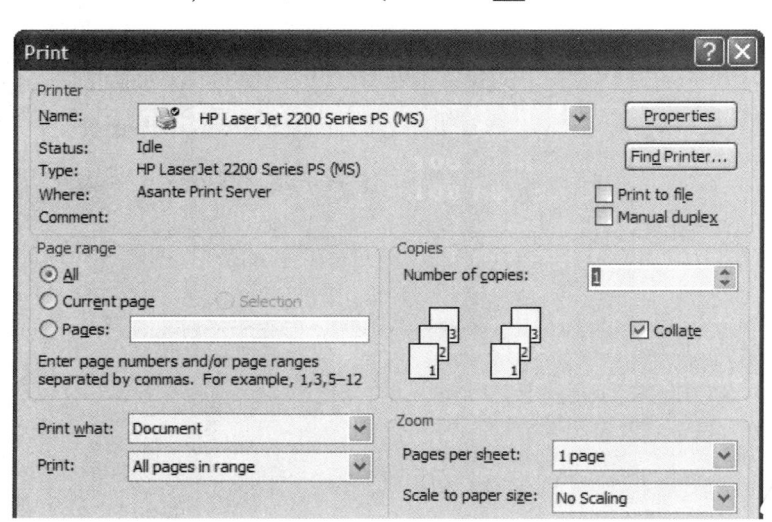

Print document *continued*

5 Notice standard settings

In **Printer** area, notice **Name**. Make sure it is printer you want to use. (If not, click ▼ button and select printer from list.)

Near bottom of dialog box, verify that **Print what** item is **Document**.

You can also print information about document (see figure at left).

Verify that **Print** item is **All pages in range**.

You can also print odd or even pages.

Verify that **Pages per sheet** item is **1 page**.

You can also print multiple miniature pages on sheet.

Verify that **Scale to page size** item is **No Scaling**.

If printer allows, you can reduce or enlarge image.

6 Choose range of pages and number of copies to print

In **Page range** area, leave **All** selected, but notice other options.

Leave **1** as **Number of copies**.

You can use arrows to select number; or type number you want inside Copies *box.*

7 Send document to printer, or cancel print command

Click **OK** button (or **Cancel** button if you're not ready to print).

8 Close document without saving changes

Any changes you made in Page Setup *dialog box are stored in document.*

On **File** menu, choose **Close**.

If asked whether to save changes, click **No** (or tap Ⓝ).

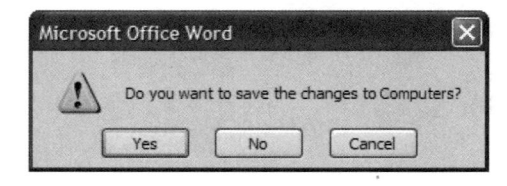

Page Setup *changes are discarded.*

STOP Computers *as completed on page 16 must be saved on disk.*

Explore views

Microsoft Word lets you choose the view that's best for you when you work on a document.

DOC / 21

1 **Open Computers document (see page 18)**

2 **Get more space for document**

If task pane is present, hide it (click ☒ on pane's title bar, or choose **Task Pane** on **View** menu).

If window doesn't fill display, click ⬜ (maximize) at right of title bar.

3 **See preview of printed document**

On **File** menu, choose **Print Preview** (or click 🔍 on standard toolbar).

Window shows how printed document will look, but you can't work on document in this view. (You'll learn more about this view on page 51.)

On new print preview toolbar, click Close.

4 **See whole page in view you can work on**

On **View** menu, make sure **Normal** is chosen.

Notice numbers and shaded area on ruler.

Zero on ruler is at start of your text. Shaded area is for right margin.

On **View** menu, choose **Print Layout**.

Now you see page border and margins around text. Vertical ruler appears at left with shading for top margin. You'll learn to change margin sizes later.

Notice blinking insertion point in text.

Insertion point means you can enter and edit text in this view.

5 **Use full screen**

On **View** menu, choose **Full Screen**.

Title bar, menu bar, toolbars, and rulers disappear, but insertion point remains. (Margins appear because you were in print layout view before.)

Move pointer to top of display.

Menu bar slides down into view.

On **View** menu, choose **Full Screen** (now selected).

View returns to print layout.

6 **Zoom out or in**

Near right end of standard toolbar, click arrow next to percentage.

On zoom drop-down list, choose **Whole Page**.

Percentage is adjusted to fit page in your window.

Explore other zoom options on list.

End with **100%**.

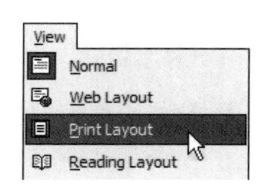

Tip

Use Full Screen view when you have a lot of text to enter and don't want to be distracted. You'll have to use keyboard shortcuts for toolbar commands you might need.

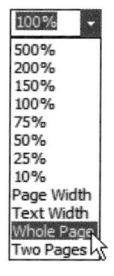

Explore views *continued*

7 *Use layout meant mainly for reading documents*

On **View** menu, choose **Reading Layout**.

Type is enlarged and text is formatted for small, side-by-side pages.

Click anywhere in text.

Insertion point means you can also work on text in this view.

On new reading layout toolbar, click [Close].

8 *Prepare to use scrolling*

In long documents, only part can be in view. Your document is short, so you'll now shrink window so you can see only part of it.

At right of title bar, click ▫ (restore).

Put pointer on bottom edge of window, and drag up so paragraph 3 is hidden.

In vertical scroll bar at right, locate scroll box and scroll buttons.

Scroll bar stands for whole document. Box stands for part you can see.

— Scroll button
— Scroll box stands for part you can see
— Later part that you can't see now
— Scroll button

9 *Scroll to see hidden text*

Watch scroll box and text as you click lower scroll button three or four times.

Text moves in from below, line by line, and out at top. Space now above box stands for part that went out.

With pointer on upper scroll button, hold down mouse button.

Text moves rapidly in from above. Scroll box goes to top of bar.

Watch text as you click anywhere in scroll bar below box.

One "screenful" of text moves in from below.

Click in scroll bar above box.

Put pointer on scroll box, and slowly drag it down and back up.

You can make large moves through any document or list this way.

10 *Return to original view and close document*

At right of title bar, click ▫ (maximize).

On **View** menu, choose **Normal**.

On **File** menu, choose **Close**.

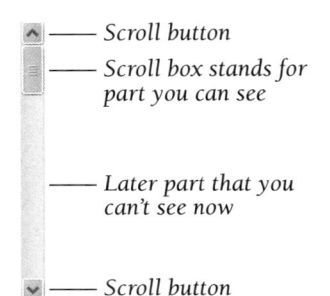

By the way

Scroll bars also appear in dialog boxes when a list of options is too long to fit. You scroll through lists the same way you scroll through a document.

> **STOP** Computers *as completed on page 16 must be saved on disk.*

Select text

Text must be selected (highlighted) before you can make changes to it.

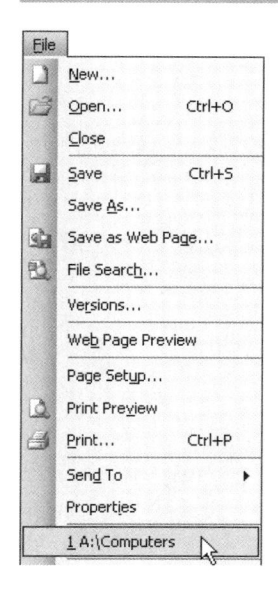

1 Open Computers document

See page 18 for details.

OR

Choose **Computers** in bottom area of **File** menu.

2 Select block of text (method 1)

Position I-beam pointer before first letter you want to select.

With mouse button down, drag pointer through text you want to select.

You can drag horizontally or in any direction through text.

Release mouse button.

3 Deselect selected text

Click anywhere in text or tap keyboard arrow key (↓ or ↑ or → or ←).

Highlighting disappears. Insertion point is positioned where you clicked.

4 Select block of text (method 2)

Position I-beam pointer to left of first letter you want to select. Click to place insertion point.

Hold down SHIFT. Move pointer after last letter you want to select, and click. Release SHIFT.

All text between places you clicked is highlighted.

5 Add to selected text

Hold down SHIFT. Click after last letter you want added. Release SHIFT.

Selection now extends from original starting place to last place clicked.

Tip
You can add text to the selection only in the same direction as before. You can remove text by clicking before the first letter you want to remove from the selection.

---

6 Select block of text (method 3)

Put insertion point in middle of paragraph 2. Hold down SHIFT while you tap arrow keys.

Click anywhere in text to deselect current selection.

7 Select one word

Double-click any word.

Notice that space (but not punctuation) after word is also highlighted.

Deselect word.

8 Select one sentence

Hold down CTRL and click anywhere in sentence.

Entire sentence, including period and space(s) after, is highlighted.

Tip
CTRL *is at lower-left and lower-right corners of main group of keys.*

Select text *continued*

9 *Select one line of text*

Position pointer to left of line.

Pointer shape changes from I-beam shape to this: ⇘.

Click.

Entire line to right of pointer is highlighted.

Click anywhere in text to deselect highlighted line.

10 *Select many lines of document*

Position pointer to left of first line you want to select.

Press mouse button and drag pointer down left side of document.

Highlighting follows pointer.

Release mouse button.

Click anywhere in text to deselect highlighted area.

11 *Select paragraph*

Position pointer to left of paragraph, and double-click.

OR

Triple-click anywhere inside paragraph.

12 *Select nonadjacent text*

Using any previous method, select some text.

Hold down [CTRL].

Again using any method, select other text not adjacent to already selected text.

13 *Select entire document (method 1)*

Position pointer to left of all text, and triple-click.

Click anywhere in text to deselect it.

14 *Select entire document (method 2)*

On **Edit** menu, choose **Select All** (or hold down [CTRL] and tap [A]).

Other menu commands often have "control key" shortcuts like this. Hereafter, key combinations like this will appear as [CTRL][A].

15 *Deselect highlighted area*

Click anywhere in text or tap any keyboard arrow key.

16 *Close document without saving changes*

🛑 Computers *as completed on page 16 must be saved on disk.*

Use clipboard editing

After entering text, you often need to erase parts of it and move sentences and paragraphs around.

DOC / 25

---

1 **Open Computers document**

2 **Select paragraph and blank line after it**

Position pointer to left of text paragraph 2, and double-click.

With (SHIFT) held down, click left of blank line after paragraph 2.

3 **Cut selection to clipboard**

On **Edit** menu, choose **Cut** (or tap CTRL X, or click ✂ on standard toolbar).

4 **View clipboard**

On **Edit** menu, choose **Office Clipboard**.

> Clipboard *task pane appears at right of window.*

In large scroll box, notice text you cut to clipboard.

5 **Paste from clipboard**

Click just before first word in paragraph 1 of document.

> *Blinking insertion point shows where cut text will be inserted. (If whole line is accidentally highlighted, repeat above step.)*

On **Edit** menu, choose **Paste** (or tap CTRL V, or click 📋 on standard toolbar, or click item on **Clipboard** task pane).

> *Text on clipboard (old paragraph 2 and blank line) is copied into document and is now paragraph 1. Text also remains available on clipboard.*

6 **Copy paragraph to clipboard**

Highlight text paragraph 3 and blank line after it.

On **Edit** menu, choose **Copy** (or tap CTRL C, or click 📋 on standard toolbar).

> *Selection remains in document, but new item appears at top of clipboard.*

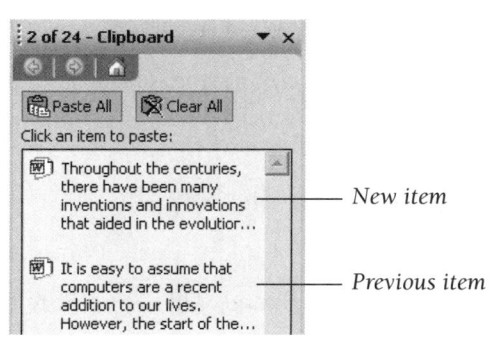

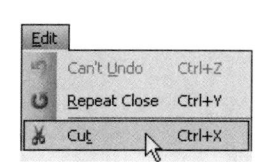

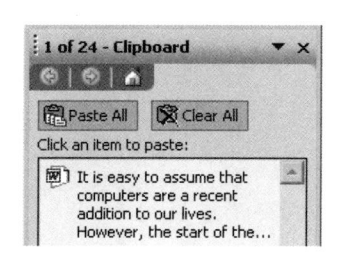

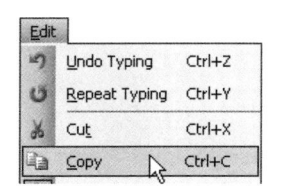

— *New item*

— *Previous item*

26 / Word Processing with Microsoft Word   ***Use clipboard editing***   *continued*

> *By the way*
> *The Office clipboard allows you to cut, copy, and paste items among all Office applications*

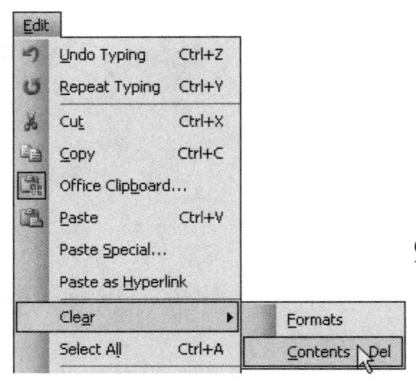

7 *Paste from clipboard*

Click just before first word in new paragraph 1 of document.

If you paste now, which item on clipboard will be pasted? Find out.

On **Edit** menu, choose **Paste** (or tap CTRL V, or click 📋 on standard toolbar) and tap ENTER to move original text down.

Paste command always pastes newest item on clipboard. Former paragraph 3 appears twice in document. Clipboard still contains two items.

8 *Delete paragraph*

Highlight new paragraph 1 and blank line after it.

On **Edit** menu, choose **Clear**; on submenu, choose **Contents** to delete highlighted text. (Or just tap DELETE or BACKSPACE.)

Look at **Clipboard**.

Clear command has no effect on clipboard.

9 *Close Computers document without saving changes*

10 *Paste into new document*

Notice both items still present on clipboard.

On standard toolbar, click 📄 (new blank document).

On standard toolbar, click 📋 (paste).

As before, newest item is pasted—this time into different document.

On **Clipboard**, click *second* icon to paste item. Then click *first* icon.

Clipboard lets you click individual items to paste them.

11 *Paste everything on clipboard*

Click just before first word in paragraph 1 of document.

On **Clipboard**, click 📋 Paste All .

Both items are pasted. Order is oldest first—bottom to top.

12 *Clear clipboard*

On **Clipboard**, click 🗙 Clear All .

On **Edit** menu, look at **Paste** command. Look at paste button on toolbar.

Both are dimmed. There's nothing to paste.

13 *Close clipboard*

Click ✕ on **Clipboard** task pane.

14 *Close document without saving changes*

Complete previous activity before going on.

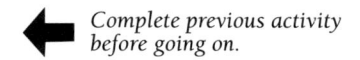

Use drag & drop editing

Here's another way to move and duplicate text in a document. Many people find it simpler and more direct.

1 Open Computers document

2 Highlight text

Select all of paragraph 2 and blank line after it.

3 Move highlighted text ahead of paragraph 1

Notice pointer shape as you move it into any highlighted text.

Pointer changes shape to this: .

With pointer in highlighted text, hold down mouse button.

Drag arrow pointer just before first word in paragraph 1.

Notice that dotted insertion point moves with arrow.

Release mouse button.

Highlighted text disappears from old location and is inserted at arrow position. You have dragged selection and dropped it before paragraph 1.

4 Place copy of paragraph 3 ahead of new paragraph 1

Highlight text paragraph 3 and blank line after it.

Put pointer in highlighted text. Hold down [CTRL] and mouse button.

Drag arrow pointer just before first word in new paragraph 1.

Release mouse button first, then [CTRL].

You have dragged a copy of paragraph 3 and blank line and dropped the copy before paragraph 1.

5 View clipboard

On **Edit** menu, choose **Office Clipboard**.

Drag and drop editing has no effect on clipboard.

Close **Clipboard** task pane.

6 Close Computers without saving changes

Computers *as completed on page 16 must be saved on disk.*

Undo changes

Microsoft Word allows you to undo actions you have performed to change content or format of text in document.

1 **Open Computers document**

2 **Select paragraph**

Position pointer to left of paragraph 1.

Pointer changes from I-beam to this: .

Double-click.

3 **Delete paragraph; undo change (method 1)**

Tap BACKSPACE.

Paragraph is deleted.

On standard toolbar, click (undo typing).

Paragraph is "undeleted."

By the way
The undo menu command is usually followed by the name of the last action you performed.

4 **Delete paragraph; undo change (method 2)**

With paragraph selected, choose **Clear**, then **Contents** on **Edit** menu.

Paragraph is again deleted.

On **Edit** menu, choose **Undo Clear** (or tap CTRL Z).

5 **Undo multiple actions**

Click anywhere in text paragraph 1 and type **AAAAA**.

Click anywhere in text paragraph 2 and type **BBBBB**.

Click anywhere in text paragraph 3 and type **CCCCC**.

Click arrow on right part of  .

Drop-down list shows changes you've made. Changes are in reverse order, with most recent at top.

On drop-down list, move pointer to **Typing "AAAAA"**.

Item and all items above it are highlighted.

Click **Typing "AAAAA"**.

Effect is to undo all changes down through item you selected.

6 **Redo changes just undone**

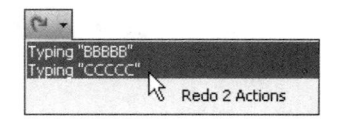

On **Edit** menu, choose **Redo Typing** (or click , or tap CTRL Y).

You should again see AAAAA in paragraph 1, but not previous changes.

Click arrow on right part of 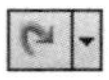 . Notice two actions you can redo.

On drop-down list, click **Typing "CCCCC"**.

Both BBBBB and CCCCC reappear.

7 **Close document without saving changes**

STOP *Computers as completed on page 16 must be saved on disk.*

Find text

You can get help in finding words you're looking for—a nice feature if your document has lots of text.

DOC / 29

1 **Open Computers document**

2 **Find word**

First, capitalize words inside quotation marks in text paragraphs 2 and 3.

Move insertion point to beginning of text (`CTRL HOME` is shortcut).

On **Edit** menu, choose **Find** (or tap `CTRL F`).

Type **Computer** (with capital C) in **Find what** box.

Keep clicking **Find Next** until search ends, moving dialog box if necessary to see matches. Click **OK** to close dialog box that reports end of search.

Seven matches were found. Notice that "computer" in "computers" was also found and that capitalization was ignored.

3 **Find whole word**

Click **More** to see additional search options in dialog box.

In **Search Options** area, click **Find whole words only**. Click **Less**.

Keep clicking **Find Next** (or tapping `F`) until search ends. Click **OK**.

Only five matches are found now because you asked for only that exact word (and not others that contain computer*).*

4 **Make case-sensitive search**

Click **More**. Click **Match case**.

Keep clicking **Find Next** (or tapping `F`) until search ends. Click **OK**.

Whole word Computer with first letter capitalized is found twice.

5 **Click Cancel to close dialog box and end Find**

By the way
Searching always begins at the position of the insertion point. If you start in the middle of a document and reach the end, a dialog box asks whether to continue the search at the beginning.

Tip
You can also click the check box for Highlight all items found in, *then click the* Find All *button. Word highlights all occurrences of that word in the document.*

Tip
The Find *command is especially useful in long documents. It allows you to go directly to words or phrases anywhere in a document.*

← *Complete previous activity before going on.*

Replace text

Sometimes you need to change one word to another in many places in a document.

1 Begin replacement

Make sure insertion point is at start of document.

On **Edit** menu, choose **Replace** (or tap `CTRL`+`H`).

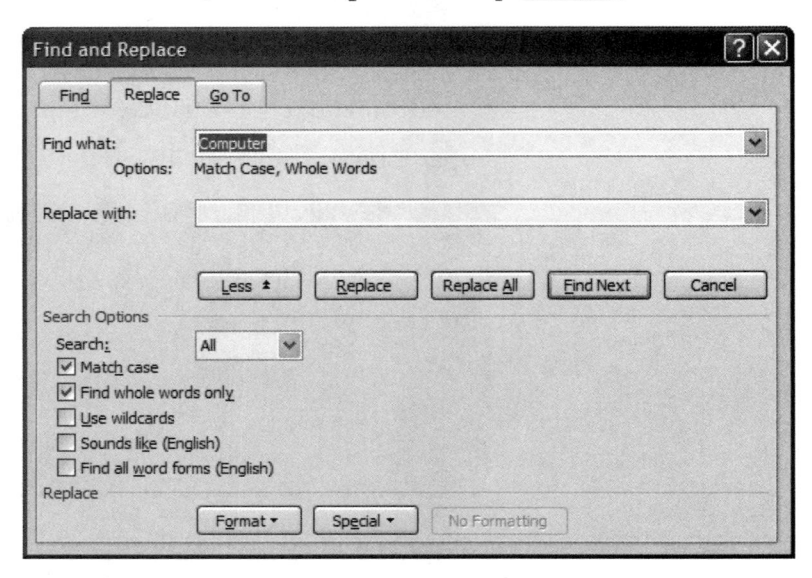

By the way
Notice that the last search text appears highlighted in the Find what *box, and all check boxes are the way you left them.*

---

2 Enter text to be replaced

In **Replace with** box, type `abacus`. Click **Match case** and **Find whole words only** to remove check marks. Click **Less**.

3 Find and replace words one by one

Click **Find Next**.

   Word computers *is highlighted.*

Click **Find Next** to avoid making change and go to next instance.

Click **Replace** to change **computer** to **abacus**.

   Next occurrence is word computers, *which you won't change.*

Click **Find Next**. Replace each remaining occurrence of **computer**.

Click **OK** to close message box reporting end of search.

By the way
Notice that the replaced text matches the case of the original text.

---

4 Find and replace words without checking

Click to right of **Computer** in **Find what** text box.

Type `s` and click **Replace All**.

   Two instances of word computers *are found and changed to* abacus.

5 End Replace

Click **OK**, then click **Close** button in dialog box.

6 Close Computers document without saving changes

Tip
It's usually wise to switch on the Find whole words only *option before using* Replace All. *That prevents replacing "cat" with "dog" in "scatter," for example.*

🛑 Computers *as completed on page 16 must be saved on disk.*

Check spelling

Microsoft Word can check your words against its spelling dictionary, and add new words to your custom dictionary.

DOC / 31

---

1 **Open Computers document**

Make sure you've set spelling options as shown on page 12, step 4.

2 **Create spelling errors in paragraphs 1 and 2**

Change *business* to *busness*. Change *revolution* to *revoluting*.

Change *recent* to *ricent*. Change *science* to *sciance*.

On new line after your name, type **Whoopdedoo**.

Put insertion point at start of document.

By the way
If any text is highlighted when you give the Spelling and Grammar *command, only the selected text is checked.*

3 **Open Spelling dialog box**

On **Tools** menu, choose **Spelling and Grammar** (or click 📝 on toolbar).

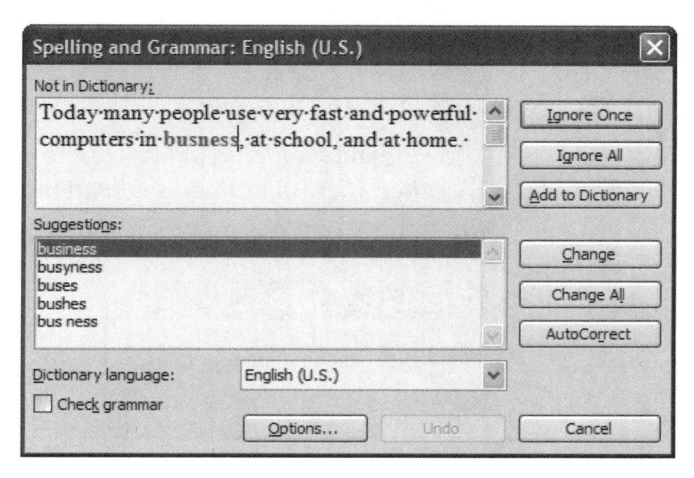

4 **Replace word not found in dictionary (method 1)**

In upper scroll box, notice **busness** in boldface and red.

In **Suggestions** scroll box, correct spelling is highlighted. Click **Change**.

Clicking Change All *would replace all similar misspellings in document.*

5 **View second word not in dictionary**

In upper scroll box, revoluting *is next problem word. In* Suggestions *scroll box, word you want is not highlighted this time.*

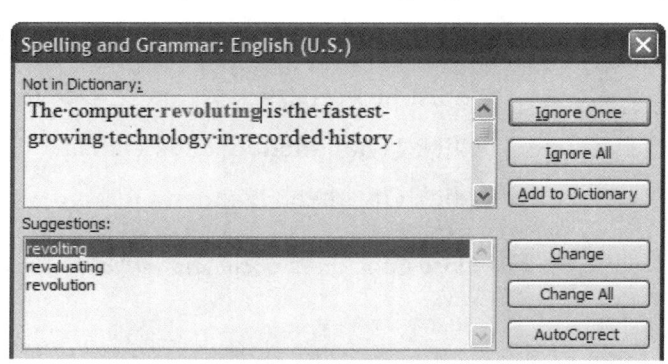

Check spelling *continued*

6 *Correct word (method 2)*

Double-click correct word in list (or click word, then click **Change**).

7 *Correct other words not in dictionary*

Use either method to correct remaining words.

If your name is flagged, click **Ignore All**.

> *Clicking* Ignore All *marks word as OK in document. It won't be flagged if you check same document again.*

Stop at **Whoopdedoo**.

8 *Add unknown word to dictionary*

> *"Whoopdedoo" is not in dictionary. You can add it so it won't be flagged in this or other documents.*

Click **Add to Dictionary**.

> *Word automatically adds word to custom dictionary, which is shared with other Microsoft Office applications.*

When told check is complete, click **OK**.

> *If* Check grammar *box was checked, you would see* Readability Statistics *report. You would close window to go on.*

9 *Remove word from dictionary*

On **Tools** menu, choose **Options**.

Click **Spelling & Grammar** tab.

> *Dialog box should look like figure on page 12, step 4.*

Click **Custom Dictionaries** button.

In **Custom Dictionaries** dialog box, click **Modify**.

> *New window opens with list of words added to custom dictionary.*

In list of words, scroll if necessary to **Whoopdedoo**.

Click **Whoopdedoo**; click **Delete**.

Click OK, then OK, then OK.

10 *Close Computers document without saving changes*

Tip

After opening the custom dictionary document, you can also add words to it. This method is useful when you have many words to add. Put each word on a separate line.

> **STOP** Computers *as completed on page 16 must be saved on disk.*

Change fonts & sizes

Text can appear in many different fonts and sizes. Each font specifies the shapes of all the letters, numbers, and symbols.

DOC / 33

1 **Open Computers document**

2 **Check current font and size of text**

Highlight any text in paragraph 1.

Near left of formatting toolbar, look at font name and size.

[Times New Roman ▾ 12 ▾]

Toolbar shows name and size of font used for selected text.

3 **Change font**

On formatting toolbar, click ▾ next to current font to see drop-down list.

Your list of fonts may be different.

On font list, scroll up and choose **Arial** (or type `arial` in box at top, and tap ENTER).

Menu command affects only highlighted text in document.

4 **Change size**

On formatting toolbar, click ▾ next to **12** (current size) to see size list.

Choose **18** (or enter size you want in box at top).

5 **Change font and size**

Make font **Courier New** and font size **9**.

6 **Change fonts and sizes, and save results**

Give words in each text paragraph different fonts and sizes.

On **File** menu, choose **Save As** (*not* Save). Type `Fonts` in **File name** box.

Click **Save**.

Close **Fonts** document.

Changed document is saved with new name. Original remains unchanged.

Complete previous activity before going on.

Apply font styles

You can easily add font styles, such as bold or italic, to selected words in the document.

1 **Open Computers document**

2 **Add single style to selected text**

Highlight all of text paragraph 2.

On formatting toolbar, click **B** (bold), or tap CTRL B.

Paragraph 2 appears in bold type. Bold tool stays boxed and highlighted.

3 **Remove same style**

On formatting toolbar, click boxed tool, or tap CTRL B again.

Command is like on-off switch, so bold style is removed when you choose command again. Box and highlighting on tool tells when it is on.

4 **Add styles one by one**

If necessary, select text paragraph 2.

On formatting toolbar, click **B**, or tap CTRL B.

On formatting toolbar, click **I** (italic), or tap CTRL I.

On formatting toolbar, click **U** (underline), or tap CTRL U.

All three tools are boxed and highlighted.

Click outside paragraph to deselect text and see styles.

Tools are no longer boxed because insertion point is not in paragraph 2 now.

5 **Remove added styles one by one**

Select all text in text paragraph 2.

Watch text as you click **B**, then **I**, then **U**.

6 **Undo removal of styles**

Click arrow on right part of (undo). On undo list, choose *first* occurrence of **Bold**.

All three styles are added back to text.

7 **Remove styles**

If necessary, select all text in text paragraph 2. Tap CTRL SPACEBAR.

8 **Apply font styles, save, and close document**

Apply a different style to words in each text paragraph of document.

On **File** menu, choose **Save As** (*not* Save). Type **Styles** in **File name** box. Click **Save**.

Changed document is saved with new name. Original remains unchanged.

On **File** menu, choose **Close**.

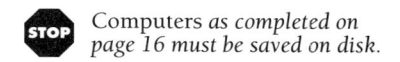

🛑 Computers *as completed on page 16 must be saved on disk.*

Use Font dialog box

A single dialog box lets you specify all character formats at the same time: the font, the size, the styles, and other details.

DOC / 35

1 **Open Computers document**

2 **Change font, size, style, and color at same time**

Highlight all text in paragraph 1.

On **Format** menu, choose **Font**. If necessary, click **Font** tab at top.

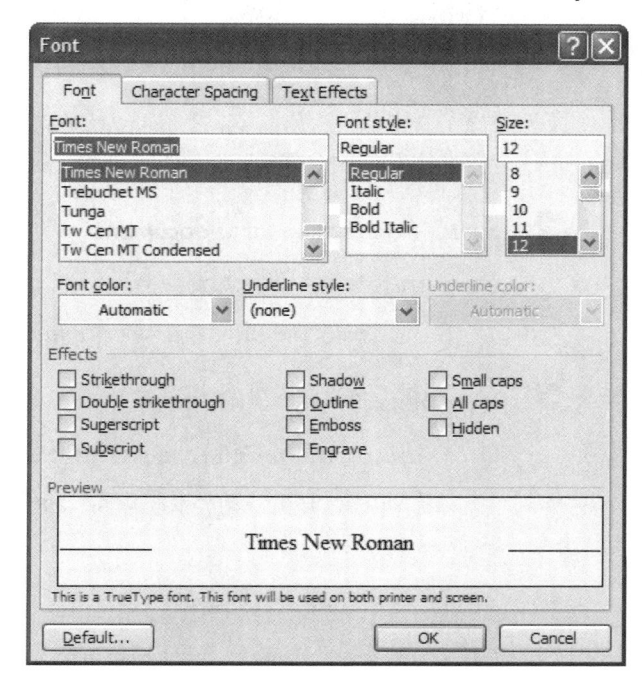

On **Font** list, use scroll bar to see fonts. Click to highlight one you want.

You can also enter font name in highlighted box at top.

On **Font style** list, click **Bold Italic**.

On **Size** list, use scroll bar to see sizes. Click to highlight one you want.

On **Font color** list, choose dark red.

On **Underline style** list, click first single line.

In **Effects** area, click **All caps** to put mark in check box.

Click **OK**. Click away from paragraph 1 to see result.

All changes happen at same time.

3 **Remove all character formats**

You could do this with Fonts *dialog box, but there's easier way.*

Highlight all text in paragraph 1. Tap CTRL SPACEBAR.

4 **Close document without saving changes**

On **File** menu, choose **Close**.

When asked whether to save changes, click **No**.

By the way
On Font style *list,* Regular *means no italic and no bold.*

🛑 *At least two Word documents must be saved on disk.*

Open many documents

As with most Windows applications, you can have several documents open in separate windows.

1 **Open documents**

Make sure floppy disk is in drive and document window is **maximized**.

On **File** menu, choose **Open**. Make sure **Look in** location is **3½ Floppy**.

Click name of first Word document on list.

With CTRL held down, click each of other Word documents on list.

All file names should be highlighted.

Click **Open**.

All documents open, but only one document is visible.

2 **Switch from document to document**

On **Window** menu, choose name of another document you want.

Because document windows are maximized, only one is visible.

3 **View all documents at one time**

On **Window** menu, choose **Arrange All**.

All four windows appear. None is maximized. One with darkest title bar is active.

4 **Activate different window**

Click any clear area in another window.

5 **View one of four documents on full screen**

Click any window to make it active.

Click ▢ (maximize button) in upper-right corner of active window.

Window fills display.

Click ▢ (restore button) in upper-right corner of active window.

Window goes back to previous size.

Click maximize button in another document window.

Chosen window fills application window, as before.

6 **Close multiple documents**

Press SHIFT and hold it down.

On **File** menu, choose **Close All**. If asked, don't save changes.

If necessary, maximize empty **Microsoft Word** window.

7 **Exit Microsoft Word**

On **File** menu, choose **Exit**. Eject floppy disk and take it with you.

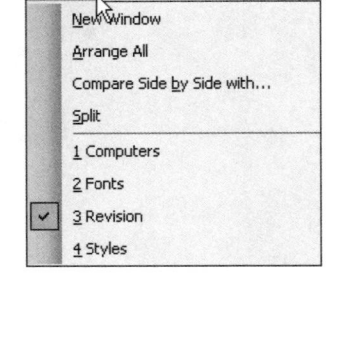

Align text

The lines of text in a paragraph can all be aligned to the left, the right, the center, or both left and right (justified).

1 **Start Microsoft Word; close task pane at right**

New blank document should appear below toolbars (if not, click 🗋 on standard toolbar).

2 **Locate alignment tools on formatting toolbar**

3 **Enter text using alignment options**

Click 🔳 (center).

Insertion point moves to center of text area.

Type `Computer History Society`.

Tap ENTER twice.

Each new line picks up previous center-alignment formatting.

Click 🔳 (align right).

Insertion point moves to right side of document.

4 **Enter automatic date**

On **Insert** menu, choose **Date and Time**.

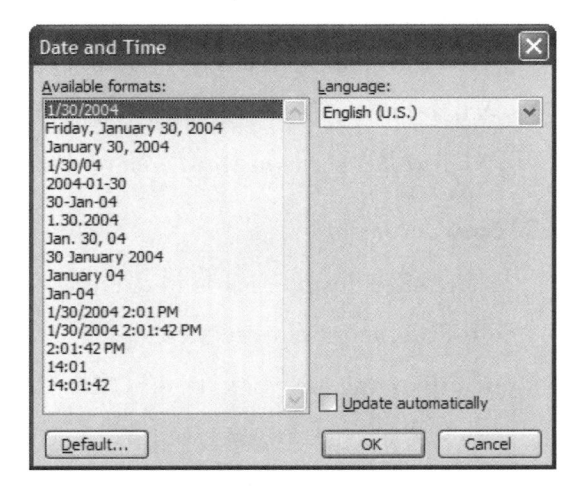

> **By the way**
> *The dates and times listed come from the settings on your computer.*
> *The* Update automatically *option inserts a date that changes to always reflect the current date.*

On **Available formats** list, choose format you like, then click **OK**.

5 **Enter additional text with left alignment**

Tap ENTER twice.

Each new line picks up previous right-alignment formatting.

Click 🔳 (align left).

Insertion point moves to left side of document.

Type `Mr. John Smith,`.

Align text *continued*

6 *Add blank lines*

Tap ENTER twice.

Each new line picks up previous left-alignment formatting.

7 *Enter body paragraph*

Type following paragraph. Do not tap ENTER at ends of lines; let text wrap.

```
How many times have you wondered about the
history of computers or about the "computer
revolution"? Is this a modern phenomenon or
simply another step in the evolution of
technology? The Computer History Society
meetings offer thought-provoking discussions
on such topics. Please join us next month.
```

8 *Check spelling*

On **Tools** menu, choose **Spelling and Grammar** (or click ABC on toolbar).

Use methods beginning on page 31 to make corrections.

9 *Change left alignment to justified alignment*

Click anywhere in body paragraph to select it.

Alignment commands (and all other paragraph format commands) affect paragraph with insertion point or with any highlighted text.

Watch ends of lines as you click ▤ (justify).

Text has even (justified) left and right margins.

10 *Save document*

Make sure floppy disk is in drive.

On **File** menu, choose **Save**.

In **File name** text box, type **CHS Note**.

Click ▾ at right of **Save in** box to see drop-down list of locations.

On list, choose **3½ Floppy**.

Click **Save**.

New document is saved on disk.

11 *Move insertion point to top of document*

Tap CTRL HOME.

← *Complete previous activity before going on.*

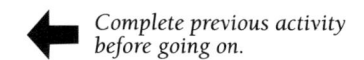

Apply indents

Other paragraph format controls let you indent lines in paragraphs from the left and right margins.

1 View indent markers at ends of ruler

If ruler is not present, choose **Ruler** on **View** menu. Locate indent markers.

First-line indent — Hanging indent — Left indent — Right indent

2 Set right and left indents

Click anywhere inside body paragraph.

For paragraph formatting, you don't have to highlight entire paragraph.

Press and drag right indent marker 2 inches to left (to 4" mark on ruler).

Text is indented from right margin only in selected paragraph (one with insertion point in it). To set indents in more than one paragraph, highlight some text in each.

Press and drag left indent marker 1 inch to right (to 1" mark on ruler).

Dragging rectangle moves first line and hanging indent markers as well.

By the way
If the ruler units are not inches, you can switch units on the Tools menu, Options dialog box, General tab.

3 Set first-line indent

Carefully press and drag first-line indent marker (*top* triangle, now above left indent marker) to right 0.5 inch (to 1.5" mark).

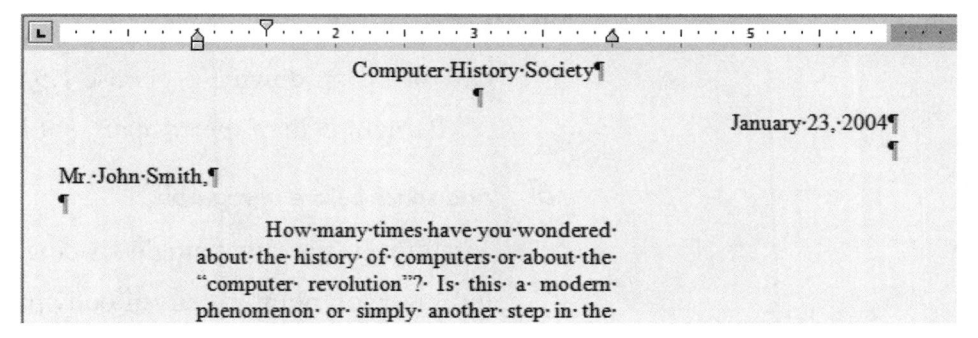

Computer History Society¶
¶
January 23, 2004¶
¶
Mr. John Smith,¶
¶
How many times have you wondered about the history of computers or about the "computer revolution"? Is this a modern phenomenon or simply another step in the

This time, first line of selected paragraph is indented more than rest.

4 Set hanging indent

Carefully press and drag first-line indent marker (*top* triangle) to left 1 inch (to 0.5" mark).

This time, first line "hangs"—begins to left of other lines. Format is useful for numbered or bulleted paragraphs.

5 Reset indents to original settings

With insertion point in body paragraph, press and drag right indent marker to 6" mark on ruler.

Press and drag first-line indent marker back to left indent marker.

Press and drag left indent marker to 0" mark on ruler.

Tip
Be careful not to drag too far to the left and into the "minus area." If you do, use the horizontal scroll bar to see the markers, and drag them back.

Complete previous activity before going on.

Apply line spacing

Additional paragraph format controls let you change vertical line spacing.

1 **View line spacing drop-down list**

On formatting toolbar, click arrow at right of (line spacing).

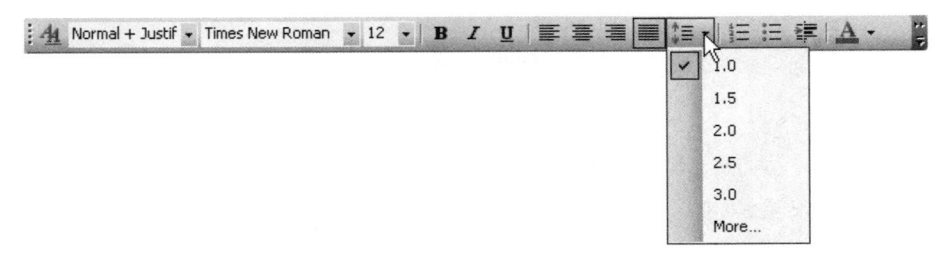

```
1.0
1.5
2.0
2.5
3.0
More…
```

2 **Double-space paragraph lines**

If necessary, click inside body paragraph.

Like alignment and indentation, line spacing affects only paragraph with insertion point (or paragraphs with some text highlighted).

On line spacing drop-down list, choose **2.0** (or tap CTRL 2).

Lines are double-spaced now.

3 **Single-space lines again**

On same drop-down list, choose **1.0** (or tap CTRL 1).

4 **Set paragraph line spacing to 1.5 lines**

On same drop-down list, choose **1.5** (or tap CTRL 5).

Paragraph lines spread apart, but less than with double-spacing.

5 **Add space before paragraph**

Tap CTRL 1 to restore single-spacing.

Put insertion point at start of body paragraph.

Tap BACKSPACE to delete blank line before paragraph.

Now you'll learn another way to put space between paragraphs.

If necessary, click inside body paragraph.

Tap CTRL 0 (zero).

One line space is added before selected paragraph. There's no paragraph mark on blank line; it's part of body paragraph format.

Double-click arrow pointer just left of body paragraph to select it.

Blank line is also selected. It is part of body paragraph.

6 **Remove space before paragraph**

With body paragraph still selected, tap CTRL 0 (zero) again.

7 **Close document without saving changes**

🛑 Computers *as completed on page 16 must be saved on disk.*

Use Paragraph dialog box

Like the Font *dialog box, this one lets you make many format changes at the same time. They affect whole paragraphs.*

DOC / 41

---

1 **Open Computers document**

2 **Delete blank lines between paragraphs**

Move pointer to left side of document.

Pointer changes to arrow pointing up and to right.

Click to left of first blank line after paragraph 1. Tap [BACKSPACE] to delete line.

Do same for blank lines after text paragraphs 2 and 3.

3 **Select some text in all paragraphs**

Click anywhere in paragraph 1.

With [SHIFT] held down, click anywhere in text paragraph 3.

4 **Open Paragraph dialog box**

On **Format** menu, choose **Paragraph**. Look at options available.

On **Alignment** list (in **General** area), choose **Justified**.

On **Special** list (in **Indentation** area), choose **First line**. On **By** list, choose 0.5" if necessary.

In **After** box (in **Spacing** area), click up-arrow twice to choose **12 pt**.

Dialog box settings should look like figure below.

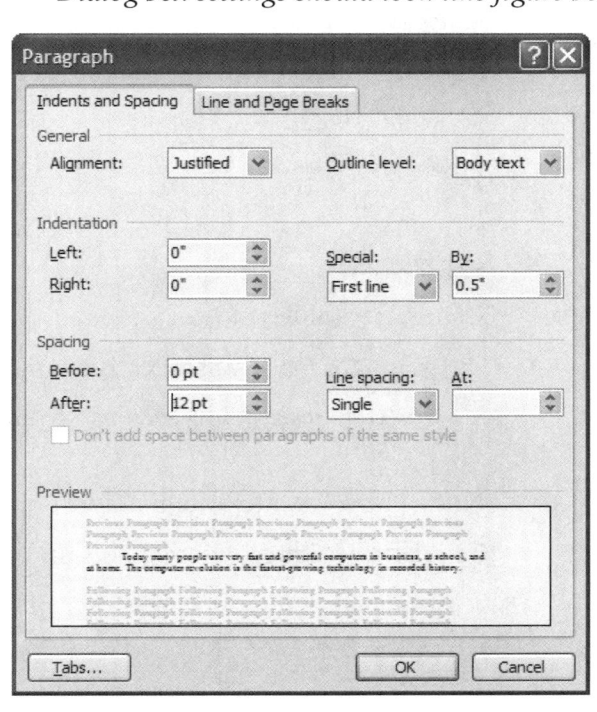

Click **OK**.

All format changes happen at once. Only paragraphs 1–3 are affected.

5 **Close document without saving changes**

Tip

Your blank lines are actually blank paragraphs. A paragraph is any text (including none) followed by a paragraph mark (¶). That's why it's a good idea to see these marks when you're editing. If yours are hidden now, click ¶ on the standard toolbar.

Use tab stops

Tab stops are another paragraph format feature. They give you control over alignment of words in columns.

1 Open new document (unless you just started Word)

On standard toolbar, click ▯ (new blank document).

2 Notice tab features on ruler

If ruler is not present, choose Ruler *on* View *menu.*

Tab stop tool ——
Default tab stops ——

Default tab stops every 0.5 inch are in effect until you place your own stops.

Click tab stop tool to rotate through four main tabs you can set—
▯ (left), ▯ (center), ▯ (right), and ▯ (decimal).

Continue to click past three other markers and return to ▯ (left tab).

3 Set custom tab stops (method 1)

With stop tool set to ▯ (left), click ruler at 0.75" mark.

Left tab stop appears where you clicked on ruler. Default tab stop to left of custom tab disappears. Default stops to right remain.

Click tab stop tool twice to select ▯ (right) tab stop.

Click ruler at 2.5".

Use same steps to set decimal tab at 3.5" and center tab at 5".

Ruler should look like this.

> **By the way**
> *Each paragraph in a document can have its own tab stop settings. When you set a tab stop, it affects only the paragraph with the insertion point or highlighted text.*

4 Use tab stops

Using `TAB` (at left side of keyboard; key may look like this: ⇥), type this:

`TAB` **Left** `TAB` **Right** `TAB` **3.0** `TAB` **Center**

You should see arrow each place you tap `TAB`. *(If not, click* ¶ *on standard toolbar.)*

Notice how each text item aligns relative to custom tab stop on ruler.

Tap `ENTER`. Notice where insertion point is. Look at stops on ruler now.

Insertion point is in new paragraph with same tab stops. Whenever you tap `ENTER`, *new paragraph "inherits" tab stops (and all other formats) from previous paragraph.*

Type this in new paragraph:

`TAB` **Apple** `TAB` **IBM** `TAB` **$999.98** `TAB` **Compaq**

Words and numbers align with ones above.

Use tab stops continued   DOC / 43

5 ***Clear all tab stops from new paragraph***

Tap [ENTER] twice to add blank line.

As before, same tab stops are in effect for new paragraph.

Press and drag left tab stop (at 0.75") down off ruler. Release mouse button.

Do same for other tab stops on ruler.

New line has default tab stops but no custom tab stops. Custom tab stops remain in paragraphs above. Each paragraph has own format settings.

> *Tip*
> *If you accidentally double-click a tab stop, the Tabs dialog box opens. Just close it for now and go on.*

6 ***Set custom tab stops (method 2)***

On **Format** menu, choose **Tabs**.

> *Tip*
> *If you don't see the Tabs command on the menu, wait a few seconds or click the arrow at the bottom to see the full menu. To turn on full menus, see page 10.*

In **Tab stop position** box, type **1**. Leave **Left** as **Alignment** setting.

Click **Set**.

In **Tab stop position** box, type **5**.

In **Alignment** area, click **Decimal**.

Click **Set**. Click **OK**, and look at ruler.

You've set a left tab stop at 1" and a decimal tab stop at 5".

7 ***Use tab stops***

Type these lines:

[TAB] **Dell** [TAB] **962.59** [ENTER]

[TAB] **Acer** [TAB] **1896.95** [ENTER]

[TAB] **Sony** [TAB] **1993.98** [ENTER]

Each new paragraph gets tab stops from previous one.

8 ***Close document without saving changes***

Use tab leaders

When you use a tab stop, you can easily put a row of dots, dashes, or underlines in the space before the tab stop.

1 **Create new blank document (unless you just started Word)**

2 **Create single tab stop with leader**

On **Format** menu, choose **Tabs**.

Duplicate this **Tabs** dialog box.

Settings put one right tab stop at 5" mark with leader number 2 (dotted). Settings will affect blank paragraph with insertion point.

Click **OK**.

3 **Enter two lines using new tab stop**

```
Chapter 1  [TAB] 1  [ENTER]
Chapter 2  [TAB] 12 [ENTER]
```

4 **Use different types of tab leaders**

Double-click tab stop at 5-inch mark on ruler.

Tabs dialog box opens. Tab at 5 inches is selected. If not, click to select.

Under **Leader**, choose **3** (dashed line). Click **OK** and type this:

```
Chapter 3  [TAB] 25 [ENTER]
```

Use same methods to complete figure below.

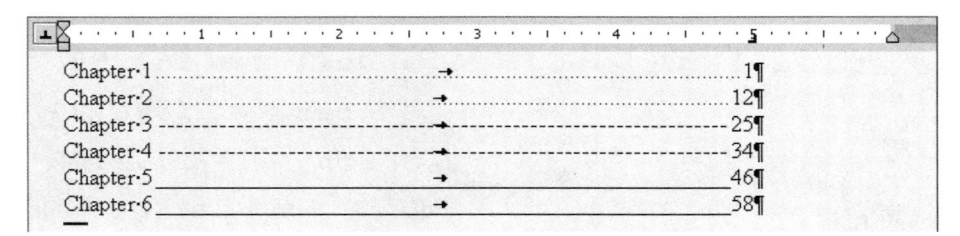

5 **Close document without saving changes**

> **Computers** *as completed on page 16 must be saved on disk.*

Define paragraph styles

You can give a name to any combination of paragraph (or character) formats. Then you can apply the formats by name.

1 **Open Computers document**

2 **See current styles in document**

At left end of standard toolbar, click ▾ to display style drop-down list.

Every new document you create comes with these named styles.

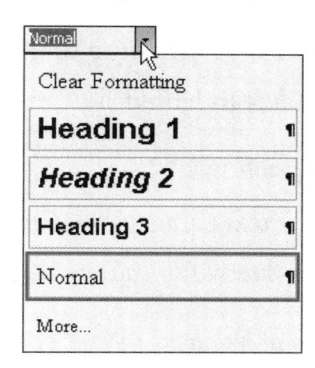

Border (around Normal*) shows style of paragraph with insertion point.*

Click ▾ again to close style list.

3 **Apply named style to selected paragraph**

Click anywhere in text paragraph 2.

On style list, choose **Heading 1**.

Notice changes in text. Whole paragraph is affected.

Click anywhere in text paragraph 3.

On style list, choose **Heading 2**.

4 **Remove applied styles**

With [SHIFT] held down, click anywhere in text paragraph 2.

Some text should be highlighted in text paragraphs 2 and 3.

On style list, choose **Normal**.

Both paragraphs return to original formatting.

5 **Apply formats, one by one, to paragraph**

Click anywhere in paragraph 1.

On **Format** menu, choose **Paragraph**.

In **Indentation** area, set **Left** and **Right** to 1".

On **Special** list, choose **First line**. Leave 0.5" in **By** text box.

On **Line spacing** list, choose **1.5 lines**. Click **OK** to see result.

Paragraph 1 should have all formats you just defined for it. Next you'll create named style that does whole job in one click.

Tip

Using named styles for all paragraphs in a document has two benefits. First, it makes headings and body paragraphs consistent throughout the document. Second, if you change the definition of a style, all paragraphs with that named style are automatically updated.

By the way

When a paragraph is selected and the top of the style drop-down list is blank, it is because mixed styles are applied to the paragraph.

By the way

Instead of Left *and* Right*, the labels in your dialog box may be* Before text *and* After text.

Define paragraph styles *continued*

Tip
Be sure to tap ENTER *after typing the style name; otherwise Word does not save the style.*

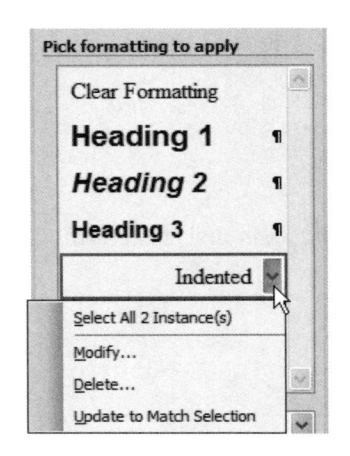

6 **Create new style based on current paragraph formatting**

At left of formatting toolbar, click **Normal + Left:** (or **Normal: Before**) to highlight all text in box.

Type **Indented** and tap ENTER.

Style named Indented *is created, using formats from current paragraph.*

Watch style name on formatting toolbar as you click in each paragraph.

Paragraph 1 has Indented *style; rest have* Normal *style.*

7 **Apply new paragraph style**

Click anywhere in text paragraph 3. On style drop-down list, choose **Indented**.

Paragraph 3 changes to Indented *style.*

8 **Change definition of Indented style**

At left of formatting toolbar, click 🅰️ (styles and formatting).

Styles and Formatting task pane appears at right of window.

In task pane, put pointer on **Indented**, and click ▼ at right.

On drop-down list, choose **Modify**.

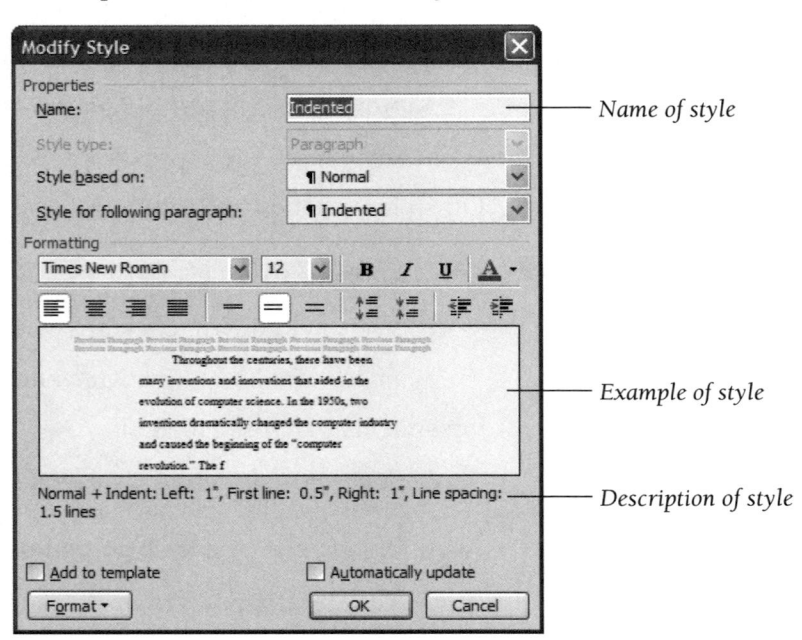

— Name of style
— Example of style
— Description of style

In **Formatting** area, on font size drop-down list, choose **14**.

In same area, click **B**, *I*, and U.

Click **OK**.

Text in both paragraphs with Indented *style show change.*

9 **Close document without saving changes; close task pane**

Tip
In addition to paragraph styles, you can also create named character styles and add them to the same drop-down list. Start by selecting some text and applying the formats you want (font, font size, and so on). Then choose the Styles and Formatting *command on the* Format *menu, click the* New Style *button, enter a name for the style, choose* Character *on the* Style type *list, and click* OK. *You can then apply the style by name to any selected text.*

CHS Note *as created on pages 37–36 must be saved on disk.*

Add graphic object

You can add a graphic object to a word processing document. Microsoft Word comes with a gallery of clip art you can use.

DOC / 47

1 *Open CHS Note document*

2 *Insert graphic*

Notice insertion point at beginning of document.

On **Insert** menu, choose **Picture**, then **Clip Art**. (If **Add Clips to Organizer** dialog box appears, click **Later**.)

Insert Clip Art task pane appears at right of window.

> **Tip**
> *If you did not do a complete installation of Microsoft Office, the clip art files may be missing. If so, click Cancel and exit Microsoft Word. Run the Office Setup program and install clip art. You'll need the original Office 2003 CDs.*

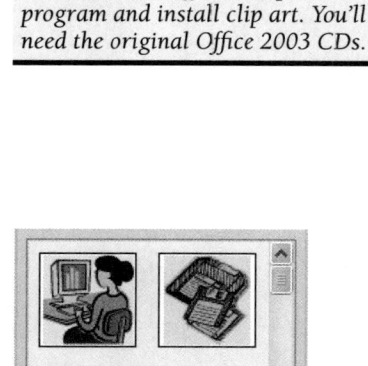

In **Search text** box in task pane, type **computer**. Click **Go**.

In task pane, use scroll bar to view results (may vary).

Click image you like.

Image is inserted into document at insertion point in first line

Tap [ENTER] to put figure in separate paragraph ahead of text.

Close **Insert Clip Art** task pane.

3 *Adjust size of graphic*

Click in middle of picture to select it and see **Picture** palette.

> **Tip**
> *If the* Picture *palette does not appear, choose* Toolbars *from the* View *menu, then select* Picture.

Toward right of **Picture** palette, click (format picture).

In dialog box, click **Size** tab.

In **Scale** area, change **Height** to **50%**.

Tap [TAB] key. Notice that **Width** changes too.

Click **OK**.

4 *Click in text away from graphic to deselect it*

5 *Close document, saving changes when asked*

Use AutoText entries

Microsoft Word has built-in text entries you can use to speed up document creation. You can also create your own entries.

1 **Create new blank document**

2 **Switch AutoText feature on**

On **View** menu, choose **Toolbars**, then **AutoText**.

If toolbar is docked at top (or other edge) of window, drag its handle (thin vertical, dotted bar at left) to middle of window.

Toolbar appears as palette titled AutoText.

At left of **AutoText** palette, click 🖐 (autotext) to see options.

If check box at top is empty, click it.

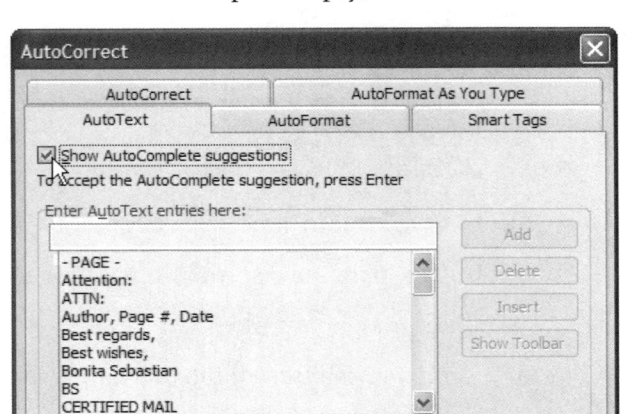

> **By the way**
> You can also reach the dialog box at the right by choosing AutoCorrect Options *on the* Tools *menu or* AutoText, *then* AutoText *again on the* Insert *menu. It's the same dialog box, no matter how you reach it.*

Scroll through list and look at collection of AutoText phrases (may vary).

If your list doesn't contain **Attention:**, **Best regards**, and **Best wishes**, type each phrase in text box at top and click **Add**.

Click **OK** to enable AutoText and close dialog box.

3 **Explore AutoText feature**

Type **best** and one space.

So far, nothing is new.

Type **r** and look at box just above line of type.

Box has tip suggesting phrase you may want.

Tap ENTER to replace your typing with phrase in tip.

If tip was not what you wanted, you'd just keep on typing as usual.

Tap ENTER to start new line. Type **atte** and tap ENTER to accept tip.

On same line, type one space. Type **atte** again.

Oops! There's no tip this time. AutoText is smart enough to know that atte *can't mean* Attention: *unless it's at start of line.*

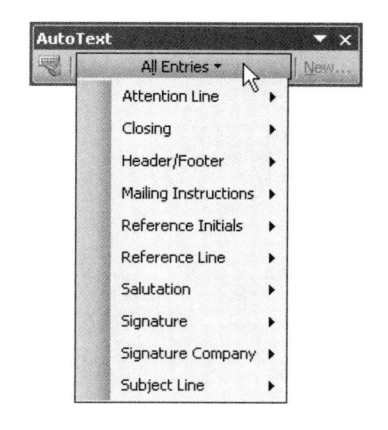

Use AutoText entries *continued* DOC / 49

4 *Insert AutoText entry manually*

Tap ENTER to start new line.

On **AutoText** palette, click ▾ to see **All Entries** drop-down list.

On menu, point to **Closing** (or **Normal** if you added entries in step 2).

Submenu of closing entries appears.

Click any submenu item to insert it in document.

5 *Create custom AutoText entry*

Tap ENTER to move to blank line in document.

Type `Computer History Society`.

Select and format text as 14 point, bold.

If necessary, select whole line, including paragraph mark at end.

Paragraph mark includes formatting in AutoText item.

On **AutoText** palette, click **New**.

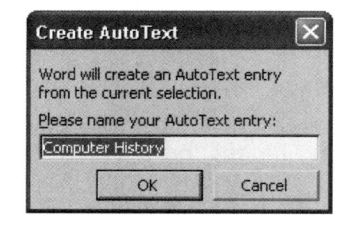

Type `chsoc` and click **OK** to add name to list.

Tip
You must use at least four characters for the name of the AutoText entry.

6 *View new AutoText item*

On **All Entries** menu on palette, point to **Normal**.

New entries you create appear here.

7 *Insert custom AutoText in document*

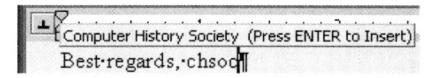

Click to right of first line of document, and type one space.

Type `chsoc` and notice tip above typing.

Tap ENTER to insert formatted AutoText entry.

8 *Delete AutoText item from list*

At left of **AutoText** palette, click 🖳 (autotext) to see options.

Scroll down and select **chsoc**. Click **Delete** button.

In **AutoCorrect** dialog box, click **Show AutoComplete suggestions** to remove check mark. Click **OK**.

9 *Close palette; close document without saving changes*

🛑 Computers *as completed on page 16 must be saved on disk.*

Insert page breaks

Microsoft Word automatically starts a new page when necessary. You can also add manual page breaks.

1 Create two-page document

Open **Computers**. If necessary, on **View** menu, choose **Normal**.

You will copy and paste existing text several times.

Drag down left margin to highlight all lines before your name.

On **Edit** menu, choose **Copy** (or tap CTRL C).

Click 🗋 to create new blank document.

On **Edit** menu, choose **Paste** (or tap CTRL V).

Repeat pasting four or five more times.

Text copied to clipboard is pasted each time.

2 Save for future use

On **File** menu, choose **Save As** (*not* Save).

Save with name **Twopages** on disk.

3 View automatic page break

Scroll up if necessary to see dotted line across page.

Dotted line shows where new page begins when document is printed.

4 Select location for manual page break

Click to put insertion point anywhere in text a few lines above dotted line.

5 Insert page break (method 1)

On **Insert** menu, choose **Break**.

If necessary, click to select **Page break**; then click **OK**.

Manual break appears as dense dotted line with words Page Break.

Notice that automatic page break has disappeared.

6 Remove page break

Click in left margin of **Page Break** line to highlight it.

Tap BACKSPACE (twice if necessary) to go back to original text.

7 Insert page break (method 2)

Tap CTRL ENTER .

Manual break appears again. Next you'll preview document to see break.

By the way

The page break line is a single nonprinting page break character. As with any other character, you can highlight, copy, paste, and delete it.

Complete previous activity before going on.

Preview document

It is always a good idea to preview a document to see page breaks before printing.

1 **Preview both pages of document**

On **File** menu, choose **Print Preview** (or click 🔍 on standard toolbar).

Preview toolbar replaces others. Page appears at reduced scale.

On toolbar, click ▦ (multiple pages). Click middle icon in first row to see two side-by-side pages.

2 **Zoom in (method 1)**

Position pointer over page you want to view more closely.

If pointer has arrow shape, tap mouse button.

Pointer changes shape to 🔍 (magnifying glass with +).

Click magnifying-glass pointer at area you want to zoom in on.

Zoom scale is 100%, and area where you clicked appears.

3 **Zoom out (method 1)**

Position pointer over enlarged page. Pointer now has minus sign: 🔍.

Click page to zoom out.

Notice zoom percentage on toolbar.

4 **Zoom in (method 2)**

To right of zoom percentage on toolbar, click ▼ to see zoom options.

Click to select **100%**.

View percentage increases.

5 **Zoom out (method 2)**

Display zoom list again.

Click to select **Two Pages**.

View percentage decreases. Two pages appear again.

6 **Explore other buttons on toolbar**

Notice 🖨 (print) on preview toolbar.

You could print document now. Instead, you'll exit preview.

7 **Exit preview**

Click [Close] on preview toolbar to return to normal view.

8 **Close document without saving changes**

> Twopages *as completed on page 50 must be saved on disk.*

Change page margins

You can set all four margins on the page. Paragraph indents automatically adjust to the new margins.

1 **Open Twopages document**

2 **View margin controls**

On **File** menu, choose **Page Setup**. If necessary, click **Margins** tab.

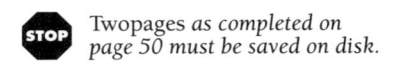

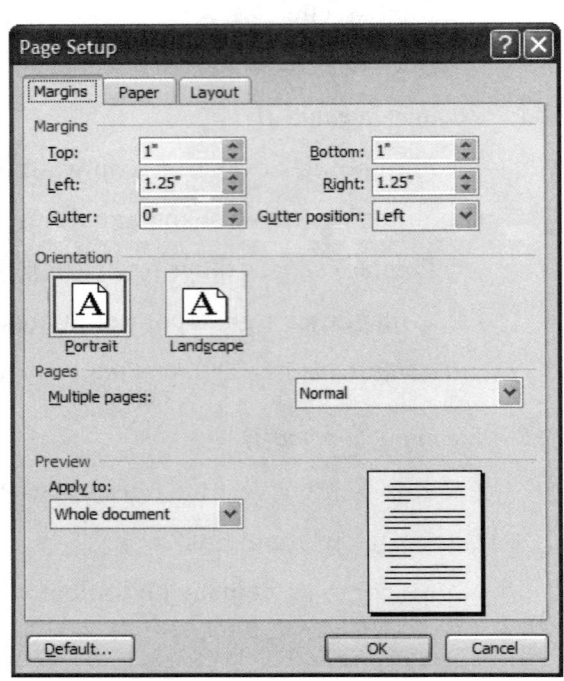

By the way
The top four numbers are the sizes of page margins now. The gutter is extra space at the edge of the page to allow for binding.

3 **Change margins and see results**

Change left margin to 1" and right margin to 3".

Notice changes in **Preview** area. Click **OK**.

On **View** menu, choose **Print Layout**. Notice new margins.

On standard toolbar, click arrow for zoom percentage. Choose **Two Pages**.

4 **Mirror even and odd pages**

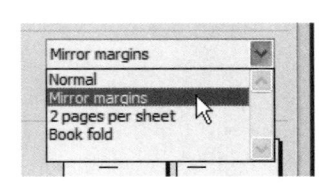

On **File** menu, choose **Page Setup**.

In **Pages** area, choose **Mirror margins** on drop-down list.

> *Margin labels change to* Inside *and* Outside. *Preview area shows two pages. Mirrored pages are used for documents to be printed on both sides.*

5 **Look at other options**

Notice options in **Orientation** area for printing portrait or landscape.

In **Preview** area, look at **Apply to** drop-down list.

> *Page setup changes can apply to whole document or just parts.*

6 **Click OK to see margins now; close document without saving changes**

> ⛔ Twopages *as completed on page 50 must be saved on disk.*

Add columns & breaks

Microsoft Word allows you to put more than one column of text on each page. You can also adjust where columns break.

1 **Open Twopages document**

2 **Create two-column layout for whole document**

Change view to **Print Layout**.

On standard toolbar, choose **Two Pages** on zoom drop-down list.

> *View shows how columns look when printed.*

On **Format** menu, choose **Columns**.

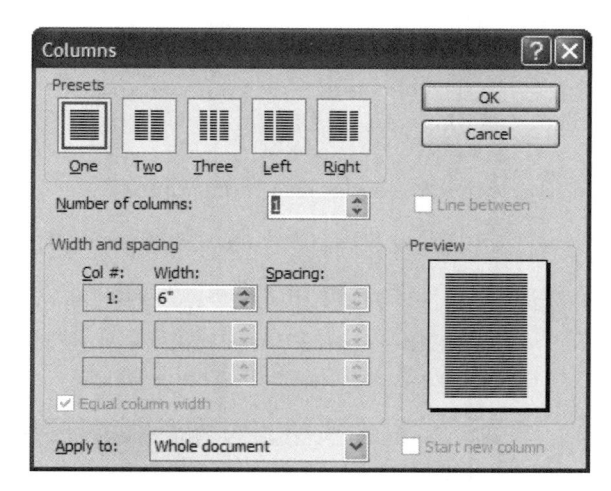

In **Presets** area, click icon labeled **Two**. Look at **Preview** area.

Click **OK** and notice effect.

3 **Insert column break**

Click before any word in text paragraph 4.

On **Insert** menu, choose **Break**, then click **Column break**. Click **OK**.

> *Column breaks where you clicked.*

4 **Return to normal view**

On **View** menu, choose **Normal**. Scroll through text.

> *In normal view, text appears as single narrow column.*

On **Format** menu, choose **Columns**. Under **Presets**, click icon labeled **One**. Click **OK**.

> *Text widens to margins. Column break now serves as page break.*

5 **Close document without saving changes**

> **STOP** Twopages *as completed on page 50 must be saved on disk.*

Add headers & footers

A header or footer can be used to put titles and page numbers at the top or bottom of each page.

1 **Open Twopages document**

2 **View two pages at maximum size**

On **View** menu, choose **Print Layout**.

On zoom percentage drop-down list (on toolbar), choose **Two Pages**.

On **View** menu, choose **Full Screen**.

Two pages fill display; menu bar and toolbars disappear.

Move pointer to top of display area.

Menus slide into view and are available. You'll use this view to explore headers and footers.

3 **Activate header and footer areas**

On **View** menu, choose **Header and Footer**.

Dashed outlines shows header and footer areas on both pages.

In **Header and Footer** palette, move pointer over each icon and read its description. *Don't click tools yet!*

4 **Enter header text**

On **View** menu, choose **Ruler**.

Notice insertion point in header area of page 1. Look at tab stops on ruler.

Ruler shows center tab stop at 3" and right tab stop at 6".

Tap TAB twice to move insertion point to right tab stop at 6".

Type **Computer History Society**.

Same text appears in header areas of both pages.

Use **View** menu to hide rulers.

5 **Move to footer and enter text**

In **Header and Footer** palette, click ▦ (switch between header and footer).

Insertion point jumps to footer area. Ruler settings are same as for header.

Tap TAB to move insertion point to center tab stop at 3".

In **Header and Footer** palette, click # (insert page number).

You should see 1 in middle of page-1 footer area, 2 in page-2 footer.

Tap TAB to move to right tab stop at 6".

In **Header and Footer** palette, click ▦ (insert date).

Current date is inserted. (Date is updated when you open document.)

Add headers & footers *continued*

6 Switch between body text and header and footer text

Double-click anywhere in body text of document.

> *Palette disappears. Header and footer text is dimmed. Body text is active.*

Double-click in any header or footer text.

> *Palette returns. You can now edit headers and footers.*

7 Make header and footer different on first page

> *Often you want different header and footer, or none at all, on first page.*

On **File** menu, choose **Page Setup**. Click **Layout** tab.

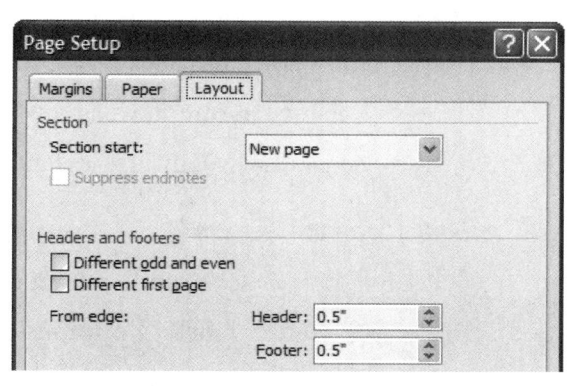

By the way
You can also set the distance headers and footers appear from the edge of the paper. Most printers cannot print closer to the edge than 0.5".

In **Headers and footers** area, click to place mark in **Different first page** check box.

Click **OK**. Look at headers and footers now.

> *Header and footer no longer appear on first page. Also, dashed boxes there say* First Page Header *and* First Page Footer.

8 Add special header on page 1

Click anywhere in **First Page Header** box.

With insertion point in header area, tap TAB and type **CHS**.

> *First page now has header, but it's different from rest.*

9 Restore normal view

On **View** menu, choose **Full Screen** (now selected).

> *Headers and footers are also visible in* Print Layout *view.*

On zoom drop-down list, choose **100%**.

On **View** menu, choose **Normal**.

> *Headers and footers are hidden in this view.*

Tip
To see and edit headers in normal view, use the Header and Footer *command on the* View *menu. The view switches to print layout and the same toolbar appears.*

10 Close document without saving changes

> ⛔ *Twopages as completed on page 50 must be saved on disk.*

Create sections

Sections are like chapters in a book. Sections can have different headers, page margins, and numbers of columns.

1 Open Twopages document

2 Add section break

Put insertion point just before first word in text paragraph 4 (Today).

On **Insert** menu, choose **Break**.

Look at four options in **Section break types** area.

All but Continuous *cause next section to begin new page.*

In **Section break types** area, choose **Continuous**.

Click **OK**.

Nonprinting section break character is inserted. Symbol for character is double row of dotted lines with Section Break (Continuous) *in middle.*

Change to **Print Layout** view. Change zoom percentage to **Two Pages**.

Because you chose Continuous, *no page break occurs at new section.*

3 Change format of section 2

Click anywhere below **Section Break (Continuous)** marker.

On **Format** menu, choose **Columns**.

Under **Presets**, click icon labeled **Three**. Click **OK**.

First three paragraphs are in single column. Rest are in three columns.

4 Change type of section break

With insertion point still in section 2, choose **Page Setup** on **File** menu.

Click **Layout** tab.

In **Section start** area, choose **New page**. Click **OK**.

Section 2 now starts new page.

5 Delete section break and see result

Click anywhere inside **Section Break (Next Page)** marker.

Tap [SHIFT]→ to select marker.

Marker isn't highlighted, but it is *selected. You delete selection as usual.*

Tap [BACKSPACE].

Entire document is now in one section with three-column format.

6 Close document without saving changes

By the way
The format change affects just the section with the insertion point (or any selected text).

Tip
Use section breaks when you want different headers in different parts of a long document. Each section can have its own headers, footers, and page numbering.

Computers *as completed on page 16 must be saved on disk.*

Insert table

You can easily add tabular information to a Microsoft Word document without setting tab stops.

DOC / 57

1 **Open Computers**

You'll insert table just below paragraph 1.

2 **Prepare to insert**

Click just before paragraph mark at end of paragraph 1.

Tap [ENTER] twice.

Insertion point should be in middle of three blank lines. You'll insert table here. It's always good to leave blank spaces around table.

3 **Insert table**

On **Table** menu, choose **Insert**, then **Table**.

Type **4** for **Number of columns**; tap [TAB]; type **4** for **Number of rows**.
Click **OK**.

Empty table with four columns and four rows appears in document. Rectangles formed by intersections of rows and columns are called "cells."

4 **Enter data in table**

Insertion point should already be in first cell.

Type `Computers in Use`. Tap [TAB] to move to next cell.

Type `1990` [TAB] `1995` [TAB] `2000`.

Tap [TAB] to move to next cell.

Insertion point moves to next row.

Continue entering text to create table shown below. Do *not* tap [TAB] after last entry.

Computers in Use	1990	1995	2000
Business	50,000	70,000	98,000
School	20,000	35,000	87,000
Home	10,000	25,000	60,000

Insert table *continued*

5 **Save document with new name**

On **File** menu, choose **Save As**. Save with name `Table` on disk.

6 **Select rows and columns**

Put arrow pointer just left of row 2. Click to select whole row.

Put pointer just above column 3. Watch pointer change to ↓. Click to select column.

Click any cell. On **Table** menu, choose **Select**, then **Row** (or **Column**).

Select submenu also allows you to select single cell or entire table.

7 **Format table**

Select row 1.

On formatting toolbar, click **B** (bold) to add bold style to column labels.

Select column 1. Watch first cell in column as you click **B**.

Button takes cue from first cell in selection; it's bold, so button removes bold.

Click **B** again to apply bold to all selected cells. Deselect cells.

8 **Adjust column width**

Put pointer on line between columns 1 and 2 (at 1.5" on ruler). Watch pointer change to vertical double line with arrows ↔.

Press and drag left to 1" mark.

Width of column 1 is reduced.

Use above steps to adjust other column widths to 1 inch also.

9 **Select columns 2, 3, and 4**

Position pointer at top of column 2. Watch for pointer to change to ↓.

Press and drag right to top of column 4, being sure to keep pointer in table.

Columns 2, 3, and 4 are selected.

10 **Change text alignment in selected cells**

On formatting toolbar, click ≡ (center).

Text is centered within cells in all three columns.

11 **Center table on page**

Select all cells in table.

On **Table** menu, choose **Table Properties**.

Dialog box like figure on next page appears.

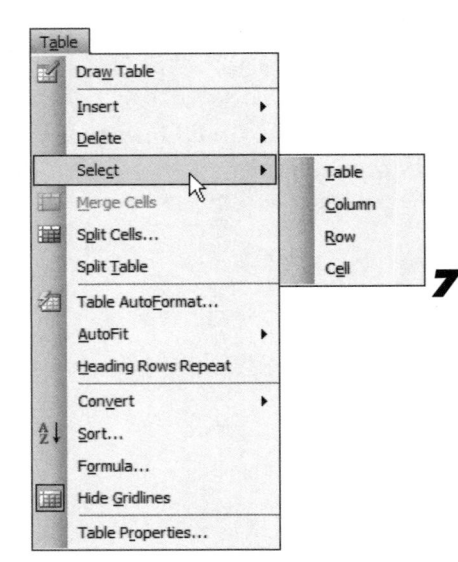

Tip
If the Table Properties *command is not on the menu, wait a few seconds or click the arrow at the bottom to see the full menu.*

Insert table *continued*

In **Alignment** area, click **Center**; then click **OK**.

Table is centered between margins.

12 Add shading

Select all cells in row 1.

On **Format** menu, choose **Borders and Shading**.

Click **Shading** tab.

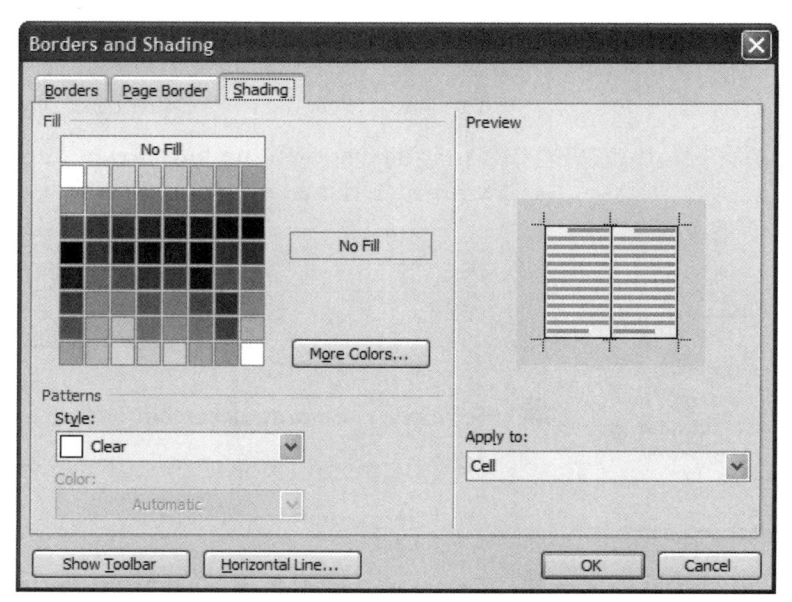

In **Fill** area, choose shade of gray at right end of first row. Click **OK**.

Click outside table to see formatting.

13 Close changed document, saving changes

> Computers *as completed on page 16 must be saved on disk.*

Set up mail merge

You can create a data document with names and addresses, link it to a form letter document, and print letters with merged data.

1 Open new document for name and address data

On standard toolbar, click ☐ (new blank document).

"Data document" for mail merge is ordinary word processor document with table containing data you want to use. First step is to insert blank table.

If necessary, switch to normal view.

2 Insert table to hold data

On **Table** menu, choose **Insert**, then **Table**.

Table must be in first blank line of document; otherwise, merge will fail.

Type **6** for **Number of columns**; tap TAB.

Type **4** for **Number of rows**.

Click **OK**.

Six columns will hold first name, last name, address, city, state, and zip code.

3 Enter headings in first row

Insertion point should already be in first cell.

Type following text:

`First` TAB `Last` TAB `Address` TAB `City` TAB `State` TAB `Zip`

Column headings are names of data fields. You'll use these field names in your form letter instead of actual data for people.

4 Enter name and address data

Tap TAB to go to first cell in next row.

Enter data shown in figure below, tapping TAB between entries. Substitute your own name and address in first row. Do *not* tap TAB after last entry.

First	Last	Address	City	State	Zip
Bonita	Sebastian	456 Pine St.	Santa Cruz	CA	95060
Bill	Gates	123 Main St.	Redmond	WA	98052
Donald	Jacobs	789 Hunt St.	Garden City	IA	50101

By the way

You can use the same data document to print mailing labels or envelopes. You do this by linking the data document to a different "main document" for each job. You'll learn about linking next.

---

5 Save and close data document

On **File** menu, choose **Save**. Save with name `People` on disk.

On **File** menu, choose **Close**.

6 Create document to become "main document" for merge

Open **Computers** from your floppy disk.

Form letter document will be based on this document.

On **File** menu, choose **Save As**. Save with name `Formltr` on disk.

Set up mail merge *continued*

7 ***View mail merge toolbar***

On **View** menu, choose **Toolbars**, then **Mail Merge**. Notice new toolbar at top.

Put pointer on first five tools (all but first two dimmed), and read names.

You'll use most of these to set up main document, link it to data document, and move placeholders for data into main document.

8 ***Make current document into main document for merge***

At left of mail merge toolbar, click 🗋 (main document setup).

In small **Main Document Type** dialog box, click **Letters**. Click OK.

9 ***Link to data document***

On mail merge toolbar, click 🗐 (open data source).

Change **Look in** location to 3½ **Floppy**. Open **People** document.

Document opens in background—no button appears on taskbar.

On mail merge toolbar, click 🗐 (mail merge recipients).

Mail Merge Recipients *dialog box shows all data from table you created in* People *document, and lets you remove some people or change sort order.*

Click **Zip** header to sort rows by zipcode. Then click **OK**.

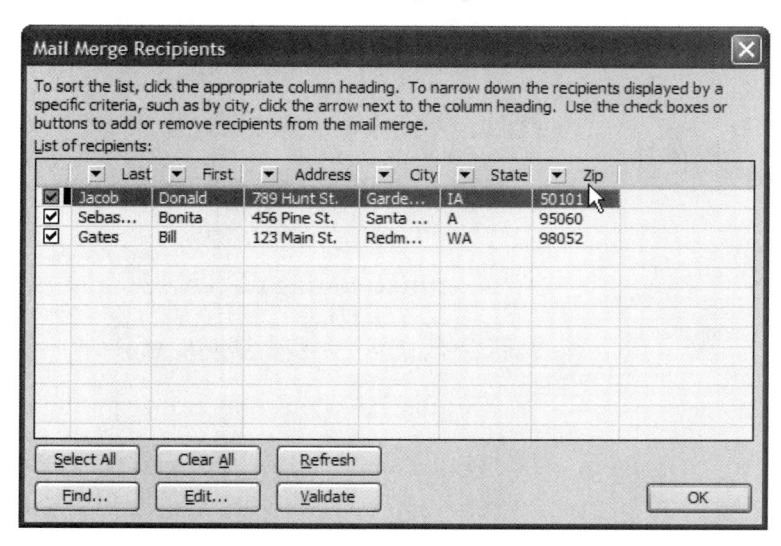

10 ***Get ready to insert placeholder fields for data***

If necessary, put insertion point at beginning of text in **Formltr** document.

Tap ENTER two or three times. Put insertion point in first blank paragraph.

Space at top of document makes it easy to rearrange placeholders after inserting them.

Set up mail merge *continued*

11 Insert placeholder fields

On mail merge toolbar, click 🖹 (insert merge fields).

Drag **Insert Merge Field** dialog box to right so first blank line can be seen.

Make sure **Database Fields** radio button at top of dialog box is selected.

In dialog box, click **First**, then **Insert** (or double-click **First**).

«First» appears at insertion point. Name came from column header in table. Data from column in table appear here in merged document.

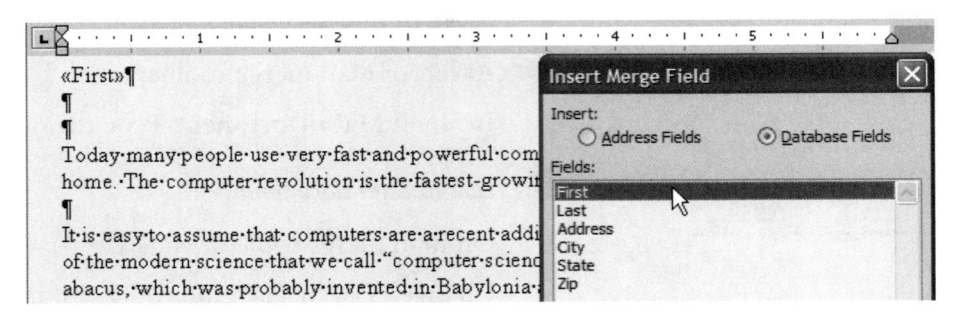

Double-click **Last** to put «Last» at insertion point.

You'll need space between names. You'll do that after all fields are inserted.

Double-click each remaining field in list. Then click **Close**.

Top of main document should look like figure below.

12 Reorganize placeholders

Put insertion point between «First» and «Last». Tap [SPACEBAR].

Put insertion point between «Last» and «Address». Tap [ENTER].

Continue editing placeholders until they look like figure at left.

13 Add salutation with placeholder

Put insertion point in empty paragraph after «Zip».

Tap [ENTER]. Type **Dear** plus space.

On mail merge toolbar, click 🖹 again.

In **Insert Merge Field** dialog box, double-click **First**. Click **Close**.

Type comma. Add or delete blank lines so only one follows salutation.

14 Save and close main document

Link to data document is saved in main document. You can do merge at any time.

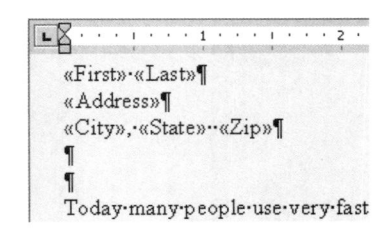

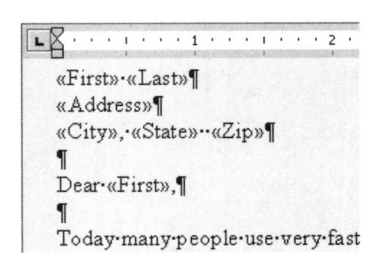

← *Complete previous activity before going on.*

Do mail merge

Once you've created a main document, linked it to a data document, and inserted placeholder fields, you're ready to merge.

1 Open main document (Formltr); if necessary, show mail merge toolbar

In dialog box asking about using SQL to update data, click **Yes**.

Process updates any changes in People *document.*

2 Check link to data document (People)

On mail merge toolbar, click 📇 (mail merge recipients).

Notice main document is still linked properly to data document, with data still in zipcode order. Click **OK**.

3 Carry out merge

On mail merge toolbar, put pointer on last four tools, and read names.

You can send merged output to different places.

Click 📄 (merge to new document) to send output to new document.

In dialog box that appears, make sure **All** is selected. Click **OK**.

Letters are merged into new Letters1 *document (in print layout view).*

If necessary, switch to normal view.

```
Donald Jacobs¶
789 Hunt St.¶
Garden City, IA  50101¶
¶
Dear Donald,¶
¶
Today many people use very fast and powerful computers in business, at school and at home.  The computer revolution is the fastest-growing technology in recorded history.¶
¶
It is easy to assume that computers are a recent addition to our lives.  However, the start of the modern science that we call "computer science" can be traced back to the dust abacus, which was probably invented in Babylonia almost 5,000 years ago.¶
¶
Throughout the centuries, there have been many inventions and innovations that aided in the evolution of computer science.  In the 1950s, two inventions dramatically changed the computer industry and caused the beginning of the "computer revolution."  The first was the transistor; the second was the integrated circuit or chip.¶
¶
Bonita Sebastian
═══════════════════ Section Break (Next Page) ═══════════════════
Bonita Sebastian¶
456 Pine St.¶
```

Scroll down and look at rest of new document. Notice section breaks.

4 Print document (optional)

5 Close files, hide toolbar, and exit Word

Close **Letters1** and **Formltr** documents without saving changes.

On **View** menu, choose **Toolbars**, then **Mail Merge** (now selected).

Exit Microsoft Word.

Tip

You could send output directly to the printer, but sending to a new document lets you preview things. If the result is OK, print it. If you need to make changes, just close the new document without saving it.

By the way

Each letter is in a separate section of the new document. Each section begins a new page and restarts any page numbers at 1.

STOP Computers *(page 16)* and CHS Note *(page 38)* must be saved on disk.

Insert hyperlink

You can create a link in one document that the user can click to go to another document.

1 Start Microsoft Word and open Computers document

2 Insert hyperlink to CHS Note document

In second line of **Computers** document, highlight **fastest-growing technology**.

On **Insert** menu, choose **Hyperlink** (or tap CTRL K).

If necessary set **Look in** location to **3½ Floppy** (or other place files are saved).

Click **CHS Note** document on list.

Document name appears in Address *text box.*

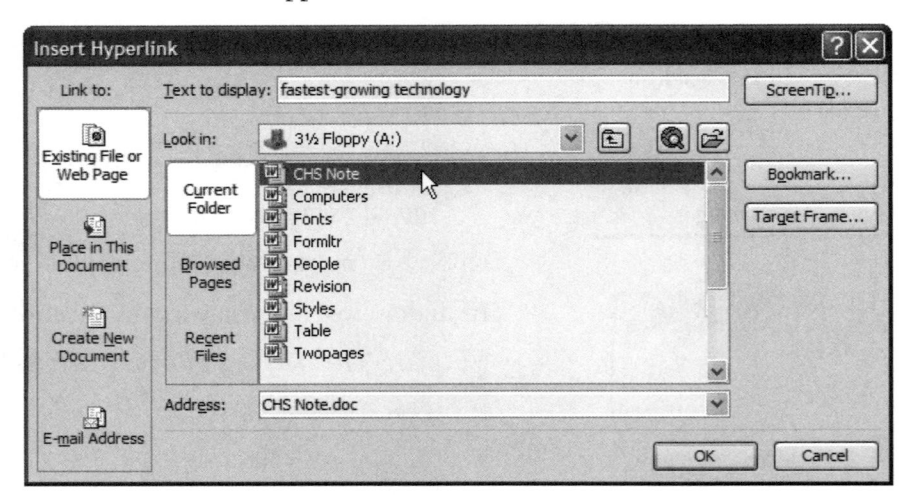

By the way
You can also create a hyperlink within the same Word document or from a Word document on your computer to a page on the World Wide Web. If you don't know the page name, or URL, you can browse the Web and find it.

Click **OK**. Notice underline and color of hyperlink text.

3 Use link

Position pointer over hyperlink. Notice text box.

With CTRL held down, click hyperlink.

Notice pointer becomes small hand when you hold down CTRL.

CHS Note *document opens and becomes active. Web toolbar appears.*

Look at buttons on taskbar.

Both Computers *and* CHS Note *are now open.*

4 Move back and forth between documents

On new Web toolbar, click (back) to see **Computers** document.

Button works like same button on Web browser.

Press CTRL and click hyperlink again to see **CHS Note** document.

5 Exit Microsoft Word without saving changes

> 🛑 Computers *as completed on page 16 must be on disk.*

Save as Web page

You can convert an existing document to a Web page document. Word creates the Hypertext Markup Language (HTML) code.

DOC / 65

1 *Start Microsoft Word and open Computers document from floppy disk*

2 *Change Computers document*

Delete all text and empty lines except paragraphs shown in figure below.

> Today many people use very fast and powerful computers in business, at school and at home. The computer revolution is the fastest-growing technology in recorded history.¶
> It is easy to assume that computers are a recent addition to our lives. However, the start of the modern science that we call "computer science" can be traced back to the dust abacus, which was probably invented in Babylonia almost 5,000 years ago.¶

Put insertion point at start of paragraph 1.

Type `Computer History Society` ENTER.

Type `Join Now` ENTER.

Click anywhere in first new line.

On styles drop-down list (at left of formatting toolbar), choose **Heading 1**.

Click anywhere in second new line. Change style to **Heading 2**.

Click in body paragraph 1. Change style to **Heading 3**.

Text should now look like figure below.

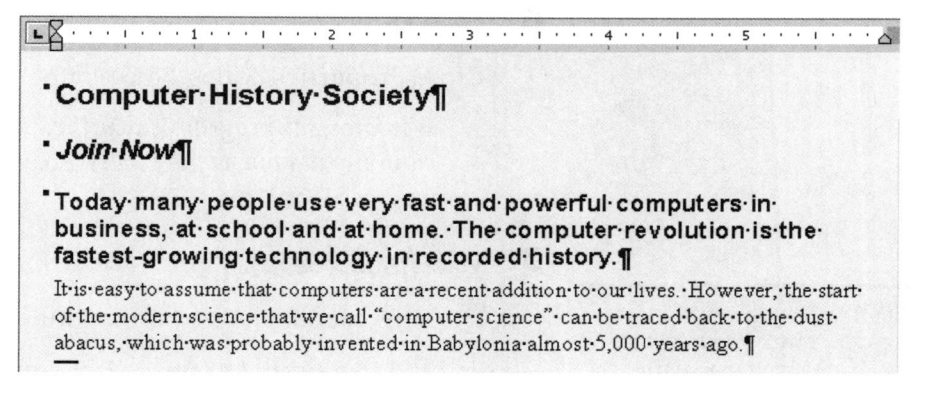

> **Computer History Society¶**
>
> *Join Now¶*
>
> **Today many people use very fast and powerful computers in business, at school and at home. The computer revolution is the fastest-growing technology in recorded history.¶**
> It is easy to assume that computers are a recent addition to our lives. However, the start of the modern science that we call "computer science" can be traced back to the dust abacus, which was probably invented in Babylonia almost 5,000 years ago.¶

3 *Rename and save document as Web page*

On **File** menu, choose **Save as Web Page** (*not* Save).

Type `CHSWeb` as file name.

Notice **Single File Web Page** in **Save as type** box.

Click **Save**.

4 *Exit Word*

On **File** menu, choose **Exit**.

By the way

If you happened to choose Save As *instead of* Save as Web Page, *you could then choose* Single File Web Page *on the* Save as type *drop-down list. The results would be the same.*

66 / Word Processing with Microsoft Word   ***Save as Web page***   *continued*

5 Check document type of file saved on disk

On desktop, click **Start** on taskbar, then **My Computer** on list at upper right of menu. (In Windows 98 or 2000, double-click **My Computer** icon.)

In **My Computer** window, double-click 3½ **Floppy** icon (or folder where you've saved files).

Scroll as necessary to see **CHSWeb** icon. Change view to **Icons**.

Icon is for file you just saved. Notice different shape from Word file icon.

Right-click **CHSWeb** icon. On shortcut menu, choose **Properties**.

Top of dialog box shows type of file is HTML or MHTML (Web page) and name of Web browser program that automatically opens file.

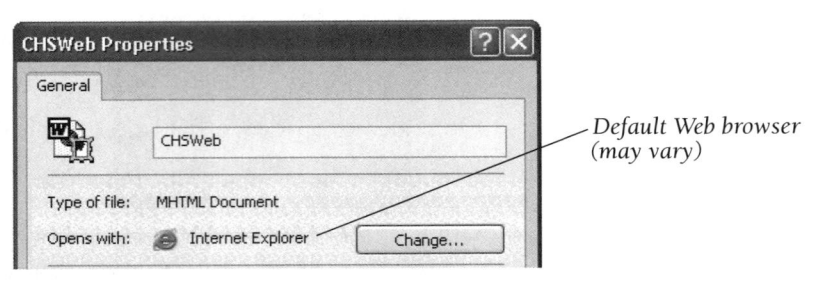

Computers — Word document
Microsoft Word Document
20 KB

CHSWeb — Web document
MHTML Document
5 KB

Default Web browser (may vary)

6 Open file in Web browser

Close **Properties** dialog box. Double-click **CHSWeb** icon.

Web browser program (identified in your Properties dialog box) begins running and opens file CHSWeb. Contents and format are same as in original Word file.

7 View HTML codes

By the way
Notepad *is a very simple text editor. Your browser program uses it to show the text and HTML codes that are the source of the Web page.*

On **View** menu, choose **Source**. Maximize **CHSWeb - Notepad** window.

Scroll down until you see **<h1>Computer History Society</h1>**.

This part of document has text (with format codes) seen on Web page.

Actual text in file (angle brackets show HTML format codes)

```
<h1>Computer History Society</h1>

<h2>Join Now</h2>

<h3>Today many people use very fast and powerful computers in business, at
school and at home. The computer revolution is the fastest-growing
technology in recorded history.</h3>

<p class=MsoNormal>It is easy to assume that computers are a recent
addition to our lives. However, the start of the modern science that we
call &#8220;computer science&#8221; can be traced back to the dust abacus,
which was probably invented in <st1:place w:st="on">Babylonia</st1:place>
almost 5,000 years ago.</p>
```

Exit NotePad program.

8 Close browser window, and shut down computer

Microsoft PowerPoint 2003
Presentations

68 Start Microsoft PowerPoint
69 Set up new document
70 Draw graphic objects
71 Move, resize & delete object
72 Use drawing aids
74 Draw more objects
75 Select objects
76 Use line tools
77 Use Basic Shapes tools
78 Modify objects
79 Duplicate objects
80 Change stacking order
81 Align objects
82 Attach text to object
84 Change object fill
86 Change outline & shadow
88 Create presentation
90 Add text to slide
91 Add new slide
92 Use outline
94 View slides
95 Add dynamic effects
97 Check spelling
98 Edit & rearrange text
100 Rearrange slides
101 Delete slide
102 Change text formats
103 Use slide master
104 Add slide with chart
106 Format chart
108 Add clip art
110 Insert WordArt
111 Add objects to master
113 Change color scheme
114 Apply design template
115 Create speaker notes
117 Create audience handouts
118 Print overheads
119 Print notes & handouts
120 Use AutoContent wizard

Start Microsoft PowerPoint

You are now ready to start the Microsoft PowerPoint application running on your computer.

> **By the way**
> On pages 68–87, you'll learn to use drawing tools to create and modify objects on a slide. If you are already familiar with drawing tools and now want to learn how to build a presentation out of a set of slides, skip ahead to page 88.

1 **Start computer, Windows, and PowerPoint**

Switch on computer and start Windows (see page 2).

Start Microsoft PowerPoint (see page 5, but choose **Microsoft Office PowerPoint 2003**).

If Office Assistant appears, do steps in tip on page 5, beside step 3.

2 **Choose customizing options**

On **Tools** menu, choose **Customize**.

Click **Options** tab. Click to put marks in first two check boxes.

Click **Close** button.

3 **Choose view options**

On **View** menu, click **Ruler** unless it is already checked.

On **View** menu, put pointer at **Toolbars**. Make sure **Standard**, **Formatting**, **Drawing**, and **Task Pane** are checked.

Window with new blank document should look similar to figure below.

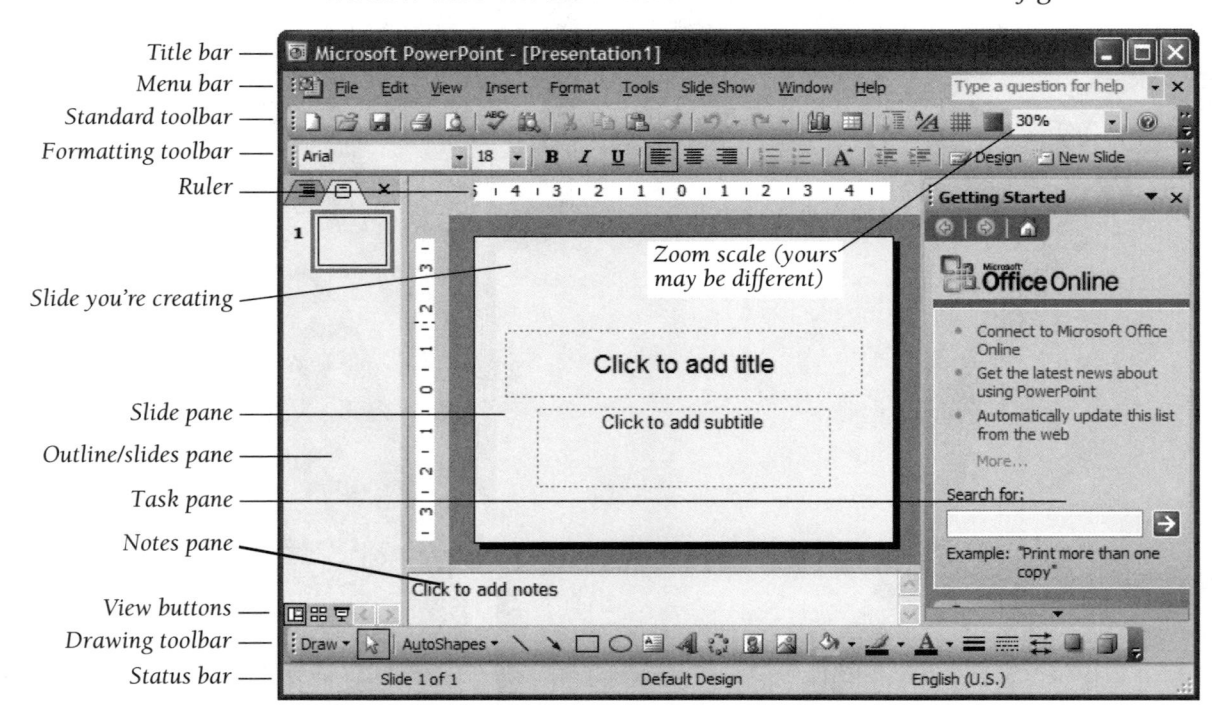

Labels on figure: Title bar, Menu bar, Standard toolbar, Formatting toolbar, Ruler, Slide you're creating, Slide pane, Outline/slides pane, Task pane, Notes pane, View buttons, Drawing toolbar, Status bar. Zoom scale (yours may be different).

4 **Set more options**

On **Tools** menu, choose **Options**.

On **Spelling and Style** tab, remove mark from first check box.

On **Edit** tab, remove mark from first check box in **Text** area.

On **View** tab, make sure marks appear in all text boxes. Click **OK**.

← *Complete previous activity before going on.*

Set up new document

PowerPoint begins with a new blank document. You'll set up a blank slide for learning to use the drawing tools.

Tip
A slide in PowerPoint is like a page in a word processing document.

1 Explore normal view of Microsoft PowerPoint window

Notice familiar items at top: standard toolbar and formatting toolbar.

In main area, notice four panes labeled in figure on page 68.

Slide pane shows reduced image of slide you'll be working on. Rulers (and zoom scale percentage) show actual slide is much larger: 10" by 7½".

At bottom, notice new view buttons at left and new drawing toolbar.

2 Change slide layout

On **Format** menu, choose **Slide Layout**. Notice changed task pane.

In **Slide Layout** task pane, use vertical scroll bar to see layout icons.

You'll use some of these later to create presentations. Blank layout is best for exploring drawing tools.

In **Content Layouts** area, move pointer over blank layout icon. Click it.

Slide is now blank.

3 Enlarge slide pane

On **View** menu, choose **Task Pane** (now checked) to hide pane.

At top of outline/slides pane at left, click ☒ to close it and notes pane.

Slide pane fills most of area between top and bottom toolbars. (If not, choose Fit *on zoom drop-down list.)*

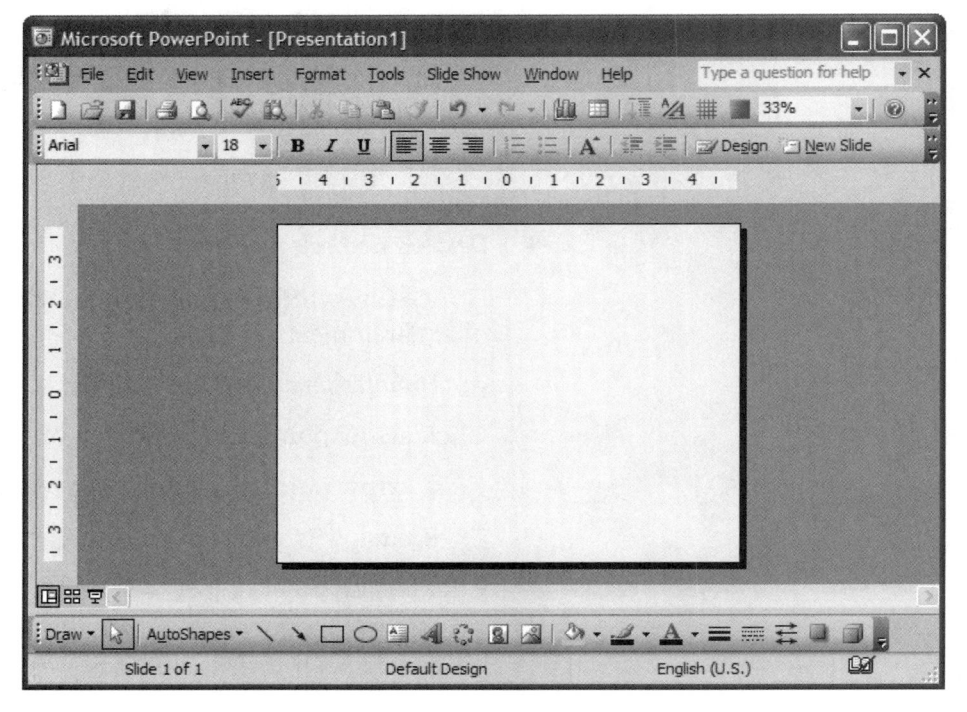

4 Save empty file with name Drawing (see page 16 for reminder of steps)

You'll need floppy disk or other place to save file.

Complete previous activity before going on.

Draw graphic objects

Microsoft PowerPoint provides tools to add simple or complex graphics that you draw for a slide or an entire presentation.

1 Look at drawing tools

If drawing toolbar is hidden, choose **Toolbars** on **View** menu, then **Drawing** on submenu.

Toolbar normally appears at bottom of screen.

Move pointer to drawing toolbar. For each tool, read name below pointer.

2 Draw simple object (method 1)

On drawing toolbar, click ▫ (rectangle tool).

Highlighted square box in toolbar shows which tool is active.

Position pointer near upper-left corner of slide area.

Pointer shape is now crosshair +.

Press mouse button and drag down and to right.

Release mouse button.

Colored rectangle with black outline appears where you drew. Active tool now is ▫ (selection tool) at left of drawing toolbar. Pointer shape is ▫.

3 Draw simple object (method 2)

On drawing toolbar, click ▫ (rectangle tool).

Click in blank area of slide.

Equal-sided rectangle (square) appears where you clicked.

4 Deselect and select object

Notice tiny white round handles on borders and green rotate handle at top of square object.

Handles mean object is selected. Rotate handle allows object to be rotated.

Click arrow pointer in clear area of slide to deselect object.

Click arrow pointer inside either rectangle. Notice handles.

Rectangle is selected.

Click inside other object to select it (and deselect first object you clicked).

You'll learn all about selecting objects on page 75.

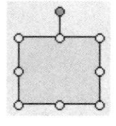

Complete previous activity before going on.

Move, resize & delete object

After you have created an object, you can modify it by moving it, changing its size or shape, rotating it, or deleting it.

PPT/ 71

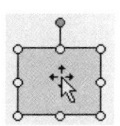

1 Move object (method 1)

If necessary, put pointer inside rectangle. Notice change in pointer shape.

Press mouse button and drag to right. Release mouse button.

Rectangle moves to new location.

2 Move object (method 2)

If object has no handles, click inside object to select it.

Watch object as you tap each arrow key on keyboard three or four times.

Object moves in small increments in direction of arrow.

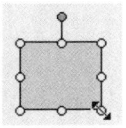

3 Make object smaller

If object has no handles, click inside object to select it.

Move pointer carefully to handle at lower right.

Pointer shape changes to ↘.

Press mouse button and drag handle up and to left. Release mouse button.

Rectangle is smaller.

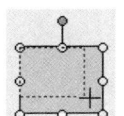

4 Make object larger

Follow step 3, except drag same handle down and to right. Release mouse button.

5 Change width of object

If object has no handles, click inside object to select it.

Move pointer carefully to handle at middle of right side.

Pointer shape changes to ↔.

Press mouse button and drag handle to right. Release mouse button.

Rectangle is wider.

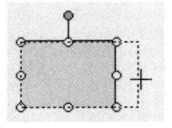

6 Rotate object

Put pointer on green rotate handle at top of selected object.

Press mouse button and drag handle partway around center of object. Release mouse button.

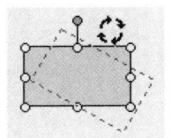

7 Delete objects

If object has no handles, click inside object to select it.

Tap [BACKSPACE].

Use same method to delete other object.

> **!** Presentation file must be open in normal view.

Use drawing aids

Freehand drawing can be difficult. Microsoft PowerPoint eases the task.

> **Tip**
> You can also create a standard-size equal-sided object by clicking with a tool in a blank area. Pressing and dragging gives you more control of the size of the object.

1 Draw equal-sided object

On drawing toolbar, click ▢ (rectangle tool).

On keyboard, hold [SHIFT] down.

Position pointer near upper-left corner of slide area.

Press mouse button and drag down and to right.

Release mouse button first; then release [SHIFT].

Equal-sided rectangle (square) appears.

2 Move object horizontally or vertically

On keyboard, hold [SHIFT] down.

Try to press object and drag to right and down.

Release mouse button, then [SHIFT].

You can move object only horizontally or vertically while pressing [SHIFT].

3 Resize object without changing shape

Make sure object is selected (has handles).

On keyboard, hold [SHIFT] down.

Move pointer to handle at lower right.

Press and drag to right and down. Release mouse button, then [SHIFT].

Object is enlarged but keeps shape.

4 Delete object

Make sure object is selected.

Tap [BACKSPACE].

5 Draw object from center out

On drawing toolbar, click ◯ (oval tool).

On keyboard, press and hold [CTRL].

Position pointer near middle of slide area.

Press mouse button and drag down and to right.

Oval grows in all directions from place where you began to drag.

Release mouse button first; then release [CTRL].

6 Delete object

With oval selected, tap [BACKSPACE].

Use drawing aids continued   PPT/ 73

7 *Draw equal-sided object from center out*

On drawing toolbar, click ▢ (rectangle tool).

On keyboard, hold down both CTRL and SHIFT.

From middle of slide area, drag down and to right. Release button and keys.

Square is drawn from center out.

8 *Use grid and guides*

On **View** menu, choose **Grid and Guides**.

In **Grid settings** area, click **Display grid on screen**. In **Guide settings** area, click **Display drawing guides on screen**. Click **OK**.

Dotted grid appears. Dashed horizontal and vertical guides also appear.

Put pointer on vertical guide (outside object); press and drag to right.

Distance (in inches from center) appears at pointer.

Watch square as you drag it near either guide.

Edge or center of square "jumps" to guide.

Delete square.

9 *Use guides to position new object*

On drawing toolbar, click ⊙ (oval tool). On keyboard, press and hold CTRL SHIFT.

Position pointer close to intersection of guides. Press mouse button and drag down and to right. Release button, then keys.

Result is perfect circle with center exactly at place guides cross.

Delete circle.

10 *Switch guides off*

On **View** menu, choose **Grid and Guides** again. Remove check marks from grid and guide settings; then click **OK**.

11 *Close file without saving changes*

Tip

If you don't see the Grid and Guides *command on the* View *menu, wait a few seconds or click the arrow at the bottom to see the full menu.*

🛑 *Drawing file as saved on page 69 must be on disk.*

Draw more objects

The drawing toolbar has many tools for creating objects. They work like the rectangle tool.

1 Open Drawing file

On **File** menu, choose **Open**.

In **Look in** box at top, make sure setting is 3½ **Floppy** (or other location where you're saving files).

Double-click **Drawing** on list of files at this location.

Make sure you see blank slide 1 in normal view. If necessary, delete any objects on slide.

2 Use steps below to draw objects in this figure

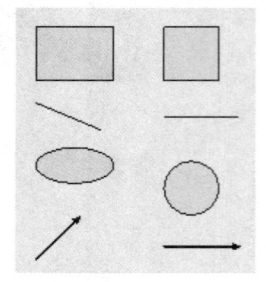

3 Draw objects shown at left side of figure

On drawing toolbar, use ▢ (rectangle tool) to draw figure at upper left.

When you release mouse button, object appears and is selected.

Use ◣ (line tool) to draw first diagonal line at left in figure.

Use ○ (oval tool) to draw third figure at left.

Use ◥ (arrow tool) to draw fourth figure at left, starting at lower left.

4 Draw objects shown at right side of figure

Use same four tools, but this time hold (SHIFT) down as you drag pointer to draw each object.

Keep holding (SHIFT) down until after you release mouse button.

With line and arrow tools, (SHIFT) forces line to be exactly horizontal, vertical, or diagonal. With other tools, (SHIFT) creates equal-sided object.

5 Save changed presentation file

On **File** menu, choose **Save**.

Next you'll use file to explore selecting multiple objects.

Tip
If you don't like the object you have drawn, tap (BACKSPACE) to delete it. Then draw it again.

Tip
To use a tool more than once, double-click it.

← *Complete previous activity before going on.*

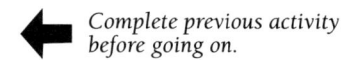

Select objects

Many commands act only on selected objects. You can select one object or several objects at once.

PPT/ 75

1 Select single objects on slide

Click pointer inside circle.

Click pointer inside square.

> *Handles show selected object.*

2 Use selection marquee to select several objects

In slide area, position pointer between rectangle and square.

Press and drag diagonally so "marquee" (dashed outline) is like figure.

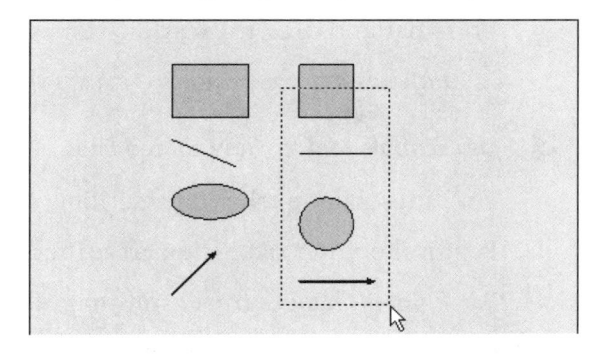

Release mouse button.

> *Square is not selected. Only objects completely inside selection marquee are selected.*

3 Add objects to selection

Hold down [SHIFT] as you click rectangle and square.

4 Remove object from selection

Hold down [SHIFT] as you click circle.

5 Delete all selected objects

On **Edit** menu, choose **Clear** (or tap [BACKSPACE]).

6 Undo change

On **Edit** menu, choose **Undo Clear** (or tap [CTRL][Z], or click ↶ on standard toolbar).

7 Select all objects

On **Edit** menu, choose **Select All** (or tap [CTRL][A]).

8 Deselect all selected objects

Click in slide area away from any object.

By the way

Selection handles on shapes other than rectangles appear on an invisible bounding rectangle.

Tip

If the Clear command does not appear on the Edit menu, wait a few seconds or click the arrow at the bottom to see the full menu.

Complete previous activity before going on.

Use line tools

In addition to the standard drawing tools, Microsoft PowerPoint provides special tools for more complex objects.

1 Add blank slide

On **Insert** menu (or formatting toolbar), choose **New Slide**.

You should see Slide 2 of 2 *at left of status bar at bottom of window.*

In **Slide Layout** task pane, choose **Blank** layout. Click ⊠ to close pane.

2 Display line tools palette

On drawing toolbar, click **AutoShapes** to see menu.

Move pointer up to **Lines**, then horizontally to bar at top of submenu.

Press bar and drag to "tear off" **Lines** palette from menu.

Palettes are like windows, except that they always stay in front.

3 Use scribble tool to draw curved lines

On **Lines** palette, click 📝 (scribble tool).

Position pointer over slide area. Press and drag to begin drawing object.

Pointer changes from arrow to pencil shape.

Continue pressing and dragging to create object. Release mouse button to end drawing.

Object is selected. Same methods as before can be used to move, resize, reshape, or delete object.

Tip
If you have trouble selecting a scribble object, click on its line.

4 Use freeform tool to draw polygons

On **Lines** palette, click 🔲 (freeform tool).

Position pointer over clear area of slide. Click to establish starting point.

Move pointer to new position and click to create first line.

Continue moving and clicking (not dragging!) to draw polygon.

Click starting point to close polygon.

Tip
You can double-click to end line drawing without closing the figure.

5 Combine methods in one object

You can combine methods to create more complex objects.

On **Lines** palette, click 🔲 (freeform tool).

Freeform tool can create curved lines like scribble tool.

Try drawing ice cream cone in figure at left (move pointer and click to draw straight lines; drag to draw curves). Double-click to end drawing.

6 Close Lines palette

Click ⊠ (close box) on title bar of **Lines** palette.

7 Save file with new slide

Complete previous activity before going on.

Use Basic Shapes tools

PowerPoint has dozens of drawing tools that automatically create complex, useful objects for your slides.

1 Add blank slide

On **Insert** menu (or formatting toolbar), choose **New Slide**.

You should see Slide 3 of 3 at left of status bar at bottom of window.

In **Slide Layout** task pane, choose **Blank** layout. Click ✕ to close pane.

2 Display Basic Shapes palette

On drawing toolbar, click **AutoShapes**. Move pointer to **Basic Shapes**.

Carefully point to bar at top of submenu; then press and drag to right to "tear off" palette.

You can press and drag title bar to move palette where you want in window.

3 Use Basic Shapes drawing tools

Click tool that looks like first object in figure below.

Draw object on slide same way you drew rectangle on page 70.

Use tools on **Basic Shapes** palette to draw other objects in figure.

4 Add new blank slide (see step 1)

5 Draw large cube

On **Basic Shapes** palette, click ▢ (cube tool).

Position pointer over clear area of slide.

With mouse button held down, press and drag diagonally, this time making cube larger.

Release mouse button.

6 Close Basic Shapes palette

Click ✕ (close box) on title bar of **Basic Shapes** palette.

7 Save file with new slide

Tip

You can also quickly create a small, standard sized basic shape on a slide. Click the basic shape tool you want, then click on the slide where you want the object to appear.

Complete previous activity before going on.

Modify objects

AutoShapes and freeform objects often have special handles for modifying their shapes.

1 Adjust shape of AutoShape object

Select cube. Notice yellow, diamond-shaped handle at left.

Many objects created using AutoShape tools have adjustment handle in addition to regular selection handles.

Press and drag adjustment handle down. Release mouse button.

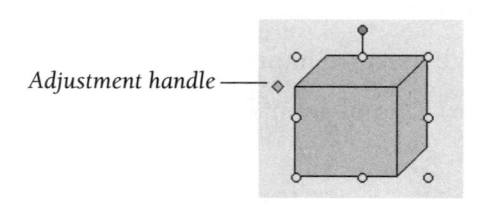

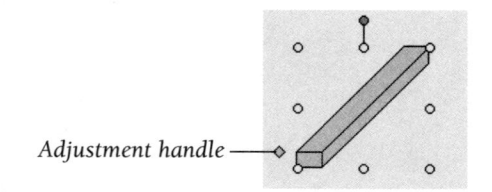

2 Undo change

On **Edit** menu, choose **Undo Adjust Object**.

3 Change object to different AutoShape

Make sure cube is selected.

On drawing toolbar, click **Draw**. On menu, choose **Change AutoShape**, then **Basic Shapes**.

Click ☺. Press and drag adjustment handle up and down.

Smiley face of same size replaces cube. Handle makes smile or frown.

4 Edit freeform object

Tap [PAGE UP] until you see slide 2 with freeform objects you drew (page 76).

Click polygon to select it.

On drawing toolbar, click **Draw**. Choose **Edit Points**.

Black square appears each place you clicked to create object.

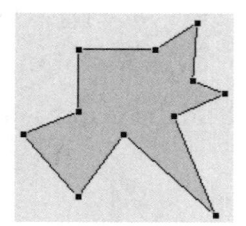

Drag squares on object to change shape.

When finished, click outside object.

5 Return to first slide; save and close file

Tap [CTRL][HOME] to go to beginning of file (slide 1).

On **File** menu, choose **Save**. On **File** menu, choose **Close**.

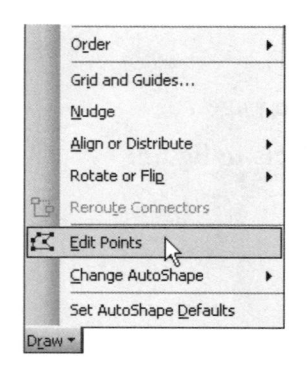

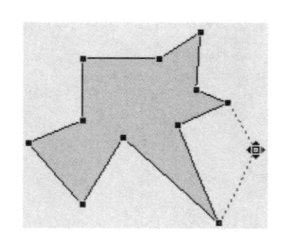

Duplicate objects

Frequently you want multiple copies of the same object. You can copy and paste objects or duplicate objects.

1 Create new presentation with blank slide

On standard toolbar, click 🗋 (new).

Notice **Slide Layout** task pane at right. In **Content Layouts** area of task pane, click **Blank** layout.

Close task pane. Close outline and notes pane.

By the way
If you've just started PowerPoint, you automatically have a new document open, and there's no need to click the toolbar button.

---

2 Copy and paste object

Use 🔲 (rectangle tool) to draw small rectangle on left side of slide.

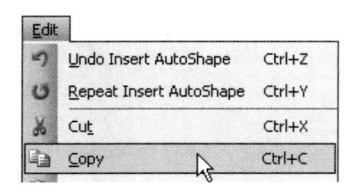

Make sure object is selected.

On **Edit** menu, choose **Copy** (or click 🗐 on standard toolbar).

On **Edit** menu, choose **Paste** (or click 🗈 on standard toolbar).

Copy appears slightly below and to right of original.

Move copy to right and line up with original.

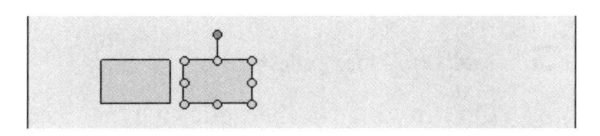

On **Edit** menu, again choose **Paste**.

Another copy appears in same place as first copy originally appeared.

3 Select and delete both copies

Original rectangle should remain on slide.

4 Duplicate object

Select rectangle. On **Edit** menu, choose **Duplicate**.

So far, effect is same as copying and pasting.

Move copy to right and line up with original.

On **Edit** menu, choose **Duplicate**.

This duplicate is pasted in relation to second as you positioned second in relation to original. Both object and its location are duplicated.

On **Edit** menu, choose **Duplicate**.

This duplicate is pasted in relation to third as third was pasted in relation to second.

Tip
If the Duplicate command does not appear on the Edit menu, wait a few seconds or click the arrow at the bottom to see the full menu.

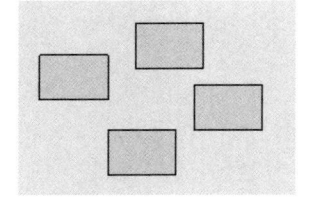

5 Move rectangles

Leave first rectangle alone. Move others so they resemble figure at left.

6 Save new file on disk

On **File** menu, choose **Save**. Save file with name `Objects`.

Complete previous activity before going on.

Change stacking order

Each new object is on a layer in front of the rest of the objects, but you can change the order of the layers.

1 Add blank slide

With document **Objects** open, on formatting toolbar, click **New Slide**.

In **Slide Layout** task pane, choose **Blank** layout. Click ⊠ to close pane.

2 Create objects in order shown by numbers in figure below

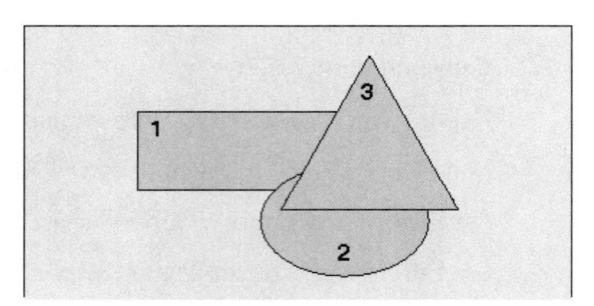

Make sizes and positions match figure. Notice stacking order.

Each new object is on layer in front of older object(s).

3 Tear off Order palette

On drawing toolbar, click **Draw** to see menu.

Move pointer up to **Order**, then horizontally to bar at top of submenu.

Press bar and drag away to "tear off" **Order** palette from menu.

4 Move triangle behind oval

Select triangle if it does not already have handles.

On **Order** palette, click 🗇 (send backward).

Layer with triangle is now behind oval but still in front of rectangle.

5 Move oval layer behind all other objects

Select oval. On **Order** palette, click 🗇 (send to back).

Layer with oval is now behind others.

6 Explore other commands

On **Order** palette, click 🗇 (bring to front).

Layer with oval is now in front.

Select rectangle. On **Order** palette, click 🗇 (bring forward).

Layer with rectangle is now in front of triangle but behind oval.

7 Use any commands to return layers to original order

8 Close Order palette

Complete previous activity before going on.

Align objects

Microsoft PowerPoint allows you to line objects up with one another at the top, bottom, middle, left, or right.

PPT/ 81

1 Tear off palette

On drawing toolbar **Draw** menu, tear off **Align or Distribute** palette.

If **Relative to Slide** button is boxed, click it.

2 Align objects by left edges

Select all objects.

You must select objects you want to line up.

On **Align or Distribute** palette, click (align left).

Left edges of all objects are now lined up with top of triangle. Leftmost object (rectangle) defines final location of alignment.

3 Undo alignment change

On **Edit** menu, choose **Undo Align Object** (or click).

4 Align objects by top edges

On **Align or Distribute** palette, click (align top).

Tops of all objects are now lined up with top of triangle. Topmost object defines location of alignment.

On **Edit** menu, choose **Undo Align Object** (or click).

5 Center all objects

On **Align or Distribute** palette, click (align center), then (align middle).

Centers of all objects are in same place.

6 Undo two alignment changes.

Click arrow to right of . On list choose *second* **Align Object**.

7 Distribute objects vertically

Deselect all objects. Drag oval down about 3".

Select all objects again.

On **Align or Distribute** palette, click (distribute vertically).

Top and bottom objects stay put. Object between moves so space between objects is same.

On **Align or Distribute** palette, click (align center).

Centers are aligned vertically and distributed vertically.

8 Close palette; close Objects file without saving changes

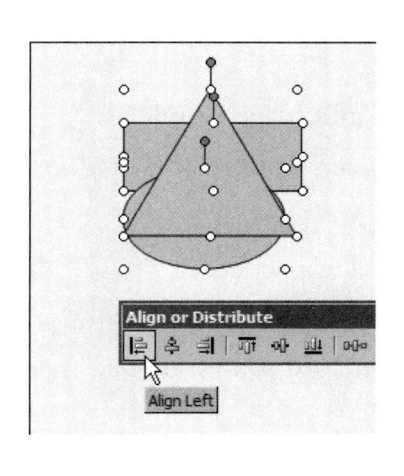

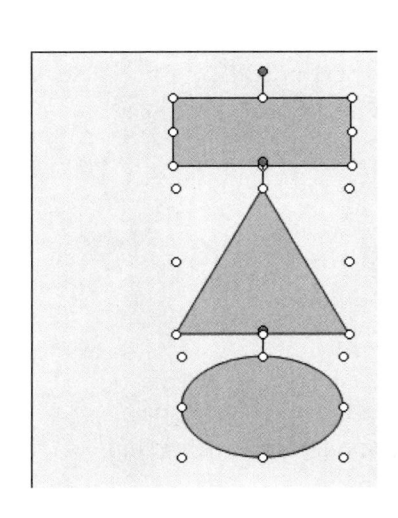

File Objects as completed on page 79 must be saved on disk.

Attach text to object

Frequently when you draw an object, you write a label on it. In Microsoft PowerPoint, you can attach the text to the object.

1 Open file Objects

Slide 1 with four rectangles appears.

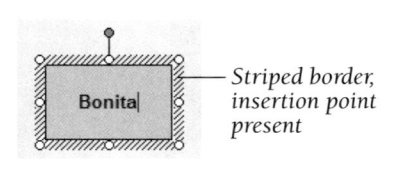

— Striped border, insertion point present

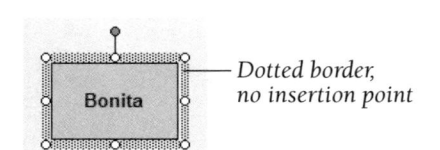

2 Attach label to first rectangle

Click left rectangle.

White selection handles indicate object is selected.

Type your first name. Notice name in rectangle and striped border.

Border means object is text box. Stripes show you're entering or editing text.

— Dotted border, no insertion point

Click inside box away from text. Notice dotted border.

Dotted border means whole box is selected as single object.

Click inside text. Notice insertion point. Notice striped border.

Box changes from graphic mode to text mode. All text in presentations is in boxes, so you need to understand how they work.

3 Explore text mode (striped border)

Drag through part of your name in text box.

Border stays striped. Mode is text.

On formatting toolbar, click **B** (bold). On font size list, choose **36**.

Only selected characters are affected in text mode. (Type appears smaller than 36 point because small zoom scale is in effect.)

Try using arrow keys → and ←.

In text mode, keys move insertion point.

4 Explore graphic mode (dotted border)

Click inside box away from text. Notice dotted border.

Mode is now graphic. Whole object is selected.

By the way

If you use the mouse to move a box now in text mode, the mode switches to graphic and is left that way.

On formatting toolbar, click **B** (bold). On font size list, choose **36**.

In graphic mode, text formatting applies to all text in box.

Try using arrow keys → and ←.

In graphic mode, keys move whole object.

5 Edit attached text

Double-click your name in rectangle.

All text is highlighted. Mode is text (striped border).

Type **1**.

Entered text replaces highlighted text. In text mode, text editing and formatting work same as in word processing.

Attach text to object continued PPT/ 83

6 *Add attached text to other objects*

Select bottom rectangle and type **2**.

Mode switches to text when you type.

Select other rectangles, and type numbers shown in figure in step 7.

7 *Format all text at once*

On **Edit Menu**, choose **Select All**.

Notice handles and borders on all objects.

All are selected in graphic mode (dotted borders).

On formatting toolbar, click **B** (bold). On font size list, choose **36**.

Click clear area of slide to deselect everything.

Slide area should look like figure below.

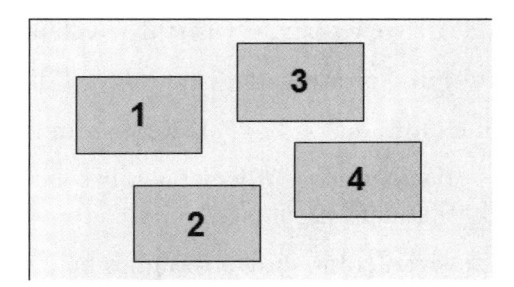

8 *Change objects*

Click object 1. Put pointer on handle at upper left; drag handle to make object bigger, as in figure below.

Mode is graphic when you change size by dragging handle.

Make object 2 wider. Make object 3 shorter.

Select object 4.

On **Draw** menu on toolbar, choose **Change AutoShape**, then **Basic Shapes**.

Click oval shape.

Object 4 changes to oval with same size and same attached text.

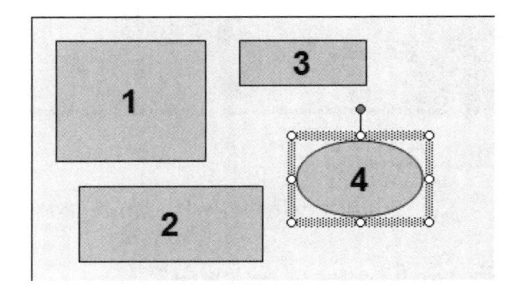

9 *Save changed Objects file*

Complete previous activity before going on.

Change object fill

New PowerPoint objects are filled with a solid light blue color. You can modify the fill attribute in several ways.

1 *Tear off fill color palette*

On drawing toolbar, click arrow at right side of ▨▾ (fill color).

Put pointer on dotted bar at top of menu; drag menu up as palette.

2 *Switch object fill off and back on*

Select rectangle 1.

On **Fill Color** palette, choose **No Fill**.

Fill color is removed. Rectangle is transparent now.

On same palette, choose **Automatic**.

— Automatic colors

Automatic (light blue) fill is added to object. Different types of objects have different automatic colors (see page 113 for more about this).

3 *Change object fill color*

Make sure rectangle 1 is still selected.

On **Fill Color** palette, click **More Fill Colors**.

In **Colors** dialog box, click **Custom** tab, then **Standard** tab.

Each tab gives different way of choosing colors. Custom gives more control. Standard is simpler.

Click red color shown in figure below.

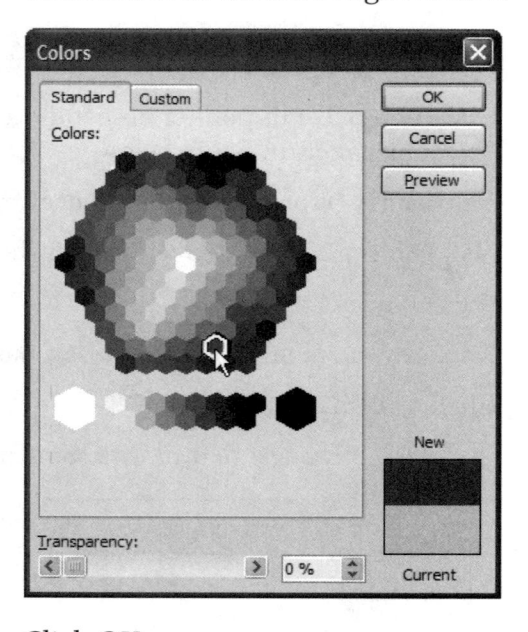

Click **OK**.

Rectangle 1 is filled with solid red. New color appears on palette.

4 *Change fill color of rectangle 2*

Select rectangle 2. Follow step 3, but choose any dark blue color.

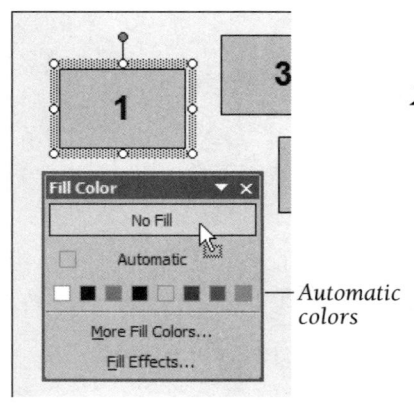

Tip

You can click the Preview *button to see the effect without closing the dialog box. If you don't like the result, you can change colors. You may have to move the dialog box to see the result. Press and drag using the dialog box title bar.*

Change object fill continued   PPT/ 85

5 *Change fill from solid to gradient*

On **Fill Color** palette, choose **Fill Effects**. If necessary, click **Gradient** tab.

In **Colors** area, choose **One color**.

You can also blend two different colors in gradient fills.

In **Shading styles** area, choose **Vertical**; then click variant you like.

Click **OK** to see fill in rectangle 2.

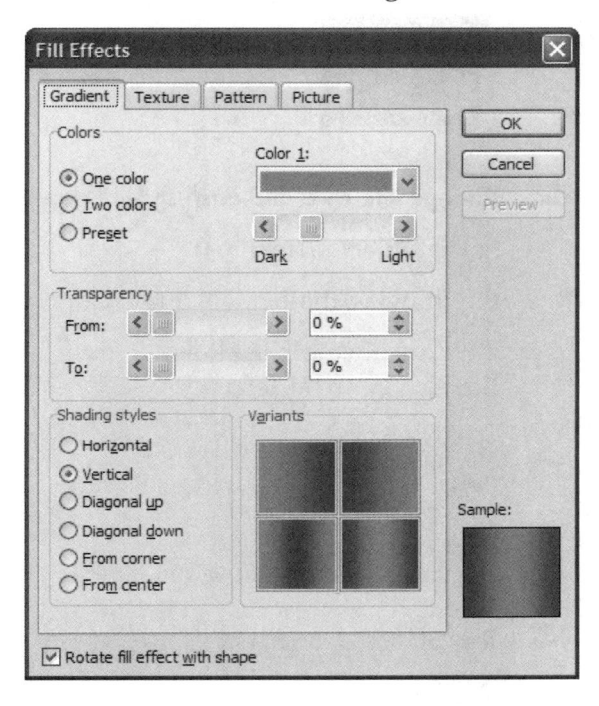

6 *Add other fills*

Select rectangle 3.

On **Fill Color** palette, choose **Fill Effects**. Click **Texture** tab to see new fills.

Choose one you like; then click **OK** to see result.

Select object 4 (oval).

On **Fill Color** palette, choose **Fill Effects**. Click **Pattern** tab to see fills.

On **Foreground** drop-down list, choose red color.

Choose pattern you like, and click **OK**.

7 *Close palette; save changed file*

By the way
In patterned fills, the current fill color appears as the foreground, with white as the default color of the background.

Complete previous activity before going on.

Change outline & shadow

In addition to modifying an object's fill, you can change the line color, style, and pattern; and you can add and adjust a shadow.

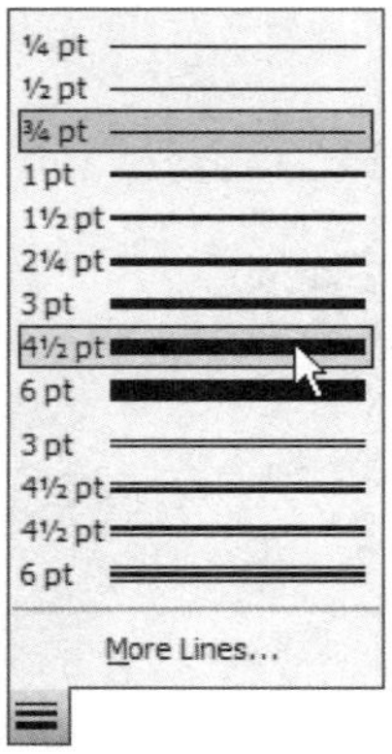

1 **Change line width of rectangle 1**

Select rectangle 1.

On drawing toolbar, click ▤ (line style). Choose *solid* line labeled **4 1/2 pt**.

Outline of rectangle is wider. (It's not as wide as on Line Style *list because you're seeing slide at reduced scale.)*

Deselect object.

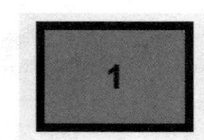

2 **Change line style and dash style of object 4**

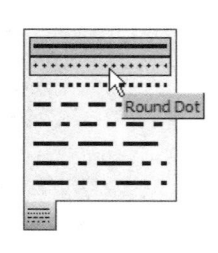

Select object 4 (oval).

On drawing toolbar, click ▤. Choose **6 pt** solid line.

On drawing toolbar, click ▤ (dash style). Choose second style from top of list (see figure at left).

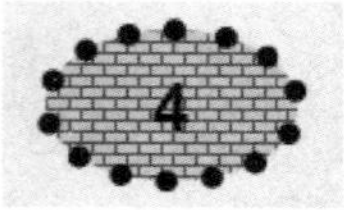

Outline is now thick and dotted.

3 **Tear off line color palette**

On drawing toolbar, click arrow at right side of ▤ (line color).

Put pointer on dotted bar at top of menu; drag menu up as palette.

Tear off **Line Color** palette.

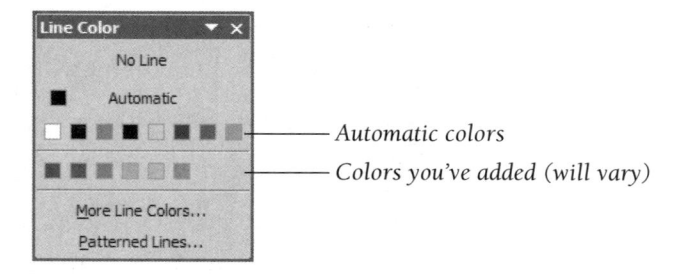

4 **Switch object outline off and back on**

Select rectangle 1. On **Line Color** palette, choose **No Line**.

On same palette, choose **Automatic**.

Outline reappears with automatic outline (black).

Tip

If you remove both line and fill from an object, it can "disappear." If this happens, choose Select All *on the* Edit *menu to see the selection handles for the missing object.*

Change outline & shadow continued

5 *Change line color*

Select object 4 (oval).

On **Line Color** palette, choose any color you like.

Close palette.

6 *Add shadow*

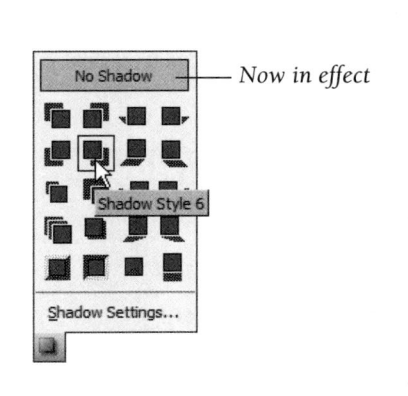

Select rectangle 2. Drag it partly in front of rectangle 1.

On drawing toolbar, click ▣ (shadow style).

Shadow options appear.

On menu, click ▣ (shadow style 6).

Deselect rectangle to see shadow.

Shadow is now semitransparent; you can see through to rectangle 1.

— *Now in effect*

7 *Change shadow transparency*

Select rectangle 2 again.

On drawing toolbar, click ▣ again. On menu, choose **Shadow Settings**.

Settings options appear as palette.

On palette, click right side of ▣▾ (shadow color).

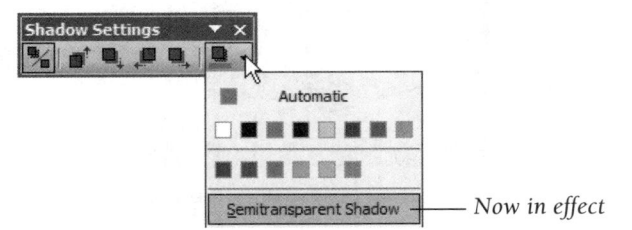

— *Now in effect*

> **By the way**
> You can also change the color of the shadow by choosing one of the color options shown here.

Click **Semitransparent Shadow** to make shadow solid color.

Deselect rectangle 2 to see result. Notice opaque shadow.

8 *Increase shadow offset*

Select rectangle 2 again.

On **Shadow Settings** palette, use ▣ (nudge buttons) to increase or decrease offset of shadow in direction of arrow.

Close **Shadow Settings** palette. Deselect rectangle 2 to see result.

9 *Remove shadow*

Select rectangle 2 again.

On drawing toolbar, click ▣ again. On menu, choose **No Shadow**.

10 *Save changed file; exit PowerPoint*

88 / Presentations with PowerPoint

Create presentation

Now you will create a slide presentation using Microsoft PowerPoint. You will begin with a new file.

1 **Start Microsoft PowerPoint (see page 68, step 1)**

2 **If necessary, set user options (rest of steps on page 68)**

You don't have to do this again if you did it earlier and logged on the computer with the same user name. Once set, user options are saved.

3 **See Microsoft PowerPoint document window in normal view**

In main area of window, notice four panes in normal view (sizes may vary).

Panes are labeled in figure below.

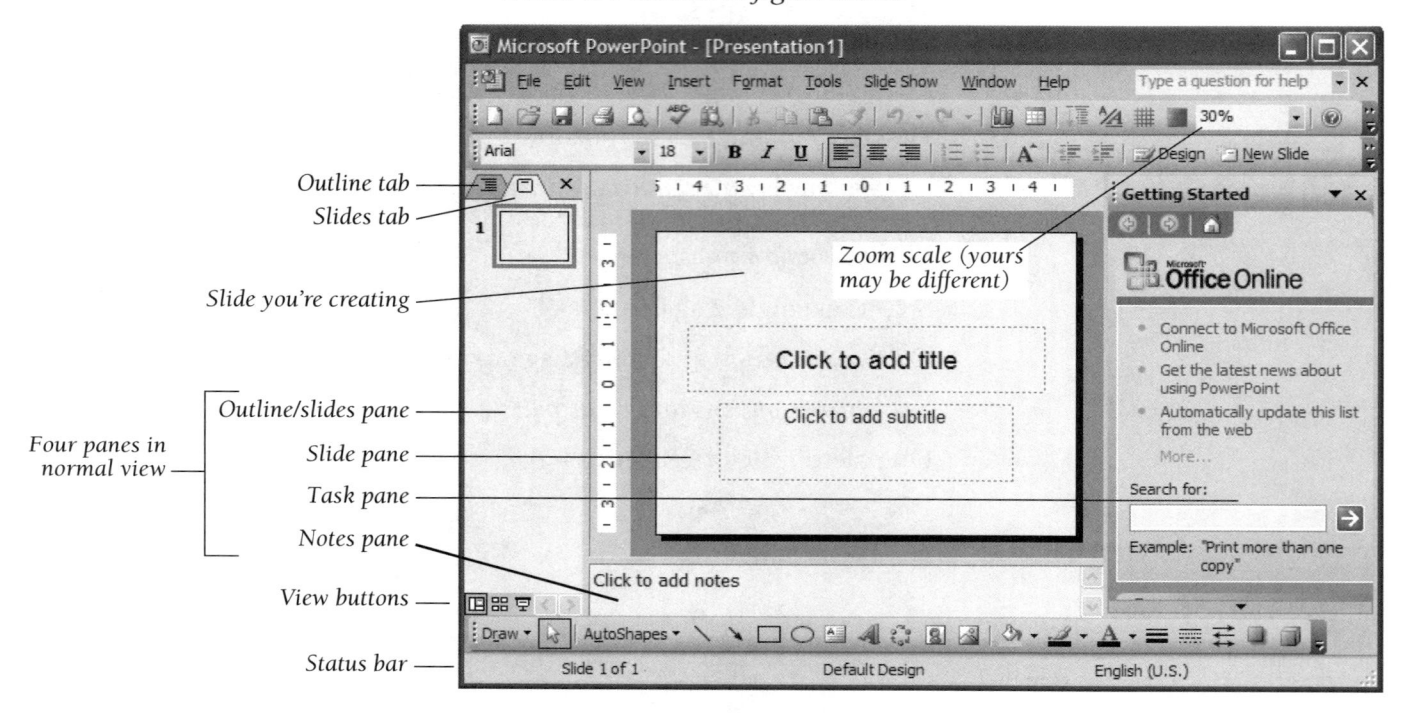

Labels on figure:
- Outline tab
- Slides tab
- Slide you're creating
- Zoom scale (yours may be different)
- Outline/slides pane
- Four panes in normal view
- Slide pane
- Task pane
- Notes pane
- View buttons
- Status bar

4 **Explore tools on standard and formatting toolbars**

Move pointer to each tool icon. Read name below pointer.

Standard toolbar contains general tools for working with files. Formatting toolbar contains tools for formatting text.

> **By the way**
> Most of the tools on the standard and formatting toolbars are identical to those on the same toolbars in Microsoft Word and Excel.

5 **Explore tools on drawing toolbar (at bottom of window)**

Drawing toolbar contains tools and menus for creating and formatting graphic objects.

6 **Explore names of view buttons (at bottom left of window)**

View buttons allow you to see same presentation in different ways.

Create presentation *continued*   **PPT/ 89**

7 *Read information in status bar (at bottom of window)*

| Slide 1 of 1 | Default Design | English (U.S.) |

Presentation documents are made up of slides. Label at left shows which slide you are viewing and working on. You'll learn about designs later.

8 *Notice outline/slides pane at left of window and notes pane near bottom*

You'll learn about these panes later.

9 *Explore layout options for first slide*

On **Format** menu, choose **Slide Layout**.

Slide Layout task pane appears. This is where you select basic format of slide. Selected layout now is Title Slide.

Selected layout (boxed) —
— *Name of selected layout*
— *Vertical scroll bar*

In task pane, click any layout icon to see its effect on slide. (Don't click anything on slide itself.)

Use vertical scroll bar to see all 27 ready-made layouts.

Scroll back to top and click icon for **Title Slide** layout.

Layout is usually best for first slide in presentation.

10 *Notice items on slide 1*

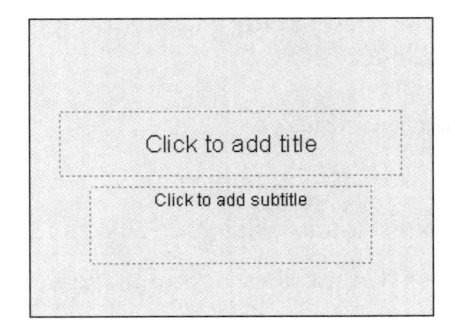

Dotted rectangles are "smart" text boxes. Labels are placeholders that show where text on slide will appear. You'll add text next.

← *Complete previous activity before going on.*

Add text to slide

Slide layouts come with placeholders for text and other objects. The next step is to replace the placeholders.

1 **Replace title placeholder**

Click I-beam pointer anywhere inside top placeholder box on slide.

Text goes away and blinking insertion point appears in box. Striped border (see page 82) means object is text box and is in text-editing mode.

Type `Computer History Society`.

Click white background area of slide above text box to deselect it.

You have replaced title placeholder with your own text.

2 **Replace subtitle placeholder**

Click I-beam pointer anywhere inside bottom placeholder box.

Text goes away and blinking insertion point appears.

Type `Dedicated to Remembering the Past While Moving to the Future`.

Notice that text "wraps" (moves to next line) within margins set by box.

Deselect text box by clicking white background area in both boxes.

> **Computer History Society**
>
> Dedicated to Remembering the Past While Moving to the Future

3 **View outline in pane at left**

At top of outline/slides pane, click [Outline] (may look like this [≣]).

Pane widens. Title and subtitle appear as main topic and subtopic of outline.

4 **Correct any mistakes**

If you made any typing error, move pointer over it on slide.

Pointer shape changes to I-beam when over text.

Click just right of error and make necessary corrections.

Tap [BACKSPACE] to delete; type characters to add.

Click white background area outside text boxes when finished.

5 **Save file with name Slides (see page 16 for reminder of steps)**

You'll need floppy disk or other place to save file.

By the way

If a red zigzag underline appears under text, PowerPoint is indicating that this word is not in the Spelling dictionary and may be misspelled. You'll learn more about checking spelling on page 97.

By the way

Once the placeholders are gone, the slide is just like one you could have created by drawing boxes and attaching text (see page 82).

Tip

You can also edit the text on a slide by making your changes in the outline.

Complete previous activity before going on.

Add new slide

Slides in a PowerPoint presentation are like word processor pages, except that you must add each slide manually.

1 **Insert new slide**

On formatting toolbar, click **New Slide** (or choose **New Slide** on **Insert** menu).

New slide appears with Title and Text slide layout selected as type for slide 2. That will be fine for this example.

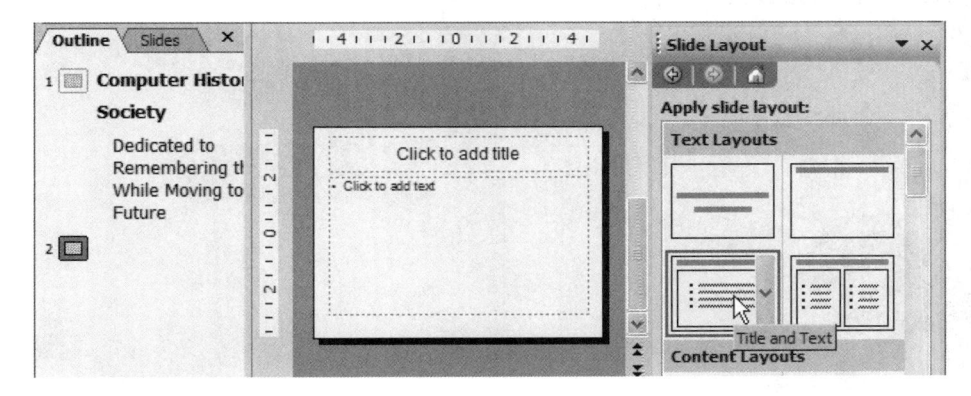

Click ✕ at upper right of **Slide Layout** task pane to hide it.

2 **Enter text for slide 2**

Click title placeholder and type `Welcome`.

Click text placeholder and type `What Can the Computer History Society Do for You?`

Tap ENTER to force new paragraph.

Type your name, comma, space, and `President`.

Each paragraph begins with bullet mark. You'll learn to change text formats later.

3 **View slide 2**

Click in white area outside text boxes.

- Welcome
  - What Can the Computer History Society Do for You?
  - Bonita Sebastian, President

4 **Correct any errors**

You can edit text in outline or on slide.

5 **Save file with added slide**

On **File** menu, choose **Save** (or click 💾 on standard toolbar).

← *Complete previous activity before going on.*

Use outline

If many of your slides are bulleted or numbered lists, you can add and edit them easily in the outline.

Tip
If the left pane is hidden, choose Normal *on the* View *menu, or click the* ▣ *view button at the lower left. If the outline is hidden, click the* Outline *tab at the top of the left pane.*

1 **If necessary, widen outline pane at left**

Carefully position pointer on border between left pane and slide pane. Watch pointer shape.

Press and drag right so outline looks like figure below.

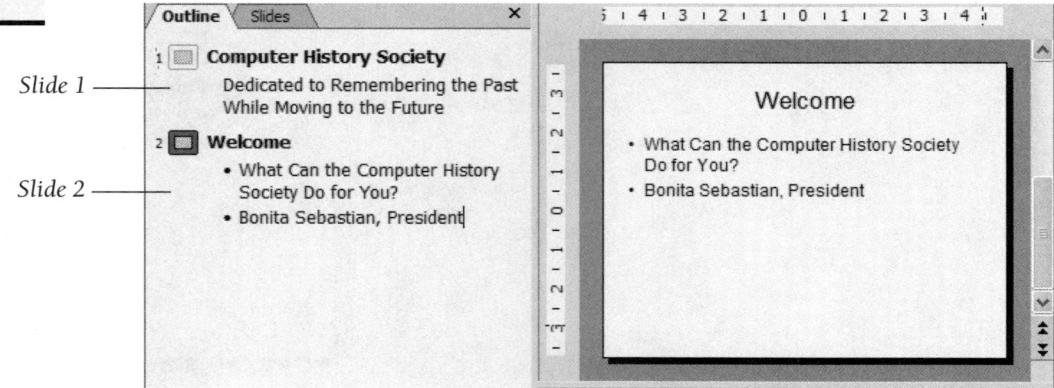

Slide 1 —
Slide 2 —

2 **Create new slide**

In outline, click at right of **t** in **President** to position insertion point.

On **Insert** menu (or formatting toolbar), choose **New Slide**.

Icon for slide 3 appears in outline. Insertion point is ready for title.

3 **Use outline to enter title on slide 3**

In outline pane, type `Topics`. Notice same text in title area of slide.

Tap ENTER.

Oops! New slide 4 is automatically added. But you haven't added bulleted list for slide 3 yet!

Tap TAB, or click ▤ (increase indent) on formatting toolbar.

Slide 4 icon is gone. Bullet appears, and insertion point moves to right.

4 **Add bulleted list for slide 3**

In outline pane, type `Introductions` and tap ENTER.

Text appears in outline and on slide. Insertion point moves down to next line at same indent level.

Type `Benefits of Membership` and tap ENTER.

Type `Services We Provide` and tap ENTER.

Type `Plans for the Future`. Do *not* tap ENTER now.

Line is last of bulleted list on slide 3.

Use outline continued PPT/ 93

5 *Create slide 4*

Tap ENTER.

Oops again! New bulleted item appears. You wanted new slide.

Tap SHIFT TAB, or click ▦ (decrease indent) on formatting toolbar.

Slide 4 appears. Bullet is gone, and insertion point moves left.

Type **Introductions** as title.

Tap ENTER, then tap TAB.

Using methods in step 4, add bulleted list shown below.

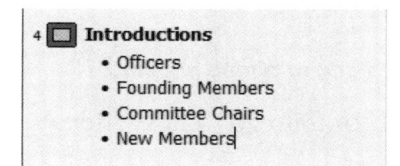

> 4 ▢ **Introductions**
> - Officers
> - Founding Members
> - Committee Chairs
> - New Members

6 *Create slides 5 and 6*

Using same methods, create slides 5 and 6 in outline view.

> 5 ▢ **Benefits of Membership**
> - Networking Opportunities
> - Fascinating Presentations
> - Leading-Edge Speakers
> - Low Dues
> - Discounts on Training Classes
>
> 6 ▢ **Services We Provide**
> - Computer History Archives
> - Community Assistance Job Bank
> - Low-Cost Training Classes
> - Informative Monthly Newsletter

7 *See results slides view*

In pane at left of window, click ▰Slides▰ (slides tab).

Miniature slides replace outline. Slide pane widens.

In left pane, click numbered slide icons to jump to different slides.

8 *Return to outline view in left pane*

Click ▰Outline▰ (may look like this ▤).

In left pane, click anywhere in text to jump to different slides.

9 *Save slides presentation file*

On **File** menu, choose **Save**.

You'll be using file you created many times in future activities.

If you're not going on, choose **Close** on **File** menu.

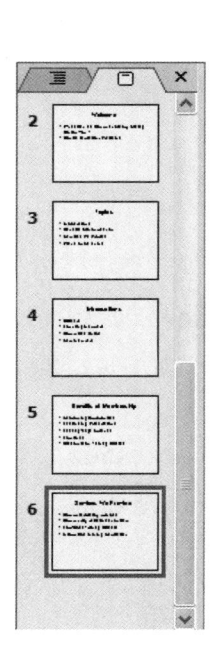

🛑 *Slides file as completed on page 93 must be saved on disk.*

View slides

There are two ways to see the slides themselves: in normal view or in slide show view. You'll explore both now.

1 View presentation in normal view

If necessary, open file **Slides** from disk; close task pane.

At top of outline/slides pane (at left), click ☒ to hide it (and notes pane).

Slide pane expands into area left by other panes.

2 Move to last slide in presentation

Tap CTRL END.

3 Move directly to slide 1

Tap CTRL HOME.

4 View slides one at a time (method 1)

Tap PAGE DOWN to go to next slide.

Continue to tap PAGE DOWN, reviewing each slide until you reach last slide.

Tap PAGE UP until you reach slide 1.

5 View slides one at a time (method 2)

Click next slide button (below vertical scroll bar at right).

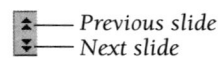

— Previous slide
— Next slide

Continue to click next slide button until you reach last slide.

Click previous slide button on vertical scroll bar.

Next to last slide appears.

6 Move to slide 1

Press and drag scroll box to top of vertical scroll bar.

Notice slide indicator near arrow as you drag.

7 View slide show

Among view buttons at bottom of window, click 🖵 (slide show).

Presentation begins, with current slide filling whole screen. You can't edit text in this view.

Tap SPACEBAR, ↓, PAGE DOWN, or mouse button to move to next slide.

Repeat until you've seen whole presentation and **PowerPoint** window returns.

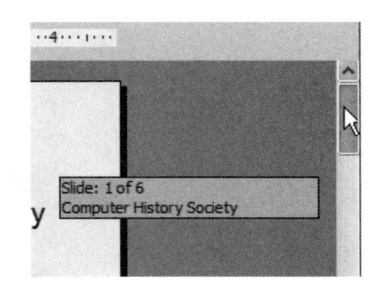

By the way

A slide show on your display is just one possible use of your presentation. You can also make color or black-and-white overhead transparencies. You can even use the presentation to make 35mm slides. If you're in a hurry to learn about this, skip to page 118.

> **STOP** Slides *file as completed on page 93 must be saved on disk.*

Add dynamic effects

You can add transitions and animations to a presentation viewed on a computer display or through a projection device.

1 Switch to slide sorter view

If necessary, open file **Slides** from your floppy disk.

Among view buttons at lower left, click ▦ (slide sorter view).

You see all slides as if on light table. New toolbar appears at top.

Put pointer on each tool to see its name.

> *Tip*
> *If slide sorter toolbar does not appear, choose* Toolbars *from the* View *menu, then choose* Slide Sorter.

2 Explore transition effects

If necessary, click slide 1 to select it.

On slide sorter toolbar, click **Transition**.

Slide Transition options appear in task pane at right of window.

In **Apply to selected slides** area, use scroll bar to see list of possible effects.

Watch selected slide as you choose any effect from list.

Figure shows how effect works when slide first appears in show.

> *Tip*
> *You can also set up an automatic advance by indicating how many seconds the slide should be displayed.*

3 Add transition effect to slide 1

On list, choose **Split Vertical Out**.

In **Modify transition** area, on **Speed** drop-down list, choose **Slow**.

4 Add different transition to slide 2

Click slide 2 image.

On **Apply to selected slides** list, choose **Fade Through Black**.

If necessary, on **Speed** drop-down list, choose **Slow**.

Add dynamic effects *continued*

5 **Add transitions to many slides at once**

Click slide 3 image. With SHIFT held down, click slide 5.

On **Apply to selected slides** list, choose **Wipe Left**.

On **Speed** drop-down list, choose **Medium**.

6 **Add animation effect to objects on slides**

Click slide 6.

On **Slide Show** menu, choose **Animation Schemes**.

List of schemes appears in task pane (list may be different).

Choose effect you like.

7 **View slide show with effects**

Click to select slide 1. Click (slide show) at bottom left of window.

Screen opens black, then splits vertically to reveal slide 1.

Move mouse slightly. Click when it appears at lower left.

On menu, choose **Felt Tip Pen**.

You can change ink or pen color on same submenu.

Use mouse to draw line under title. Tap ESC to discard tool when finished.

Tap SPACEBAR, ↓, or PAGE DOWN to move to next slide or see animation.

Screen fades to black; then slide 2 appears.

Tap ↑ or PAGE UP to move to previous slide.

Notice that line is still there. Use same pen menu to "erase all ink on slide" if desired.

Go forward through whole slide show.

Animation makes slide 6 appear with different effect.

8 **Close presentation file without saving changes; close task pane.**

Click **Discard** if asked whether to save changes.

Tip
You can go directly to any slide by typing the slide number and tapping ENTER. You can end a slide show anytime by tapping ESC.

> **STOP** Slides *file as completed on page 93 must be saved on disk.*

Check spelling

Microsoft PowerPoint can check the spelling in a presentation and add new words to your custom dictionary.

1 Open presentation file Slides

Use step 1 on page 74, but double-click **Slides** now.

2 Make spelling errors

Make three or four spelling errors in words on various slides.

3 Begin spelling check

On **Tools** menu, choose **Spelling** (or click the icon on standard toolbar).

If Microsoft PowerPoint detects errors, Spelling *dialog box appears.*

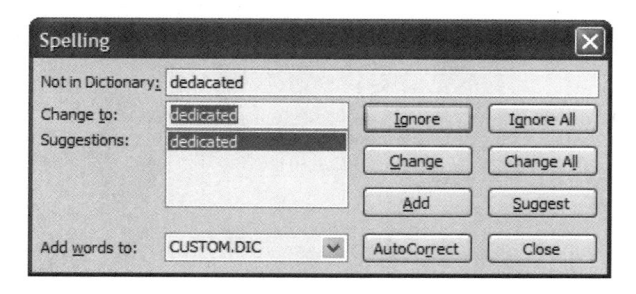

> *By the way*
> *If no words are misspelled, the* Spelling *dialog box does not open at all. Only the message box in step 6 appears.*

4 Change any misspelled words

On **Suggestions** list, click to highlight desired replacement word.

Click **Change**.

You can click Change All *to replace all occurrences of misspelled word in entire presentation.*

> *Tip*
> *If spelling options are set so you see red zigzag lines under misspelled words, you can right-click such a word and choose a suggested spelling from the shortcut menu that appears at the word.*

5 Work with flagged proper names

If your name is flagged by spelling checker, click **Ignore**.

You can click Ignore All *to skip other occurrences of flagged word in entire presentation. Or you can click* Add *to put flagged word in custom dictionary so it is never flagged again.*

6 End spelling check

When spelling check is finished, message appears.

Click **OK**.

7 Save presentation file with changes

On **File** menu, choose **Save**.

Slides file as completed on page 93 must be saved on disk.

Edit & rearrange text

You can edit text in normal or outline view. You can also easily rearrange the text on a slide in these views.

1 *If necessary, open Slides file*

File opens in normal view of slide 1 with outline in left pane.

2 *Edit text on slide 1 in normal view*

On slide, double-click to select word **Moving**.

Type `Racing`. Click in clear area of slide.

Change appears on slide and also in outline.

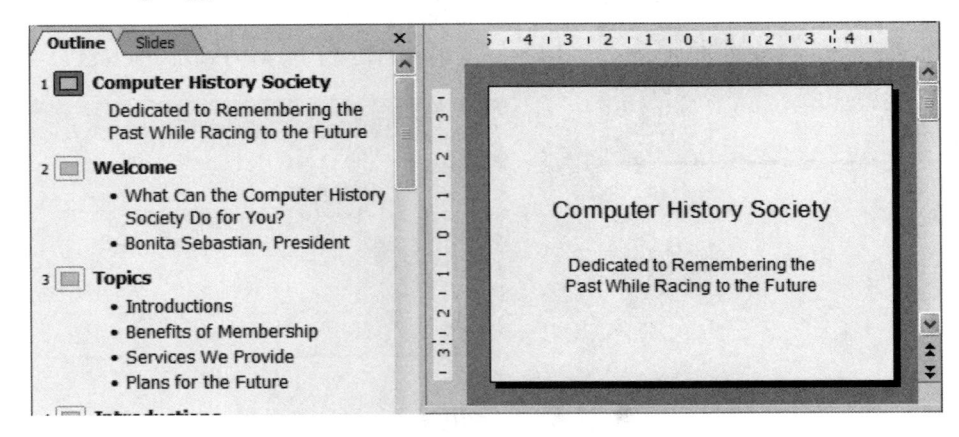

3 *Rearrange bulleted items on slide 2 in outline*

In left pane, click in bulleted item of slide 2 that contains your name.

Position pointer at bullet mark at left side of text.

Pointer changes shape: ✥.

Press and drag up to move text under **Welcome** title of slide 2.

Horizontal line across pane marks new location.

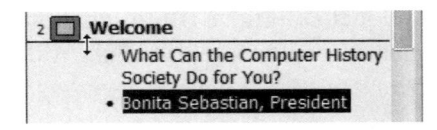

When line is at correct location, release mouse button.

Highlighted item moves to new location.

4 *Add bulleted line to slide 2 in outline pane*

Click to right of **You?** in second bulleted item.

Tap `ENTER`.

New line at same outline level is created when you tap `ENTER`.

Type `What Can You Do for the Society?`

Tip

You can also move lines up or down with the move-up and move-down tools on the outline toolbar. If the toolbar is hidden, use the View *menu to see it.*

Edit & rearrange text *continued*

5 *Combine two bulleted items on slide 5*

In outline, locate slide 5.

Click to put insertion point just left of **Leading**.

Tap [BACKSPACE] twice.

Tap [SPACEBAR]. Type `by` and tap [SPACEBAR] again.

6 *Add new level of bullets*

In slide 5 outline, click to put insertion point just right of **Dues**.

Tap [ENTER]; then tap [TAB].

New line is indented another level.

Type `Regular $50/year`.

Different bullet mark appears on slide, but same mark is on outline.

Tap [ENTER].

Another bulleted line at new level is created. [ENTER] always creates new line at same level as line above.

Enter second line as shown in figure.

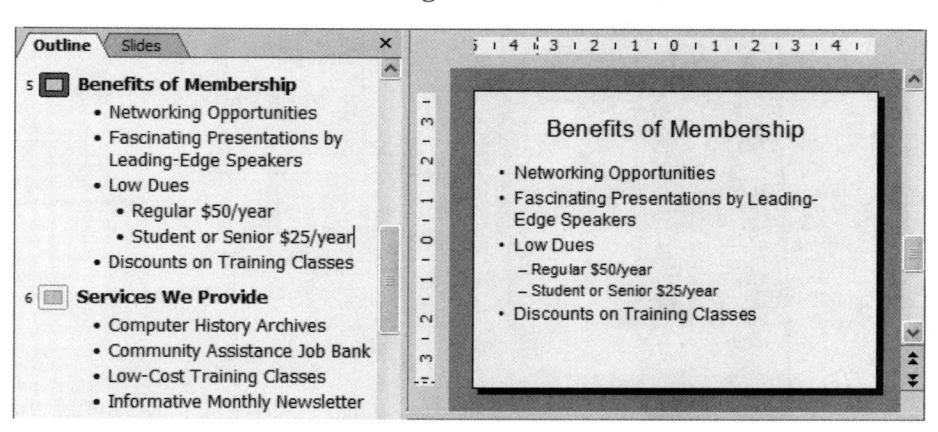

7 *Review edited presentation as slide show*

Tap [CTRL][HOME] to move to slide 1.

At bottom left of window, click ▣ to view slide show.

Tap [PAGE DOWN] to browse though slides one by one.

8 *Close presentation file without saving changes*

🛑 Slides file as completed on page 93 must be saved on disk.

100 / *Presentations with PowerPoint*

Rearrange slides

After reviewing slides, you may want to rearrange the order in which information is presented.

1 **Open Slides file**

2 **Switch to slide sorter view**

Click 🔲 (slide sorter view) at bottom left of window.

Slides appear in miniature, as if on light table.

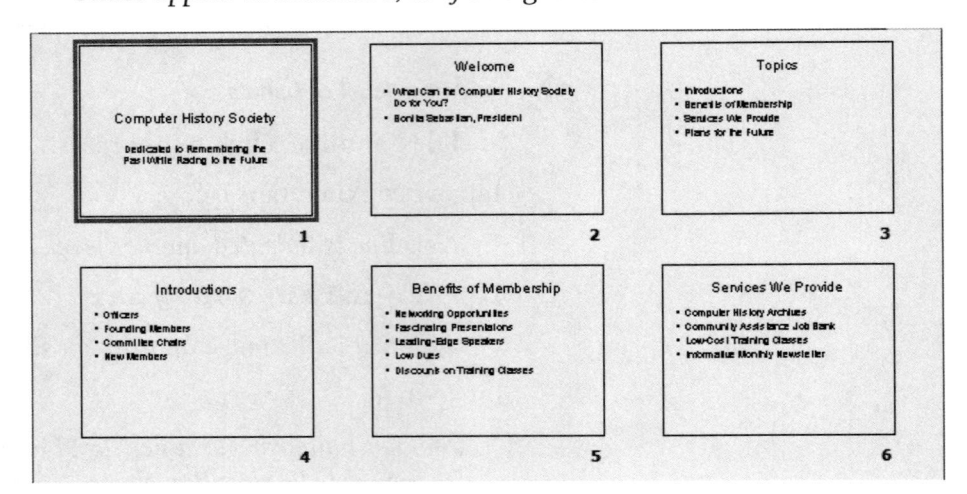

Tip
Although you can rearrange slides by dragging the icons up or down in the left pane in normal view, it's easy to make mistakes. The icons are small, and it's hard to read the text on them. The two methods here are safer.

By the way
Your screen may not look exactly like this one. The appearance depends on the size of your display and the current view percentage.

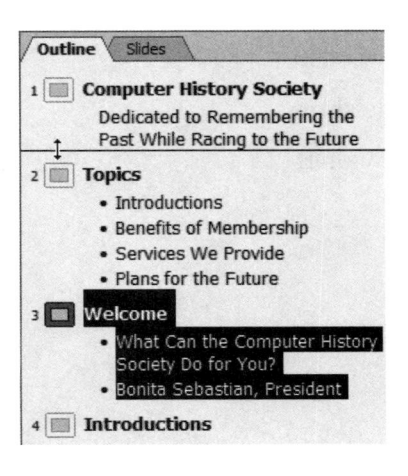

---

3 **Change order of slides (method 1)**

Put pointer in slide 3 and drag to left of slide 2.

Notice pointer shape and position marker near pointer.

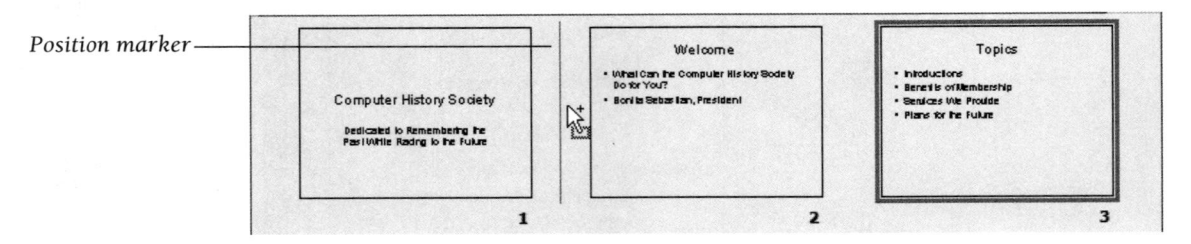

— Position marker

When position marker is to left of slide 2, release mouse button.

Slide 3 becomes slide 2, and slide 2 becomes slide 3.

4 **Change order of slides (method 2)**

On **View** menu, choose **Normal**.

Outline also shows new order. Order of slides is same in all views.

Put pointer at small slide icon to left of slide 3 title.

Press mouse button and drag up until long horizontal position marker is just above slide 2 title. Release mouse button.

Slides 2 and 3 swap places and are renumbered.

5 **If you're not continuing, close presentation file without saving changes**

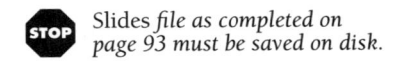

A presentation file must be open.

Delete slide

Sometimes you simply want to get rid of a slide in your presentation. That's easy to do (and undo).

PPT/ 101

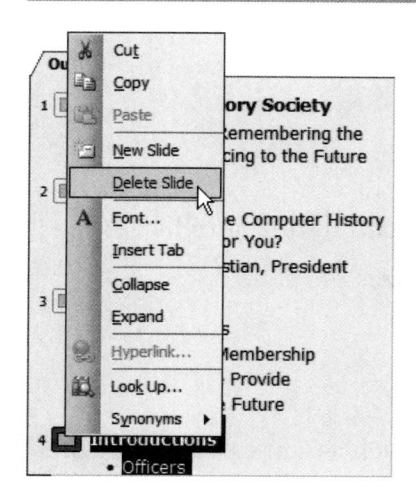

1 **Delete slide (method 1)**

If left pane is missing, click ▣ (normal view).

If outline is not present at left, click *Outline* at top.

In outline, position pointer over slide icon or any text in slide 4.

Tap *right* mouse button to see shortcut menu.

On menu, choose **Delete Slide**.

Entire slide is deleted, and later ones are renumbered.

2 **Undo action (method 1)**

On **Edit** menu, choose **Undo Delete Slide**.

Slide is "undeleted." Most PowerPoint actions can be undone.

3 **Delete slide (method 2)**

At top of left pane, click *Slides*.

Outline disappears, and column of tiny slides replaces it.

Right-click slide 3 in list.

Slide 3 appears in slide pane at right, and shortcut menu appears where you clicked.

On shortcut menu, choose **Delete Slide**.

You can also tap [DELETE] *or* [BACKSPACE] *after selecting slide.*

4 **Undo action (method 2)**

Click ↶ (undo) on standard toolbar.

Slide 3 reappears and is selected.

5 **Delete slide (method 3)**

At bottom left of window, click ▦ (slide sorter view).

Tap ← to move selection to slide 2.

Tap [BACKSPACE] to delete selection.

6 **Undo action (method 3)**

Tap [CTRL][Z].

Slide 4 reappears.

7 **Close presentation file without saving changes**

By the way

You can click the arrow on the side of the undo tool to display a list of recent actions you can undo.

> Slides file as completed on page 93 must be saved on disk.

Change text formats

You can easily change the font, size, and style of any text you select on a slide.

1 Open Slides file

Slide 1 appears in slide pane in normal view.

2 Check current font, size, and style of title

Click slide 3 icon in left pane. Highlight any text in title at right.

On formatting toolbar, notice current font, size, and style.

3 Change font, size, style, and color of title

Select all text in title line.

Use formatting toolbar to choose new font, such as **Times New Roman**.

You can move quickly to font you want by typing first letters of name in font box on formatting toolbar.

Change font size to **54**, and add bold and italic styles.

On formatting (or drawing) toolbar, click arrow at right of [A] (font color).

On menu, choose **More Colors**.

On **Standard** tab, choose any red, and click **OK**.

Click in clear area of slide to deselect title and see changes.

4 Change all text in subtitle

Tap [TAB] twice to select subtitle block.

Thick dotted border shows whole text block is selected.

Change text style to bold and text color to dark blue.

All text in block is changed.

5 Add background color

On **Format** menu, choose **Background**.

You may have to wait for command to appear.

Toward bottom of **Background** dialog box, click arrow to right of empty box.

On drop-down list, choose light blue in row of eight colors.

Click **Apply** (*not* **Apply to All**).

Slide 3 now has red and dark blue text on light blue background.

6 Go to slide 1 and view slide show

Slide 3 has "custom" format. Other slides are unchanged. In next activity, you'll apply format changes to many slides at once.

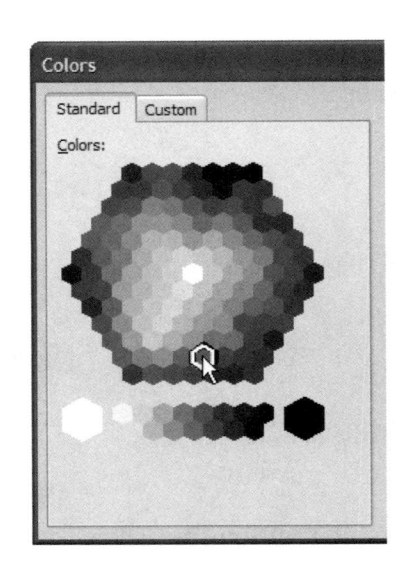

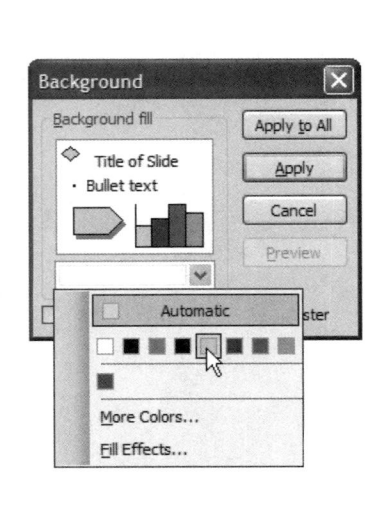

Complete previous activity before going on.

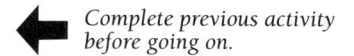

Use slide maste

Every presentation has a "slide master. Format changes you make on the slide master affect all similar slides.

PPT/ 103

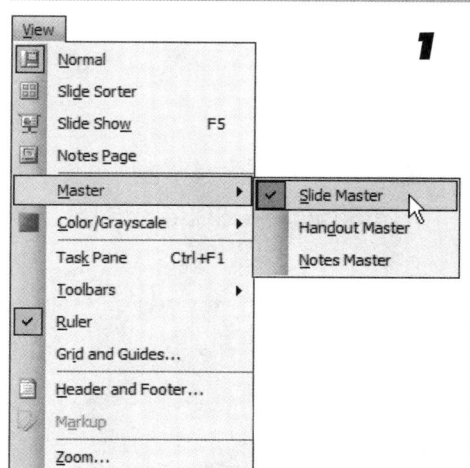

1   Switch to view of slide master

On **View** menu, choose **Master**; on submenu, choose **Slide Master**.

Slide master and small palette appear. Slide master contains placeholders for formatting all slides (except ones with custom format).

2   Format title on slide master

Click anywhere in text in box at top. Notice all text becomes selected.

Formatting will apply to all title text on slides.

Use formatting toolbar to add bold and italic styles and light blue text color.

3   Format body text on slide master

Click any text in body box (below title box).

Carefully click thick dashed border that appears. Notice border becomes dotted.

Dashed border means some text in box is selected. Dotted border means whole box is selected.

Use formatting toolbar to add bold style and dark blue text color.

4   Add background color

On **Format** menu, choose **Background**.

Toward bottom of **Background** dialog box, click arrow at right of empty box.

On drop-down list, choose **More Colors**.

Choose light yellow, and click **OK**. Click **Apply** (*not* **Apply to All**).

5   See results

On **Slide Master View** palette, click **Close Master View**.

Go to slide 1. Click 🖳 to view slide show.

All slides except slide 3 now have formats you gave to slide master. (You gave slide 3 custom formats in previous activity.)

6   Rename, save, and close file

On **File** menu, choose **Save As**. Name file **Formatted**. Click **Save**. Close file.

By the way

You can also apply different formats to different indent levels in the body text of your slides. Just click one line at a time in the body box, and apply formats to it.

By the way

PowerPoint assumes that if you added custom colors, you would want to preserve them, so it does not overwrite them when you apply master changes.

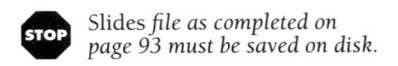

⛔ Slides *file as completed on page 93 must be saved on disk.*

Add slide with chart

You can add a chart to a slide. Charts in Microsoft PowerPoint are similar to the ones you'll create in Microsoft Excel.

> **Tip**
> You can also create a chart on any existing slide by using the Chart command on the Insert menu.

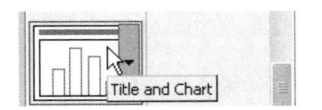

1 **Open Slides file**

2 **Add new slide with chart layout**

Tap `CTRL END` to go to last slide.

On formatting toolbar, click **New Slide** (or choose **New Slide** on **Insert** menu).

In **Slide Layout** task pane, click **Title and Chart** layout (at end).

Click ⊠ to close task pane.

3 **Add title**

Click title placeholder, and type `Computers in Use`.

4 **Add chart**

Double-click chart placeholder.

Look at names on menu bar near top of screen. Look at toolbar.

> Data *and* Chart *menus are new.* Slide Show *menu is gone. Items on menus are also changed. Menu bar and toolbar are for working with charts.*

Look at **Datasheet** window. (If window is not present, choose **Datasheet** on **View** menu.)

> *Datasheet holds data for chart. Data are in cells arranged in rows and columns. You'll replace default data with your data.*

		A	B	C	D	E
		1st Qtr	2nd Qtr	3rd Qtr	4th Qtr	
1	East	20.4	27.4	90	20.4	
2	West	30.6	38.6	34.6	31.6	
3	North	45.9	46.9	45	43.9	

5 **Enter category labels**

If necessary, move **Datasheet** window so you see chart.

Click to select cell in row 1 containing word **East**.

Type `Business` and tap `ENTER`.

> *Active cell is now* West.

Type `School` and tap `ENTER`.

> *Active cell is now* North.

Type `Home` and tap `ENTER`.

Notice changes in legend at right of chart.

Add slide with chart *continued* PPT/ 105

6 *Enter series labels*

Click to select cell containing words **1st Qtr.** Type **1 9 9 0** and tap `TAB`.

Active cell is now 2nd Qtr.

Type **1 9 9 5** and tap `TAB` to move to next cell to right.

Type **2 0 0 0** and tap `ENTER` to end text entry.

7 *Enter data*

If necessary, scroll **Datasheet** contents up so you can see row 1.

Watch columns on chart as you select cells and add data shown in figure.

			A	B	C	D	E
			1990	1995	2000	4th Qtr	
1		Business	50,000	70,000	98,000	20.4	
2		School	20,000	35,000	87,000	31.6	
3		Home	10,000	25,000	60,000	43.9	

8 *Remove column D data from chart*

Double-click ▢ D ▢ (header of column D).

Data is dimmed in window and disappears from chart.

9 *Close Datasheet window and see whole slide*

On **View** menu, choose **Datasheet** (now with boxed icon).

Selecting Datasheet *again would bring window back.*

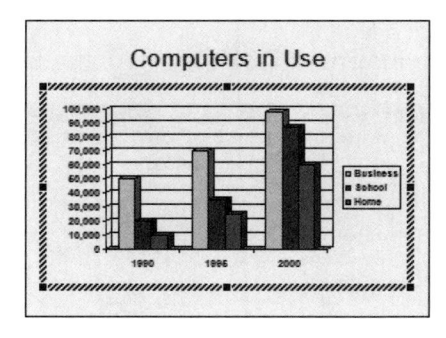

10 *Leave charting tools*

Click anywhere outside shaded border around chart.

Familiar menus and toolbars reappear. Chart remains on slide.

11 *Save presentation file*

On **File** menu, choose **Save**.

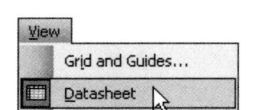

← *Complete previous activity before going on.*

Format chart

Charts in Microsoft PowerPoint can be formatted using methods similar to those you'll use in Microsoft Excel.

1 Return to charting tools

Double-click anywhere inside chart area.

Chart toolbar and menus appear. (If datasheet appears, do step 9 on page 105.)

2 Add label to value axis

On **Chart** menu, choose **Chart Options**.

> **Tip**
> *This dialog box allows you to put a title on the graph, However, it is best to put the title on the slide (as you did earlier). There's more space, and the title will not change size with the graph.*

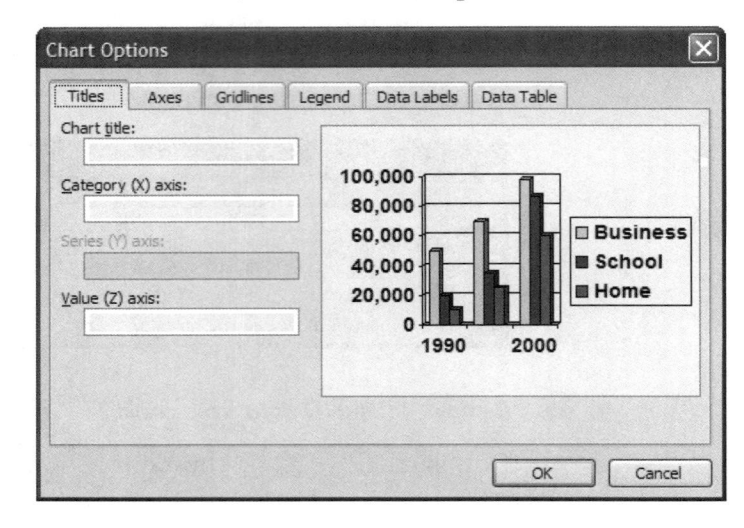

Click text box for **Value (Z) axis**. Type **Computers**. Click **OK**.

> **Tip**
> *Do not click outside the graph area on the slide. If you do, you will return to the Microsoft PowerPoint application. If this happens, double-click the graph to return to the Microsoft Graph application.*

3 Format axis title

On **Format** menu, choose **Selected Axis Title**.

In **Format Axis Title** dialog box, click **Alignment** tab.

In **Orientation** area, drag red diamond to top (see figure).

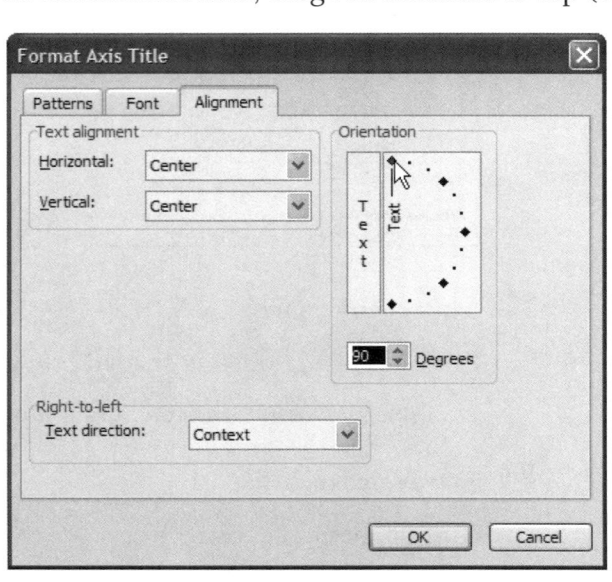

Click **OK**.

Format chart continued

4 Remove border from legend and put legend at bottom

Double-click legend (at right of chart).

If necessary, click **Patterns** tab. In **Border** area, click **None**.

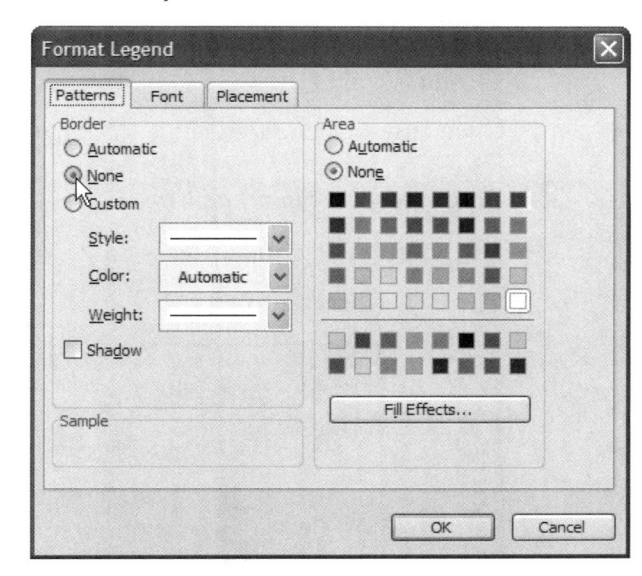

Click **Placement** tab. In **Placement** area, click **Bottom**. Click **OK**.

5 Change data being charted

On **View** menu, choose **Datasheet**.

Click cell C3 containing 60,000 home users.

Watch chart as you type **100,000** and tap `TAB`.

On **View** menu, choose **Datasheet** again to close **Datasheet** window.

6 View finished chart

Click anywhere outside chart area on slide.

You exit charting tools and return to standard PowerPoint tools.

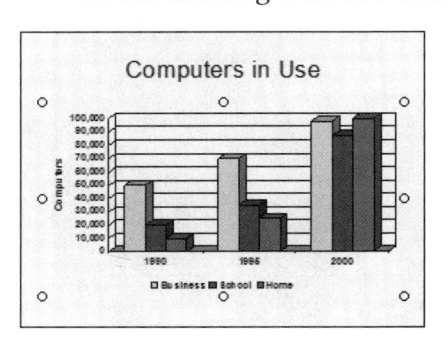

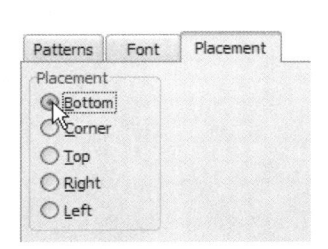

7 Save presentation with new slide

By the way

The graph is now an object on the slide. It can be deleted, moved, or resized by applying the same techniques used with other objects. See page 71.

> A presentation file must be open in normal view.

Add clip art

You can add a graphic object to a slide. Microsoft PowerPoint contains a gallery of clip art you can use.

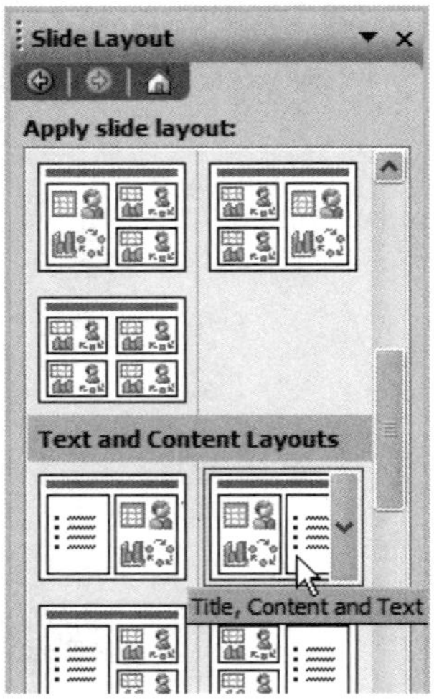

1 Create new slide

If necessary, tap `CTRL END` to go to last slide.

With slide 7 selected, on formatting toolbar, click **New Slide**.

In **Slide Layout** task pane, click **Title, Content and Text** icon.

Close task pane.

Click title placeholder. Type `Computers for All`.

2 Open and view clip art gallery

Put pointer on icons to see what things you can add to slide.

Click (insert clip art).

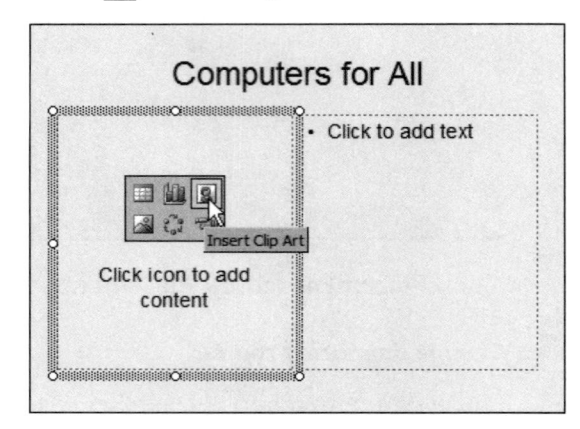

Clip art gallery appears.

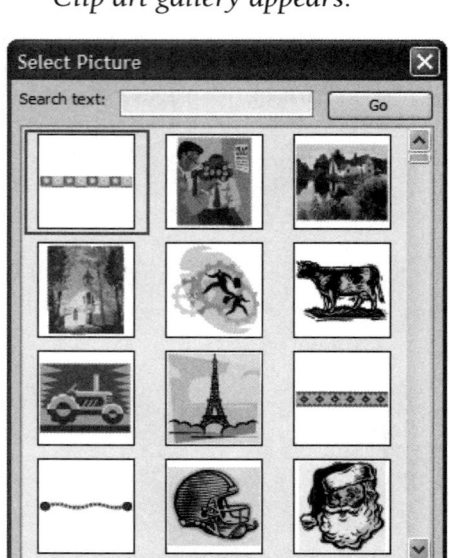

Scroll through pictures in dialog box.

By the way

The amount of clip art displayed is determined by the installation. If you do not have the entire collection, substitute other images.

The first time the clip art gallery is opened, a dialog box may appear asking whether to add new images. If this happens, you can say yes. Be aware, however, that the process takes time

Add clip art *continued*

3 *Find picture of computer*

Click in **Search text** box and type `computer`.

Click **Go**.

Scroll through images of computers; then click one you like.

Click **OK** to accept clip art and add it to slide.

By the way

The clip art is now an object on the slide. It can be deleted, moved, or resized by applying the same techniques used with other objects. See page 71.

---

4 *Adjust size and position of picture on slide*

See steps on page 71.

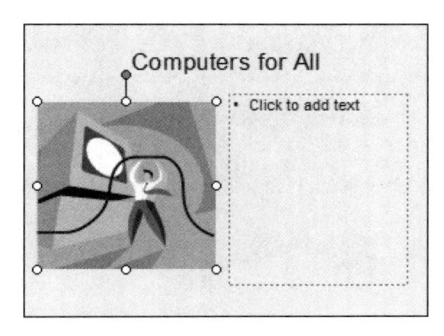

5 *View Picture palette*

Picture *palette contains buttons for modifying picture.*

Tip

If the Picture *palette does not appear when you select the clip art image, use the* Toolbars *submenu on the* View *menu to display it.*

With image selected, put pointer on each button and read description.

6 *Add clip art to existing slide without placeholder*

Go to slide 2.

On **Insert** menu, choose **Picture**, then **Clip Art**. (If **Add Clips to Organizer** dialog box appears, click **Later**.)

Clip Art *task pane appears on right.*

In **Search text** box, type `people` and click **Go**.

Browse through results; then click one you like.

Click ☒ to close clip art pane.

7 *Save presentation*

> A presentation file must be open in normal view.

Insert WordArt

You can add a text graphic to a slide. Microsoft Office includes a WordArt application for this.

1 **Create new blank slide at end of presentation**

Select last slide in presentation.

On formatting toolbar, click **New Slide**. In **Slide Layout** pane, click **Blank**.

Click ⊠ to close task pane.

2 **Add WordArt to slide**

On drawing toolbar, click 🅐 (insert WordArt).

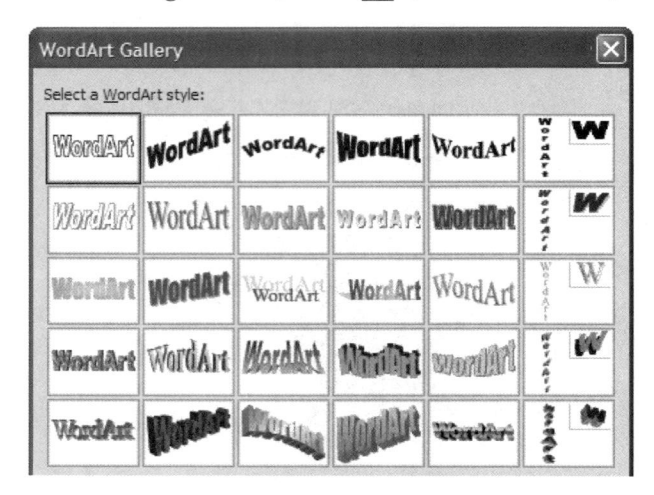

Choose style in fourth row, fourth column. Click **OK**.

3 **Add text**

Type `Computer History Society`.

In dialog box, click **B** to add bold.

Click OK.

4 **Explore buttons on WordArt toolbar**

5 **Adjust size and positioning of WordArt object**

To edit text or design, double-click object to return to WordArt window.

6 **Save changed file**

By the way

The WordArt is now an object on the slide. The text cannot be edited without returning to WordArt. However, the object can be deleted, moved, and resized by applying the same techniques used with other objects. See page 71.

> A presentation file must be open in normal view.

Add objects to master

Frequently you want a label or a graphic on all slides in a presentation. Just add the label or graphic to the slide master.

PPT/ 111

> **Tip**
> You can also move to the slide master by holding down SHIFT and clicking the normal view button.

1 Move to slide master view

On **View** menu, choose **Master**, then **Slide Master**.

2 Enter footer text

Set zoom scale to **66%**. Scroll to bottom of master.

On master, click **<footer>** placeholder in **Footer Area** text box.

Type `Computer History Society`.

3 Format text

Carefully click edge of footer box.

On formatting toolbar, choose **Times New Roman** from font list.

On formatting toolbar, click *I* (italic).

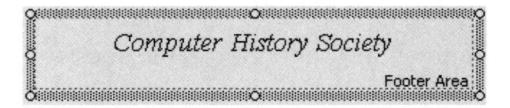

4 View text on slides

On **Slide Master View** palette, click Close Master View.

Tap CTRL HOME to go to slide 1.

Click view button, and see slide show.

5 Switch back to slide master

On **View** menu, choose **Master**, then **Slide Master**.

Set zoom scale to **Fit**.

6 Add graphic object to slide master

On **Insert** menu, choose **Picture**, then **Clip Art**. (If **Add Clips to Organizer** dialog box appears, click **Later**.)

In **Clip Art** task pane, locate and insert appropriate image.

Close task pane.

Add objects to master *continued*

7 *Resize and position object in upper-right corner as in figure*

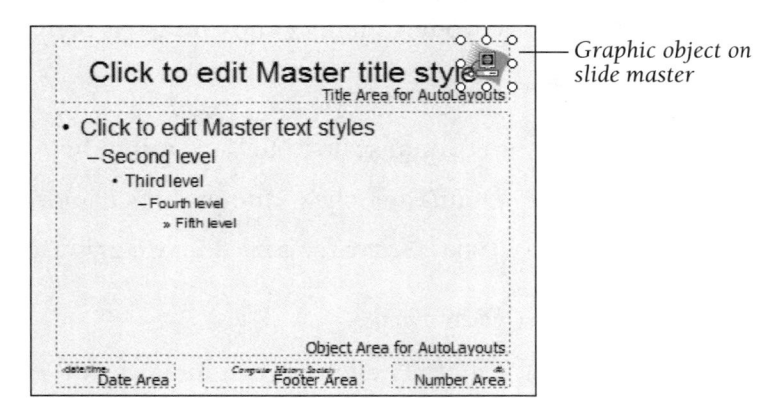

Graphic object on slide master

8 *View text and graphic object on all slides*

Click **Close Master View** to return to normal view.

Go to slide 1, and view slide show.

9 *Suppress display of object on first slide*

Make sure slide 1 is in view.

On **Format** menu, choose **Background**.

Object you added is on background layer of slide master.

Click **Omit background graphics from master** to put mark in check box.

Click **Apply** (*not* Apply to All).

10 *View presentation*

Click ▣ view button. Notice graphic object (and footer) are missing from slide 1.

Headers and footers are considered part of background.

View rest of slides. Notice graphic object on others.

11 *When show has ended, close presentation without saving changes*

> 🛑 Slides *file as completed on page 93 must be saved on disk.*

Change color scheme

The objects you put on slides are "automatically" colored a certain way. You can change all the coloring in a few clicks.

PPT/ 113

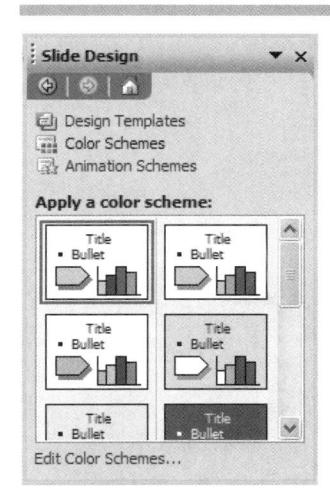

1 **Open Slides file**

2 **View available color schemes**

On **Format** menu, choose **Slide Design**. In task bar, click **Color Schemes**.

Scroll box shows color schemes you can use. Current scheme is boxed.

3 **Apply different color schemes**

Scroll through color schemes. Click one with dark blue-green background.

Click 🖳 to run slide show. On each slide, notice colors of background, title text, and other text.

You easily changed colorings of these items on all slides.

4 **Explore automatic coloring**

At bottom of **Slide Design** task pane, click **Edit Color Schemes**.

On **Custom** tab, look at labels of eight **Scheme colors**.

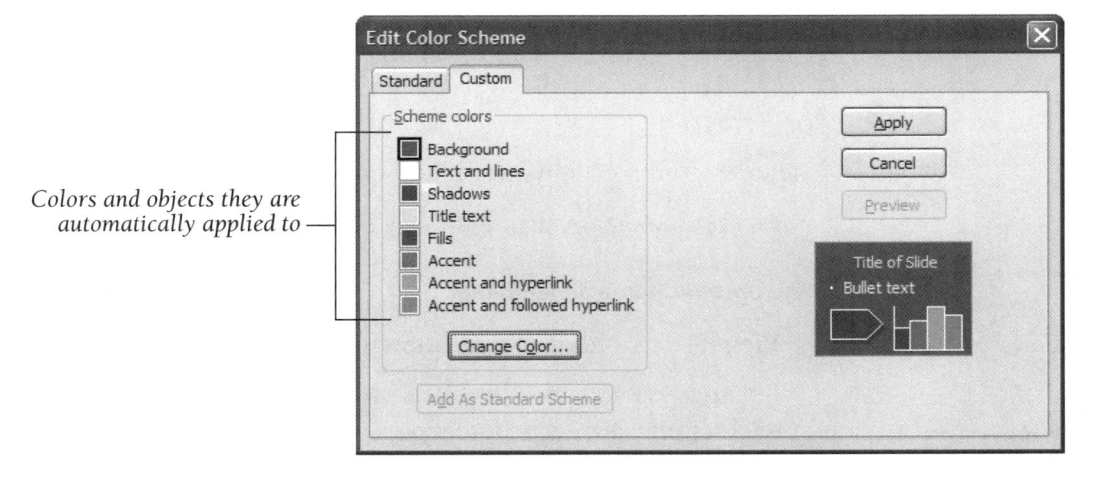

Colors and objects they are automatically applied to

5 **Define new scheme**

In **Edit color scheme** dialog box, click **Title text** color box.

Click **Change Color** button.

Title Text Color dialog box appears, ready for a color change.

On **Standard** tab, choose any light red. Click **OK**.

6 **Save your new scheme**

Click **Add As Standard Scheme** button.

Click **Standard** tab. Notice new scheme selected at bottom of others.

Click **Apply**. Close dialog box, and run slide show.

7 **Close file without saving changes; close task pane**

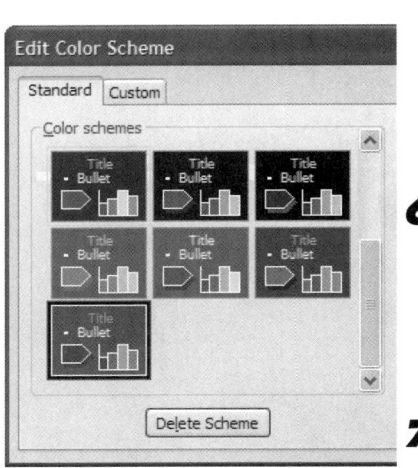

> **STOP** Slides *file as completed on page 93 must be saved on disk.*

Apply design template

Microsoft PowerPoint contains built-in color and black-and-white templates for slide shows, overheads, and slides.

1 Open Slides file

2 View available slide show templates

On **Format** menu, choose **Slide Design**.

> Slide Design *task pane shows current template and others you can use.*

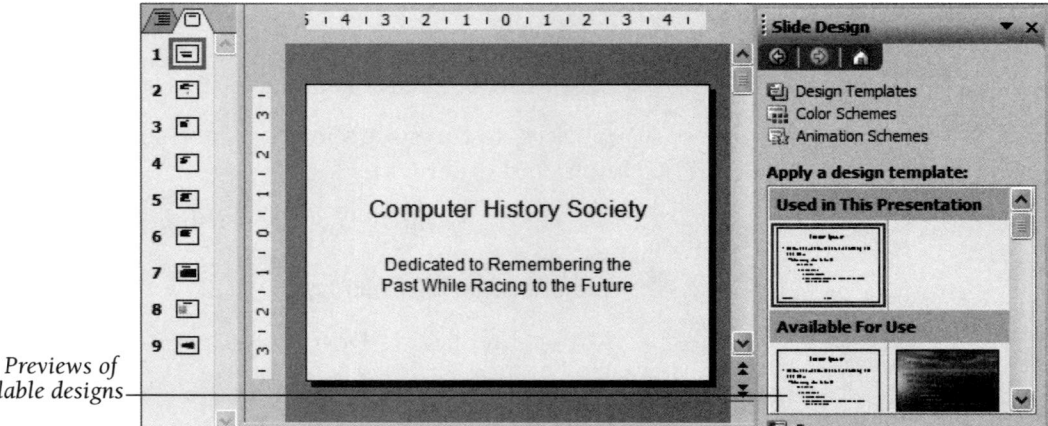

Previews of available designs

In task pane, scroll through available design templates.

3 Apply template

Click design template you might want to use.

> *Presentation is updated with new template.*

By the way

Applying a template creates a new slide master with all the format details. Any previous slide master changes you've made are lost.

Tip

It's usually a good idea to keep the original presentation file on your disk (as here). That makes it easier to undo changes and get back to your original.

---

4 View presentation with template

On **View** menu, choose **Slide Show** (or click 🖳).

> *If you do not like template, you can follow above procedure to apply another one. New template replaces previous one.*

5 Save presentation with new design as new file

On **File** menu, choose **Save As** (*not* Save).

Save with name `Design` on disk.

6 Close presentation file and task pane

On **File** menu, choose **Close**.

On **View** menu, choose **Task Pane** to close it.

🛑 Slides *file as completed on page 93 must be saved on disk.*

Create speaker notes

Each slide has a speaker's notes page where you can write anything you want to be reminded of during the presentation.

PPT/ 115

1 Open file Slides

File opens in normal view of slide 1. Notes pane is below slide pane.

2 Enlarge notes pane

Carefully place pointer on bar between slide pane and notes pane. Drag bar up about 1 inch.

3 Enter speaker notes for slide 1

Click in notes pane. Type following text. Tap ENTER between sentences.

```
This first slide should be displayed as the
audience enters.
Take a deep breath and count to 10 before
proceeding.
```

4 Add more notes

Go to next slide. Add helpful note for slide 2.

Repeat for one or two more slides.

5 View page containing slide 1 with its note

Go to slide 1.

On **View** menu, choose **Notes Page**.

Scaled-down view of first page appears. (You'll print actual pages on page 119.)

Set zoom scale to **66%**. Scroll to top of page if necessary.

Use PAGE DOWN to browse through notes pages.

There's one notes page for each slide, with slide at top, notes area below. You can enter and edit notes here or in bottom pane of normal view.

Go back to first page.

6 Enlarge font size of notes on all pages

On **View** menu, choose **Master**, then **Notes Master**.

Changes made on notes master affect all notes pages.

On notes master, click inside notes body area but away from any text.

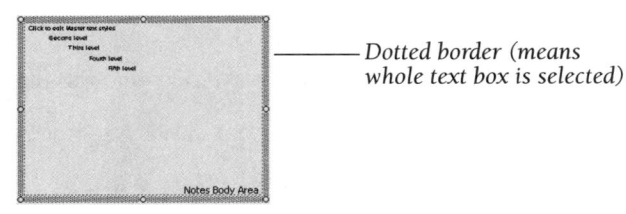

— *Dotted border (means whole text box is selected)*

On font size list on formatting toolbar, choose **18**.

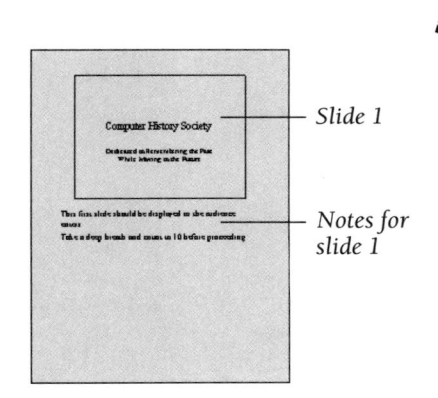

— Slide 1

— Notes for slide 1

7 Add header to all notes pages

Change zoom scale to **66%**. Scroll to top of page if necessary.

Text on master is easier to read.

Click **<header>** placeholder in **Header Area** text box.

Type `Computer History Society`.

Click outside text box to end editing.

8 Add current date to all notes pages

Click **<date/time>** placeholder in **Date Area** text box.

On **Insert** menu, choose **Date and Time**.

Choose format you want. Click **Update automatically**. Click **OK**.

9 View individual notes pages

On Notes Master View palette, click [Close Master View].

Use [PAGE DOWN] to see each notes page. Scroll down to see notes on each.

Changes you made on master affected all notes pages.

Tap [CTRL][HOME] to move to notes page 1.

Change zoom scale to **Fit**.

Notes pages are now reduced to fit in window.

10 Return to normal view with smaller notes pane

Among view buttons, click ▦ (normal view).

Carefully drag bar above notes pane back down so only one line of text is seen.

11 Rename, save, and close presentation file

On **File** menu, choose **Save As** (*not* Save).

Save file with name `Notes`.

On **File** menu, choose **Close**.

Note
PowerPoint automatically inserts a page number on each notes page.

> **STOP** Slides file as completed on page 93 must be saved on disk.

Create audience handouts

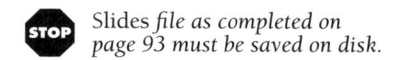

To assist note takers, you can create audience handouts with two, three, four, six, or nine slide miniatures on a page.

1 Open Slides file

2 View handout master

On **View** menu, choose **Master**, then **Handout Master**.

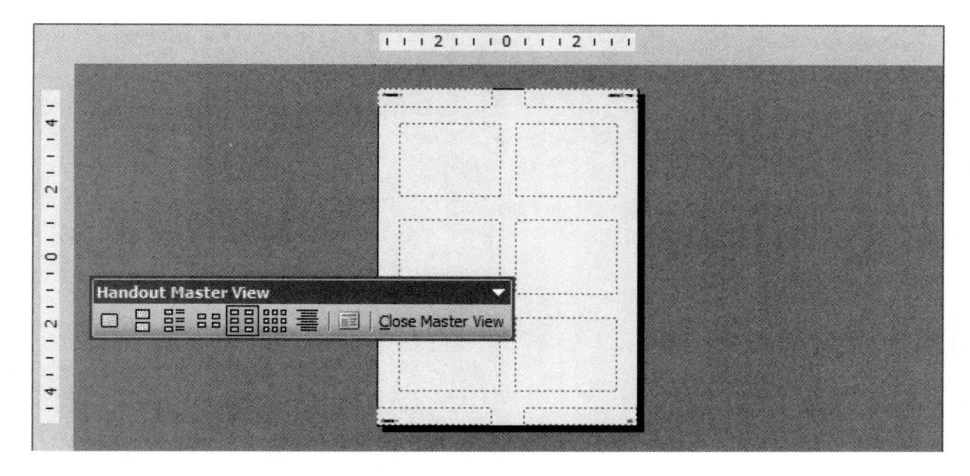

Changes you make on handout master affect all handout pages when they're printed.

> **By the way**
> You can change the layout when you print handouts, but the header, footer, and any other additions you make on the handout master will appear in all layouts.

3 View different slide layouts on handout pages

Click first six buttons on **Handout Master View** palette to see different slide layouts. Choose one.

Seventh button replaces slides with outline of whole presentation.

4 Add header and date to handout pages

Do step 7 on page 116.

Do step 8 on page 116.

On **Handout Master View** palette, click [Close Master View].

5 Preview, then return to normal view

On **File** menu, choose **Print Preview**.

On **Print What** drop-down list, choose type of handout you want.

Click **Close** when finished.

6 Rename, save, and close presentation file

On **File** menu, choose **Save As** (*not* Save).

Save file with name `Handouts` on disk.

On **File** menu, choose **Close**.

> **STOP** Slides *file as completed on page 93 must be saved on disk.*

Print overheads

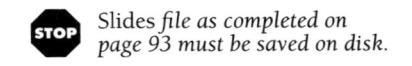

With transparency film in your printer, you can print overhead slides. You can also create a file for making 35mm slides.

1 Open Slides file

2 View Print dialog box

On **File** menu, choose **Print**. Notice all options available.

Items in Printer *area depend on printer you're using.*

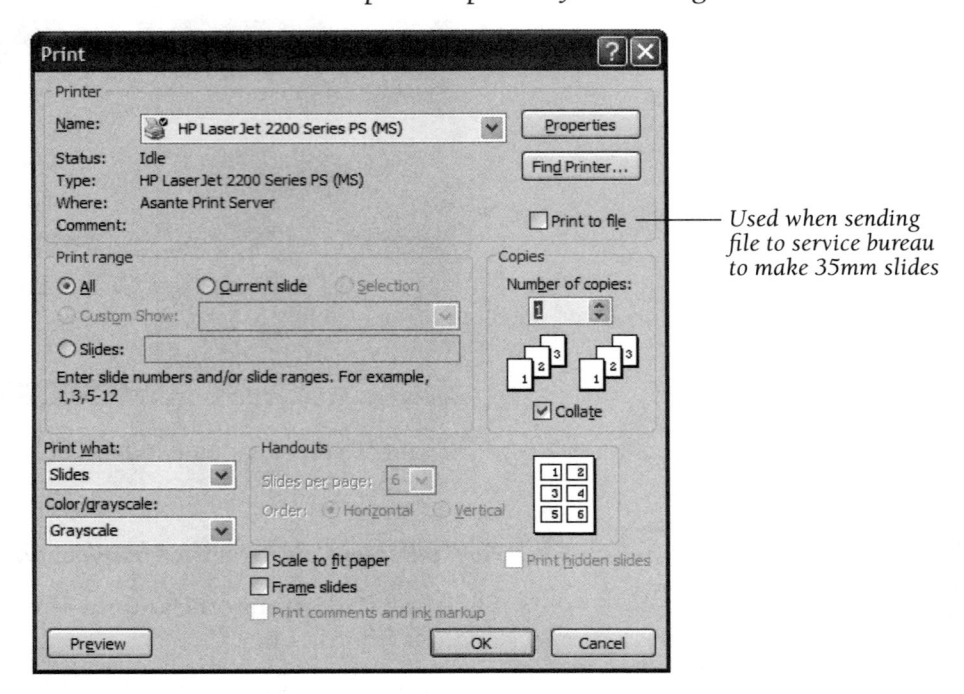

Print to file — Used when sending file to service bureau to make 35mm slides

> **By the way**
> You can click the Preview *button to see how the slides will look when printed.*

3 Choose how many copies and which slides to print

In **Print range** area, select **All** or **Current slide**, or enter slide range or numbers.

In **Number of copies** text box, use arrows or type number.

4 Choose other options

Make sure **Print what** is set to **Slides**.

Look at options on **Color/grayscale** drop-down list.

Make sure **Color/grayscale** is set for type of printer you're using.

5 Check printer's paper supply

For overheads, you need transparency film in paper tray you're using.

6 Click OK to start printing (or Cancel if you're not printing now)

7 Close file without saving changes when finished

> ⛔ Notes and Handouts (pages 115–117) must be saved on disk.

Print notes & handouts

You can also print the speaker notes and audience handouts you created earlier.

1 Open Notes file

2 Say that you want to print speaker notes

On **File** menu, choose **Print**. Click down-arrow to see **Print what** list.

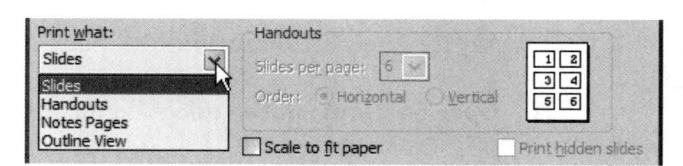

You must issue one print command for each type of output you want.

Click **Notes Pages**.

3 Choose how many copies and which slides to print notes pages for

In **Copies** text box, use arrows or type number.

In **Print range** area, select **All** or **Current slide**, or enter range.

Make any check box changes you want.

> *By the way*
> You can click the Preview button to see how the notes or handouts will look when printed.

4 Click OK to start printing (or Cancel); close file without saving changes

5 Open Handouts file

6 Say that you want to print audience handouts

On **File** menu, choose **Print**.

Click down-arrow to see **Print what** list. Click **Handouts**.

Choose **Slides per page** option you want to use.

For **Order**, click **Horizontal** or **Vertical**.

7 Choose how many copies you want

In **Copies** text box, enter number of people you want handouts for.

OR

Leave **1** as number if you'll use copy machine for duplication.

Notice setting of **Collate** check box. Change it if you like.

> *If box is checked and you're making several copies, all pages are printed once, then a second time, and so on.*

Change any other settings you want.

8 Click OK to start printing (or Cancel if you're not printing now)

9 Close file without saving changes when finished

Use AutoContent wizard

Now that you know how Microsoft PowerPoint works, you may find that an AutoContent wizard is a useful shortcut.

1 Create new presentation

If PowerPoint is running, choose **New** on **File** menu (don't click 🗋 on toolbar).

Otherwise, start Microsoft PowerPoint.

Notice **New Presentation** task pane at right.

2 Open new presentation using AutoContent wizard

In **New** area of task pane, click **From AutoContent wizard**.

3 Use AutoContent Wizard

Click **Next** button to proceed.

Continue through all steps, choosing desired options.

You may have to install any templates you choose that are not currently installed. You will need the original Microsoft Office CDs.

Click **Finish** to end. Close task pane.

4 Replace text and see slide show

Use PAGE DOWN to view slides. Click any placeholders to add your text.

Add any slides and graphic elements you like.

View slide show.

5 Exit Microsoft PowerPoint and save file

On **File** menu, choose **Exit**.

Click **Yes** when asked whether to save changed file.

Name file `Wizard`.

6 Shut down Windows and switch off computer (see page 2, step 3)

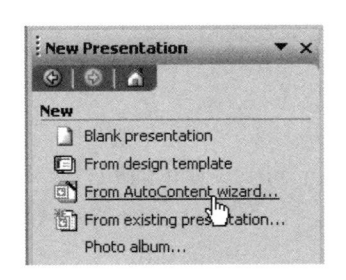

By the way

The AutoContent Wizard *can be accessed only when you are starting a new presentation.*

Microsoft Excel 2003
Spreadsheets

/ 121

122 Start Microsoft Excel
123 Explore cells
124 Enter text
126 Enter numbers & save
127 Select cells
128 Enter simple formulas
130 Use function to add
132 Copy formula (relative)
133 Create data series
134 Copy formula (absolute)
136 Insert function
138 Paste special
139 Format text
140 Change fonts & sizes
141 Change text alignment
142 Set column width & row height
143 Insert & delete cells
144 Format cell borders
146 Add cell shading
147 Format numbers
149 Enter & format dates
151 Sort data
153 Divide window into panes
154 Lock cells & protect worksheet
156 Create pie chart
159 Create column chart
161 Format chart text
162 Format chart objects
164 Reorganize sheets

Start Microsoft Excel

You are now ready to start the Microsoft Excel application running on your computer.

Tip

If Office Assistant (paper clip with eyes) appears, click it. Click Options *button. Click* Use the Office Assistant *check box to remove mark. Click* OK.

1 Start computer, Windows, and Excel

Switch on computer and start Windows (see page 2).

Start Microsoft Excel (see page 5, but choose **Microsoft Office Excel 2003** this time).

2 View maximized document window for Microsoft Excel

If task pane appears at right, choose **Task Pane** on **View** menu to hide it.

If **Microsoft Excel** window doesn't fill display, click 🗖 in its title bar.

If separate window titled **Book1** appears inside, click 🗖 in its title bar.

If formatting toolbar is to right of standard toolbar, do step 4 on page 10.

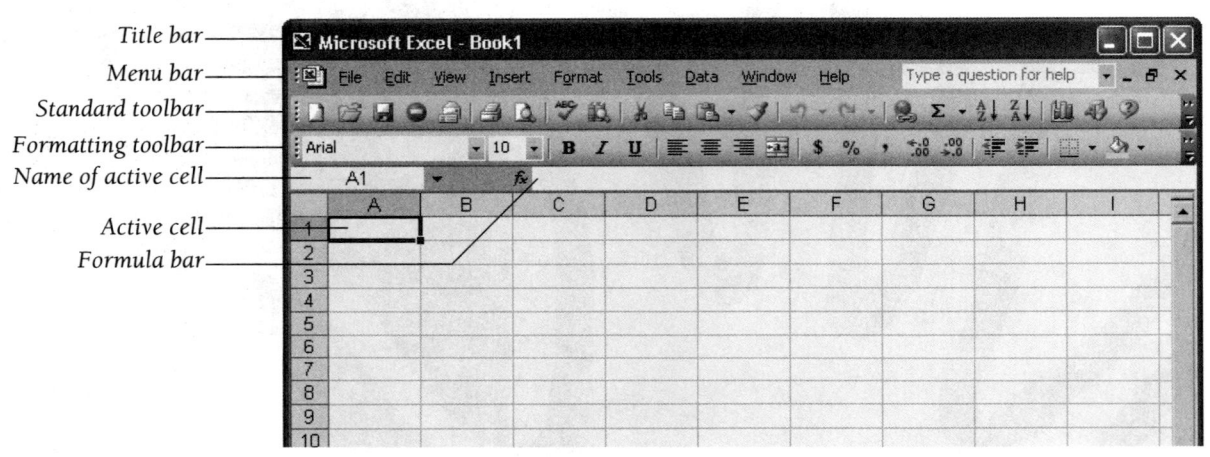

Title bar
Menu bar
Standard toolbar
Formatting toolbar
Name of active cell
Active cell
Formula bar

Move pointer tip inside new icons at right of toolbars. *Do not click!*

Name of tool appears below pointer.

3 Set user options if necessary

On **Tools** menu, choose **Options**. Click **View** tab.

Make sure all check boxes are marked *except* **Page Breaks** and **Formulas**.

On **Edit** tab, make sure all check boxes are marked *except* **Fixed decimal**.

On same tab, make sure you see **Down** in **Direction** box. Click OK.

4 Explore workbook sheets

Microsoft Excel files are called workbooks. Each new workbook normally contains three blank worksheets. You'll usually use just one.

By the way

Notice the four buttons at the bottom of the screen: |◀ ◀ ▶ ▶|. *They allow scrolling hidden sheet tabs into view if you have more tabs than will fit in the space available.*

To switch to different sheet, click its tab once.

Active worksheet tab is white; others are gray. All are empty now.

Click **Sheet1** to make first worksheet active.

← *Complete previous activity before going on.*

Explore cells

A worksheet displays columns and rows. The intersection of a column and a row forms a rectangle called a cell.

1 Select one cell

Move pointer over worksheet. Notice big plus-sign shape: ✚.

Click pointer in any cell.

Active cell border moves to cell you selected.

Click cell in column A, row 1.

2 Notice active cell name at left of formula bar

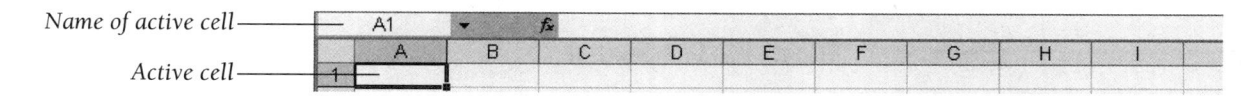

Name of active cell ⎯⎯
Active cell ⎯⎯

Name is column letter plus row number of active cell.

Click another cell.

New cell name appears at left of formula bar.

By the way
Notice that the column letter and row number headings of the active cell are darkened.

3 Practice keyboard moves

Tap ENTER to move *down* one cell. Tap SHIFT ENTER to move *up* one cell.

Tap TAB to move *right* one cell. Tap SHIFT TAB to move *left* one cell.

Tap →, ←, ↑, ↓ to move one cell in direction of arrow.

4 Select range of cells (method 1)

With pointer inside cell A1, press mouse button and drag pointer to cell C3.

Tip
When dragging, start with the pointer in the center of the first cell. Avoid the tiny square at the lower-right corner of the cell. You'll learn about this feature on page 132.

Rectangular range (multiple cells) is selected (highlighted). First cell remains white and has its name in formula bar. A1 is active cell.

5 Deselect range

Click any cell on worksheet.

6 Select range of cells (method 2)

Click cell at upper left of range, hold down SHIFT, and click lower-right cell.

7 Select range of cells (method 3)

Click cell at one corner of range.

With SHIFT held down, tap arrow keys to "paint" (or "unpaint") highlighting in direction of arrow.

> **!** *A new worksheet must be open.*

Enter text

Entering data is usually the first step in creating a spreadsheet. You enter text by selecting a cell and then typing.

1 **Begin text entry in cell A1**

Click cell A1.

Watch formula bar as you type `Computer Purchase Projections`.

> Use [BACKSPACE] to erase typing errors.

Notice ☒ (cancel) and ☑ (enter) buttons now on formula bar.

> Entry is not complete yet.

2 **Accept entry in cell**

Click ☑ on formula bar.

> Active cell stays A1. Cancel and enter buttons go away. They appear only when you enter data.

Tip
Remember that your entry is not complete until you click the enter button (or go to another cell). If some Excel commands don't seem to be working, look at the formula bar. If you see the cancel and enter buttons there, it means you forgot to complete your entry.

3 **Begin entry; then change your mind**

With cell A1 still active, type `Planned Purchases`.

Click ☒ on formula bar, or tap [ESC] on keyboard.

> Entry is cancelled, and cell A1 is unchanged.

4 **Select new cell and enter text**

Click cell A3, and type `IBM`.

> As before, cancel and enter buttons appear when you begin typing.

Tap [ENTER] on keyboard.

> Data is entered, but active cell changes to A4, cell below entry. Cancel and enter buttons go away.

5 **Enter more data**

Type `Dell` and tap [ENTER] to enter data and move to cell A5.

Type `Appel` (yes, it's misspelled). Tap [ENTER] to enter data.

> Active cell should be A6.

Tip
Tapping [TAB] also completes data entry, but makes the cell to the right become active.

Type `Acer`. Tap [CTRL][ENTER] to end data entry and leave cell active.

> [CTRL][ENTER] is equivalent to clicking ☑.

	A	B	C	D	E	F	G	H	I
1	Computer Purchase Projections								
2									
3	IBM								
4	Dell								
5	Appel								
6	Acer								

6 Correct errors; delete characters (method 1)

Click cell with error to be corrected (A5).

In formula bar, click I-beam pointer just right of error (**el**).

Insertion point appears where you clicked.

Tap [BACKSPACE] twice to erase error characters; then type **le**.

Tap [CTRL][ENTER] or click ✓ on formula bar to accept editing.

7 Replace data already in cell

Tap [↓] or click cell A6.

Once cell is selected, just type new information.

Type **Sonny** and tap [ENTER] to accept change.

Sonny replaces Acer in cell A6.

8 Correct errors, delete characters (method 2)

Sony is spelled incorrectly.

Double-click cell A6 on worksheet.

This time, insertion point appears in cell, not on formula bar.

Position I-beam pointer just right of either **n**.

Tap [BACKSPACE] to erase error.

Tap [ENTER] to accept change.

9 Delete data in cell

Click cell A1.

On **Edit** menu, choose **Clear**; on submenu, choose **Contents**.

You can also use [DELETE] for this.

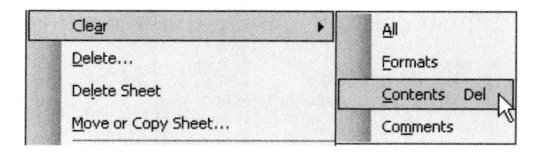

By the way

Notice that the Undo command names the step you just did. You can also undo multiple actions by using the drop-down list on the undo button on the standard toolbar.

Tip

If the Redo command is not on the menu, wait a few seconds, or click the arrow at the bottom to see the full menu.

10 Undo and redo previous change

On **Edit** menu, choose **Undo Clear** (or tap [CTRL][Z], or click ↶ on standard toolbar).

On **Edit** menu, choose **Redo Clear** (or tap [CTRL][Y], or click ↷).

Text is cleared again.

Use any method to undo change once more.

Clear is undone, and text reappears.

Complete previous activity before going on.

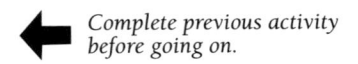

Enter numbers & save

As you'll soon see, the power of spreadsheets lies in their ability to do calculations with numerical data.

1 Save workbook file

Save on disk as Microsoft Excel workbook with name `Computers`.

For reminder of steps, see page 16.

2 Enter numbers in column B

Column B will contain the quantity of computers to be purchased in first month.

Click cell B3.

Type `11`.

Tap ENTER.

Active cell is now B4.

Type `10` and tap ENTER.

Active cell is now B5.

Type `17` and tap ENTER.

Active cell is now B6.

Type `15` and tap ENTER.

Data should appear as in figure to left.

3 Add more numbers in column C

Click cell C3.

Type `14` and tap ENTER.

Type `9` and tap ENTER.

Type `12` and tap ENTER.

Type `20` and tap ENTER.

4 Enter numbers in column D

Finish entering data to duplicate this worksheet.

	A	B	C	D	E	F	G	H	I
1	Computer Purchase Projections								
2									
3	IBM	11	14	9					
4	Dell	10	9	12					
5	Apple	17	12	16					
6	Sony	15	20	14					

5 Save changed workbook

On **File** menu, choose **Save** (or click 🖫 on standard toolbar).

No dialog box appears this time. Changed workbook file replaces previously saved version on disk. Original is permanently erased!

Tip

You can enter numbers using the keys at the top of the standard keyboard or on the numeric keypad on the right side of the keyboard.

	A	B	C
1	Computer Purchase Projections		
2			
3	IBM	11	
4	Dell	10	
5	Apple	17	
6	Sony	15	

	A	B	C
1	Computer Purchase Projections		
2			
3	IBM	11	14
4	Dell	10	9
5	Apple	17	12
6	Sony	15	20

← *Complete previous activity before going on.*

Select cells

Most commands affect only the cells that you select before giving the command. Selected cells are highlighted.

1 **Select cells with data for computers**

Click cell A3.

Hold (SHIFT) down, and click cell D6.

Shift-clicking extends selection. A3 remains active cell.

2 **Move active cell through selected block**

Watch active cell as you tap (TAB) repeatedly. Try same with (ENTER).

This is convenient when entering data in table.

3 **Select one whole column**

Click down-arrow pointer in header for column A: [A↓].

First cell in column is active cell.

4 **Select several whole columns**

With pointer inside column B header, press mouse button and drag to right to highlight columns C and D.

Notice box telling number of columns selected. Release mouse button.

5 **Select one row, then several rows**

Click right-arrow pointer in header for row 3: [→ IBM].

Whole row is highlighted. First cell is active.

Press inside row 3 header (*not* line between row headers) and drag down to highlight rows 4, 5, and 6. Notice which cell is active.

6 **Select separated rows**

Click header for row 1.

Hold down (CTRL) and click headers for rows 4 and 6. Notice active cell.

(CTRL) lets you add any cells you want to current selection.

Click any cell to deselect block.

7 **Select whole spreadsheet**

Click empty box above row 1 and to left of column A: .

All cells are selected. Different highlighting (white) shows A1 is active.

8 **Close workbook**

On **File** menu, choose **Close**. (If asked whether to save changes, click **No**.)

Tip

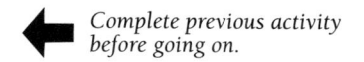

If you just start typing, the data goes into the active cell only. If you apply a menu or toolbar command, all cells in the selected block are affected.

Enter simple formulas

You can enter simple formulas in spreadsheets by using the keyboard or mouse.

1 **Create new workbook file**

On standard toolbar, click ☐ (new).

2 **Enter numbers to create following worksheet**

	A	B	C	D	E	F	G	H	I
1									
2									
3	123	321	741	1417					
4	456	654	852	2582					
5	789	987	963	3693					

3 **Save workbook**

On **File** menu, choose **Save**.

Save on disk with name `Numprac`.

4 **Enter formula (method 1)**

Click cell A7 and type `=`.

Formulas always begin with =.

Type `a3+a4`.

You don't have to type capital letters for cell names.

In cell A7, notice colors of cell names. Notice matching colors of new borders on cells A3 and A4.

Colored borders show which cells are referred to in your formula.

Click ✓ (enter) on formula bar to complete entry.

5 **Look at formula and results**

Look at formula bar and worksheet cell A7.

Cell A7 has two things in it. You see formula you entered (=A3+A4) in formula bar. You see result (579) on worksheet.

Click outside cell A7.

Result stays on worksheet, but formula is not in formula bar now.

Click cell A7 to see formula again.

6 **Enter formula (method 2)**

Click cell B7 and type `=`.

Click cell B3 (or use arrow keys to make B3 active cell).

Type `+`.

Click cell B4 (or use arrow keys to make it active).

Click ✓ to accept entry.

Tip

If you see a number in a cell, how can you tell whether the entry in the cell is the number itself or a formula that results in the number? Simple: Just click the cell and look at the formula bar. The formula bar always shows what was entered in the cell.

Enter simple formulas *continued*

7 *See results*

Formula bar should contain =B3+B4. Cell B7 should contain 975.

8 *Enter subtraction formula*

Click cell B8 and type   =.

Tap [↑] or click to select cell B7.

Type   -.

Tap [↑], then [←]; or click to select cell A7. Notice borders and colors.

Click [✓]. Check formula and result.

Formula should read =B7–A7. Result in cell B8 should be 396.

9 *Enter multiplication formula*

Click cell B10. Use any method to enter formula   =B7*B8.

For asterisk (*), tap [SHIFT][8], or use key on numeric keypad.

Click [✓].

Check formula and result.

Result in cell B10 should be 386100.

10 *Enter division formula*

Click cell B12. Use any method to enter formula   =B7/A7.

Slash (/) is on both main keyboard and numeric keypad.

Click [✓].

Check formula and result.

Result in cell B12 should be 1.683938.

11 *Enter more complex formula*

Click cell B14.

Use any method to enter formula   =A3+A4+B3+B4.

Differently colored borders show each cell referred to in formula.

Click [✓].

Check formula and result.

Result in cell B14 should be 1554.

12 *Close workbook without saving changes*

On **File** menu, choose **Close**.

Click **No** in message box when asked whether to save changes.

Tip

If you type the wrong cell name in a formula, you can drag the border with the same color to the correct cell. (Be sure to drag using an edge of the border.) The name in the formula changes.

> Computers file as completed on page 126 must be on disk.

Use function to add

Microsoft Excel has many functions you can use in formulas for such tasks as adding up a column or a row of numbers.

1 **Open Computers workbook file**

On **File** menu (in bottom area), choose **Computers**.

At bottom of File *menu, Microsoft Excel lists recently used files.*

2 **Enter formula with function (method 1)**

Click cell B8, where result of formula will appear.

Type `=sum(b3:b6)`. Notice colored items in column B.

Colon (:) is on key to right of L. *Formula uses SUM function to add numbers in cell range B3:B6. (You don't have to use capital letters when typing function names or cell names.)*

Click ✓. Check formula and result.

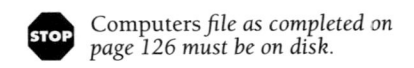

> **By the way**
> As you type the formula, Excel outlines in blue the range to be used. The corresponding cell names in the formula are also blue.

— Formula with SUM function
— Result

3 **Enter formula with function (method 2)**

Click cell C8, where result of second formula will appear.

Type `=sum(`.

Put pointer in cell C3. Press and drag down to cell C6. Release mouse button.

When you're entering formulas, dragging through cells enters cell range.

Click ✓. Notice that Excel enters closing parenthesis for you.

Check formula and result.

— Formula with SUM function
— Result

4 **Delete both formulas**

Highlight cells B8 and C8.

On **Edit** menu, choose **Clear**, then **Contents** (or tap DELETE).

Use function to add *continued*

5 *Enter formula with function (method 3)*

Click cell B8, where result of formula will appear.

On standard toolbar, click ∑ (AutoSum).

> *Formula =SUM(B3:B7) appears in formula bar (and on worksheet) with cell range highlighted. Entry isn't complete yet.*

Click ✓. Check result.

> *Results are same as in step 2.*

By the way
The extra cell in the range (B7) does not contain a number and will not affect the result. The SUM function ignores blank cells and cells containing text.

---

6 *Use AutoSum again*

Click cell C8, where result will appear.

On standard toolbar, click ∑ again.

Check formula.

> *Formula =SUM(C3:C7) should appear.*

Click ✓. Check result.

> *Results are same as in step 3.*

7 *Use AutoSum once more*

Click cell D8, where result will appear.

On standard toolbar, click ∑ again.

Check formula.

> *Oops! Formula this time is not correct: =SUM(B8:C8). AutoSum picks closest data range (to its left this time). Cell range is already highlighted in formula, so it's easy to change.*

On worksheet, press and drag from cell D3 down to cell D7.

> *Notice that formula in formula bar (and on worksheet) changes. Formula should be =SUM(D3:D7). If not, press and drag again.*

Click ✓. Check result.

> *Correct sum is 51.*

By the way
You can also edit the formula by typing in corrected ranges.

---

8 *Enter label for sums*

Click cell A8.

Type **Total** and tap ENTER.

9 *Save workbook file*

On **File** menu, choose **Save**.

> *Edited version of* Computers *replaces previous version on disk.*

← *Complete previous activity before going on.*

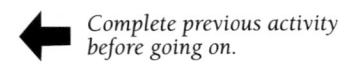

Copy formula (relative)

Microsoft Excel's AutoFill feature allows you to copy formulas from one cell to many other cells quickly and easily.

1 **Enter title for totals in column E**

Click cell E2. Type `Totals by Computer` and tap ENTER.

Tip
You can also select other common functions from the AutoSum drop-down list.

---

2 **Enter another addition formula using AutoSum**

With cell E3 active, click Σ (AutoSum) on standard toolbar.

Formula should be =SUM(B3:D3), since B3:D3 is closest range of numbers.

Click ✓ to accept formula. Check that result on worksheet is **34**.

3 **Copy formula to other cells (method 1)**

Position pointer over small square in lower-right corner of active cell border.

Small square is AutoFill handle. Pointer changes to cross.

Tip
The pointer must be in a precise location for AutoFill to work. Watch for the proper pointer shape.

2					Totals by Computer
3	IBM	11	14	9	34
4	Dell	10	9	12	

Press and drag down to cell E6. Notice outline showing range of copying.

Release mouse button.

Formula is copied down. You can also use AutoFill to copy up, copy left, and copy right. Direction depends on where you drag AutoFill handle.

By the way
The tiny box at the lower left of the selection lets you choose to copy just the formats or just the contents of the original cell. If you ignore the box, you're copying both.

	A	B	C	D	E	F	G	H	I
1	Computer Purchase Projections							
2					Totals by Computer			
3	IBM	11	14	9	34			
4	Dell	10	9	12	31			
5	Apple	17	12	16	45			
6	Sony	15	20	14	49			

Click any cell containing copied formula. Look at formula bar.

Cell names have changed from original (B3:D3) to be "relative" to location of copy of formula. For example, if copy is in row 4, range is B4:D4.

By the way
You must use method 2 when the cell where you want the copy is not next to the cell with the original.

---

4 **Copy formula (method 2)**

Click cell D8. Notice formula in formula bar.

On **Edit** menu, choose **Copy**.

Click cell E8. On **Edit** menu, choose **Paste** (or simply tap ENTER).

Verify that result is **159** and that cell names have changed in copy so formula sums numbers in column E.

5 **Save changed workbook file**

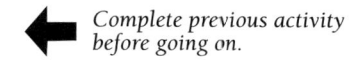

Create data series

The AutoFill feature also helps you enter standard data in a series, such as months, years, or quarters.

> **By the way**
> *AutoFill also works with days of the week. If you begin the series with an abbreviation, such as Jan or Wed, or if you use all capital letters, the rest of the series follows your example.*

1 **Enter first item in series**

Click cell B2. Type **January** and tap ENTER.

2 **Create series of months**

Select cell B2 again.

Press AutoFill handle carefully and drag to surround range B2 through D2.

	A	B	C	D
1	Computer Purchase Projections			
2		January		
3	IBM	11	14	March
4	Dell	10	9	

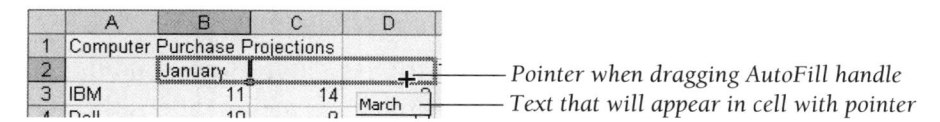

— *Pointer when dragging AutoFill handle*
— *Text that will appear in cell with pointer*

Notice box below pointer.

Release mouse button to see series.

Cell C2 now contains February, *and D2 contains* March.

3 **Save changed workbook file**

4 **Try another data series**

Click cell B2. Type **2004** and click ✓.

Press and drag AutoFill handle to surround range B2 through D2.

Release mouse button. Look at cells C2 and D2.

Both contain 2004. AutoFill tool simply copies numbers.

> **By the way**
> *Did you notice the little green "message" triangle at the upper-left corner of cell B8 when you entered 2004 in cell B2? If you click the triangle, then move the pointer to the little box that appears, you can read the message. It warns that you've put a number in a cell just outside the range used in the formula in cell B8. If that were an error (it isn't), you could fix it now.*

5 **Use Fill Series command to create series of years**

Cells B2 through D2 should still be selected.

On **Edit** menu, choose **Fill**; then, on submenu, choose **Series**.

Type of series is Linear *and Step Value is* 1. *That's what you want now.*

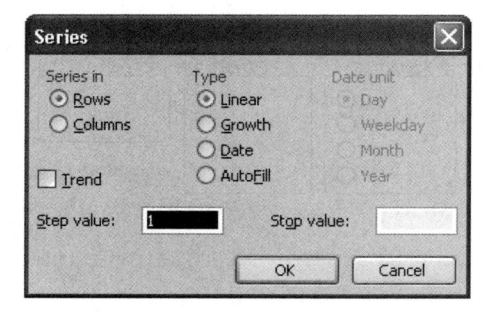

Click **OK**, or tap ENTER.

Cell C2 now contains 2005, *and D2 contains* 2006.

6 **Close workbook file without saving changes**

On **File** menu, choose **Close**. Click **No** in dialog box asking whether to save changes.

> **Tip**
> *You can also add your own series to the built-in lists. On the Tools menu, choose Options. Then click the Custom Lists tab, and use the Add button to add your own list.*

← *Complete previous activity before going on.*

Copy formula (absolute)

Relative change of cell names is normally what you want in a copy of a formula—but not always. Here's an example.

By the way
When text is entered in cell F2, text in E2 appears truncated. It is still there but is no longer displayed. You will fix this later.

---

1 Open Computers workbook file

2 Create new column title

Click cell F2. Type `Percent of Total` and tap ENTER.

3 Calculate percentages

Column F will show each computer's total projected sales as percentage of grand total (159 in cell E8).

With cell F3 active, use any method to enter formula `=E3/E8`. Notice colors of cell names and cells they refer to. Then click ✓.

Result is 0.213836. You want this shown as percentage.

With cell F3 active, click % (percent style) on formatting toolbar.

Same number now appears as 21%. You've only changed format.

4 Copy formula down column

Press and drag **AutoFill** handle down to cell F6. Release mouse button.

	January	February	March	Totals by C	Percent of Total
3 IBM	11	14	9	34	21%
4 Dell	10	9	12	31	#DIV/0!
5 Apple	17	12	16	45	#DIV/0!
6 Sony	15	20	14	49	#DIV/0!

Oops! Something is wrong!

Click cell F4. Move pointer over ⊕ error message icon to left of F4.

	January	February	March	Totals by C	Percent of Total
3 IBM	11	14	9	34	21%
4 Dell	10	9	12	⊕	#DIV/0!
5 Apple	17	12	16		#DIV/0!
6 Sony	15	20	14	The formula or function used is dividing by zero or empty cells.

Error message #DIV/0! means formula is trying to divide number by zero.

5 View formulas in cells on worksheet

Tap CTRL `.

By the way
CTRL ` *is a shortcut for an option you can also set by choosing* Options *on the* Tools *menu, clicking the* View *tab, and clicking the* Formulas *check box.*

` is usually at left of row of number keys on main keyboard. CTRL ` switches between viewing results and viewing formulas.

If necessary, scroll so columns E and F are both in view.

	C	D	E	F	G
1					
2	February	March	Totals by Computer	Percent of Total	
3	14	9	=SUM(B3:D3)	=E3/E8	
4	9	12	=SUM(B4:D4)	=E4/E9	
5	12	16	=SUM(B5:D5)	=E5/E10	
6	20	14	=SUM(B6:D6)	=E6/E11	
7					
8	=SUM(C3:C7)	=SUM(D3:D7)	=SUM(E3:E7)		
9					

Copy formula (absolute) *continued* XLS/ 135

6 *View formulas causing errors*

Look at formula in cell F4. Notice green color of empty cell C9.

Formula is =E4/E9. There is no number in cell E9.

Look at formulas in cells F5 and F6.

You wanted E3 to change relative to new location, but E8 needs to remain constant in each copy so formulas all refer to grand total.

7 *Make divisor stay same in copies*

Double-click cell F3.

Put insertion point between E and 8.

Type **$** (SHIFT 4), and click ✓.

Formula should be =E3/E$8. Dollar sign makes 8 absolute. 8 won't change in copies. 3 in E3 is still relative. It will change in copies in other rows.

Press and drag AutoFill handle again to surround range F3:F6.

Release mouse button and look at copies this time.

8 in E8 remains constant ("absolute") in all copies of formula.

	C	D	E	F
1				
2	February	March	Totals by Computer	Percent of Total
3	14	9	=SUM(B3:D3)	=E3/E$8
4	9	12	=SUM(B4:D4)	=E4/E$8
5	12	16	=SUM(B5:D5)	=E5/E$8
6	20	14	=SUM(B6:D6)	=E6/E$8
7				
8	=SUM(C3:C7)	=SUM(D3:D7)	=SUM(E3:E7)	

8 *View results in worksheet cells*

Tap CTRL ` again to see results of formulas.

Scroll so that column A is back in view.

	A	B	C	D	E	F	G	H	I
1	Computer Purchase Projections								
2		January	February	March	Totals by	Percent of Total			
3	IBM	11	14	9	34	21%			
4	Dell	10	9	12	31	19%			
5	Apple	17	12	16	45	28%			
6	Sony	15	20	14	49	31%			
7									
8	Total		53	55	51	159			
9									

Percentages appear correctly with new formulas.

9 *Save changed workbook*

On **File** menu, choose **Save**.

By the way

Cell names in formulas are often called "references" because they refer to the data in the cell. A dollar sign before a row letter or a column number makes it an "absolute reference."

← *Complete previous activity before going on.*

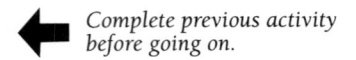

Insert function

If you forget the exact name of a function, you can find it on a list and paste it directly into a formula.

1 Add another text label to worksheet

Click cell A9. Type **Average** and tap TAB.

2 Enter formula in cell to right of label

In cell B9, type **=** to begin formula.

This is cell where average sales for January will appear.

On **Insert** menu, choose **Function**.

Insert Function dialog box appears. It lists all available functions.

In **Search for a function** text box, type **average**. Click **Go**.

You could also select Statistical *on Or select a category list.*

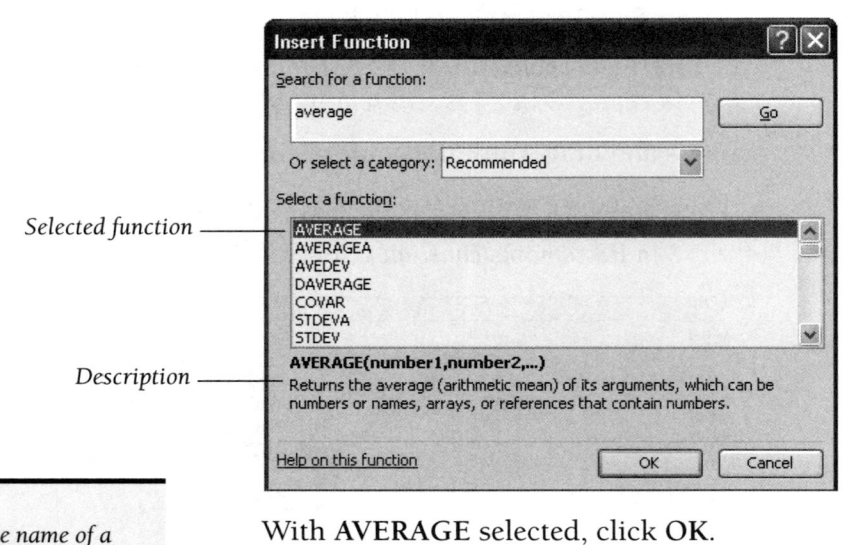

Selected function — AVERAGE

Description — AVERAGE(number1,number2,...) Returns the average (arithmetic mean) of its arguments, which can be numbers or names, arrays, or references that contain numbers.

With **AVERAGE** selected, click **OK**.

New dialog box appears.

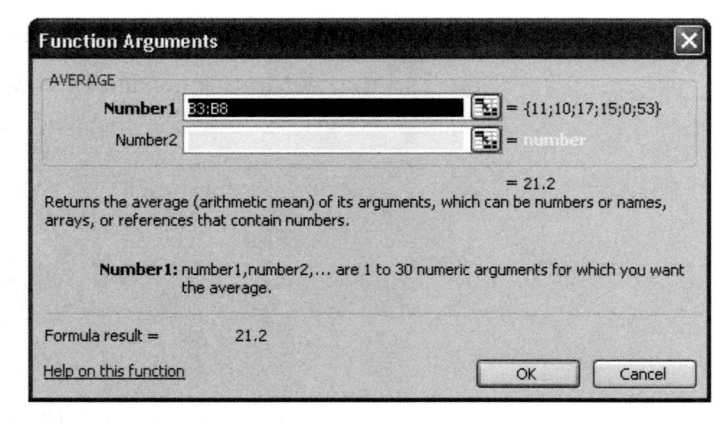

At right of **Number1** box, click (collapse dialog) to hide dialog box.

On worksheet, drag to highlight range B3:B6 (January cells to be averaged).

Click (expand dialog) to see whole dialog box. Click **OK**.

Formula is inserted, and result, 13.25, appears on worksheet.

Tip

If you don't know the name of a function but you have an idea of the kind of function you want, you can choose the category on the drop-down list below the search box. The Average function is in the Statistical category, for example.

Tip

For more information about a specific function, click the Help on this function *text link at the lower left of the dialog box.*

Insert function *continued*

3 *Copy formula to other months, and total*

Press carefully and drag AutoFill handle to surround range B9:E9.

Release mouse button.

Verify that results are **13.75**, **12.75**, and **39.75** and that cell addresses have changed to be relative to new locations of copies.

4 *Add another label to worksheet*

Click cell A10.

Type **Maximum** and tap TAB.

Cell B10 is selected.

5 *Add MAX function*

On formula bar, click *fx* (insert function).

In **Search for a function** text box, type **maximum**. Click **Go**.

On **Select a function** list, click **MAX**. Click **OK**.

Click upper (collapse dialog) to hide rest of dialog box.

On worksheet, drag to highlight range B3:B6.

Click (expand dialog) to display dialog box; then click **OK**.

Formula is inserted, and result, 17, appears on worksheet.

Copy formula to range C10:E10.

Verify that results are **20**, **16**, and **49** and that cell addresses have changed to be relative to new locations of copies.

6 *Add another function in next row*

Type **Minimum** label in cell A11.

Click cell B11.

Click *fx* on formula bar.

In **Search for a function** text box, type **minimum**. Click **Go**.

On **Select a function** list, click **MIN**. Click **OK**.

Follow steps above to add range B3:B6.

Copy formula to range C11:E11.

Verify that results are **10**, **9**, **9**, and **31** and that cell addresses have changed to be relative to new locations of copies.

7 *Save and close changed workbook file*

On **File** menu, choose **Save**.

On **File** menu, choose **Close**.

> **STOP** Numprac file as saved on page 128 must be on disk.

Paste special

You can paste copied data using many special formats. Here you will practice a few of them.

1 **Open Numprac workbook file**

2 **Use formula to add multiple columns of numbers**

Select range A7:D7. On standard toolbar, click Σ.

Formulas to sum numbers above selected range are automatically entered.

By the way
Excel allows you to complete the Paste command only once with each copied item. It does not maintain copied information on the clipboard as Word does.

---

3 **Copy cells with formulas**

With range A7:D7 still selected, on **Edit** menu, choose **Copy**.

4 **Paste values only**

Click cell A9. On **Edit** menu, choose **Paste Special**.

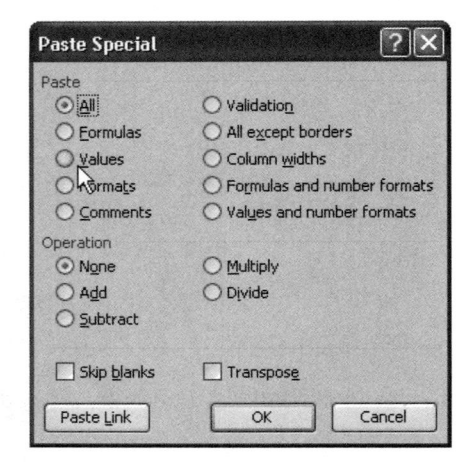

Click **Values**; click **OK**. Tap ESC to clear clipboard. View results.

Result of formula (value) is pasted, not formula.

Tip
Paste Special *does not clear the clipboard as the standard* Paste *command does. That is why you see the blinking copy range on the worksheet. Be sure to tap* ESC *to clear this range or you could accidentally delete or overwrite it.*

11	123	456	789
12	321	654	987
13	741	852	963
14	1417	2582	3693

5 **Transpose data (switch data in rows to columns and vice versa)**

Select range A3:D5. On **Edit** menu, choose **Copy**.

Click cell A11. On **Edit** menu, choose **Paste Special**.

Click **Transpose**; click **OK**. Tap ESC to clear clipboard. View results.

F	G	H	I
124	323	744	1421

6 **Add values (add copied data to data in paste range)**

Select range A3:D3. On **Edit** menu, choose **Copy**.

Click cell A4. On **Edit** menu, choose **Paste Special**.

Click **Add**; click **OK**. Tap ESC to clear clipboard. View results.

Three selected numbers in row 3 were added to ones already in row 4.

Look at formula bar for cell A4.

No formula is involved. Addition happened when you pasted.

7 **Close numprac workbook without saving changes**

> **STOP** Computers file as saved on page 133 must be on disk.

Format text

After entering data, you may want to format text to emphasize and clarify. You can use menu commands or toolbar buttons.

1 Open Computers workbook file from your disk

2 Add bold style to labels (method 1)

Highlight range A1:F2 (title in row 1 and column labels in row 2).

Pointer shape is big outlined plus sign, not small AutoFill cross.

On formatting toolbar, click **B** (bold).

Text in highlighted cells is bold. Bold tool stays boxed.

> **By the way**
> Not all text in a cell must be formatted the same way. To make some characters bold, for example, click the cell with the text, go to the formula bar, and highlight just the characters you want to be bold. Then apply bold format.

3 Remove bold using bold tool

Click cell A1. Click boxed bold tool.

4 Add bold labels (method 2)

Click column A header (above cell A1) to select whole column.

On **Format** menu, click **Cells**. Click **Font** tab in dialog box.

> **By the way**
> As you can see, the Format Cells dialog box lets you apply many different formats to the data in a cell. You'll use more of them soon.

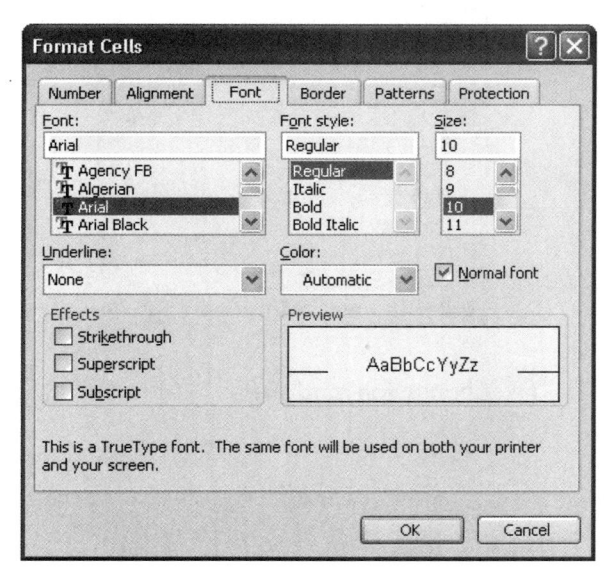

On **Font style** list, click **Bold**. Click **OK**.

5 Add bold to other labels (method 3)

Click any cell with bold text.

On standard toolbar, click (format painter).

Click header for row 8 (row of totals).

Format painter copies all formats from original cell (or block of cells) and "paints" them in whatever other cells you select.

6 Add italic to bold

Select cells A3 through A6. On formatting toolbar, click **I** (italic).

7 Save changed workbook file

← *Complete previous activity before going on.*

Change fonts & sizes

Text can appear in many different fonts and sizes. Each font specifies the shapes of letters, numbers, and symbols.

1 **Choose cell to apply format change to**

Click cell A1.

> *Notice that text flows into cells B1 and C1 but is actually contained in cell A1. (Check formula bar.) Overflow appears when neighbor cell is empty.*

2 **Check current font and size**

On formatting toolbar, notice **Arial** font in size **10**.

> *These are defaults on new worksheets.*

On formatting toolbar, click down-arrow to display font list.

> *Your list of fonts may be different.*

Tip
If the font is not Arial 10, Choose Options *on the* Tools *menu. Use the* General *tab to set the font and size.*

3 **Change font and size**

Type `tim` to move quickly down font list. Click **Times New Roman**.

> *Command affects only text in selected cell.*

On formatting toolbar, click down-arrow to display font size list.

On font size list, click **14**.

> *Row height adjusts to font size.*

4 **Change font size of another range**

Highlight cells in range A8:E8.

> *This is row of totals (if you did activity on pages 130–131).*

On font size list, click **12**.

5 **Save changed workbook file**

> Computers *workbook file* must be open.

Change text alignment

Text can be aligned left, right, or center within a cell. It can also be centered over a range.

XLS/ 141

By the way
Text labels normally align to the left, and numbers normally align to the right. But you can change that with the tools you learn here.

1 Align data within cells (method 1)

Highlight range B2:F2 (column labels you began entering on page 133).

On formatting toolbar, locate four alignment tools.

Click ≡ (center).

Select range A8:A11 (labels you entered for functions, if you did activity beginning on page 136).

On formatting toolbar, click ≡ (align right).

2 Align data within cells (method 2)

Highlight range B3:F11 (cells with numbers).

On **Format** menu, choose **Cells**. Click **Alignment** tab.

Standard alignment settings and many other options are available.

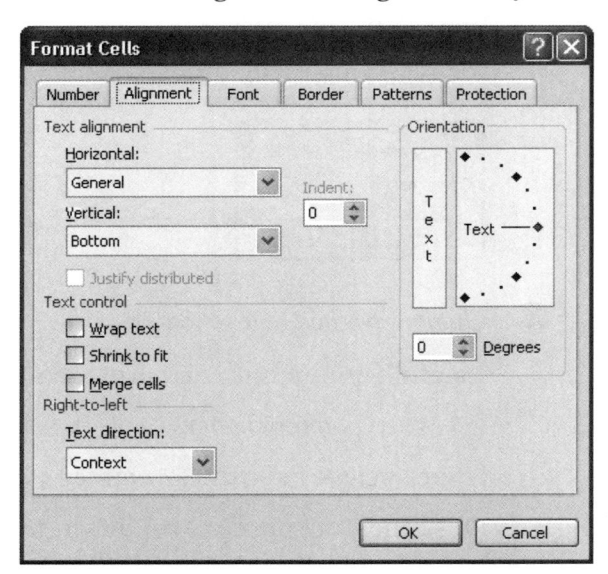

On **Horizontal** drop-down list, choose **Center**.

Click **OK**.

3 Center title on selected columns

Select range A1:F1.

On formatting toolbar, click ▦ (merge and center).

Cells are merged into one large cell. Text is centered.

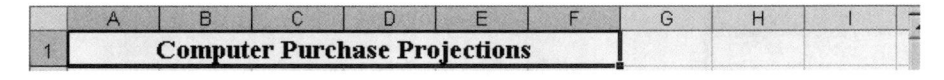

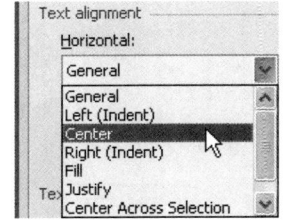

	A	B	C	D	E	F	G	H	I
1			Computer Purchase Projections						

4 Save changed workbook file

> Computers workbook file must be open.

Set column width & row height

You can easily change column widths and row heights, either one at a time or as a group.

1 Change column width (method 1)

Position pointer on right border of column E header.

When pointer changes to ↔, you can change width of column E.

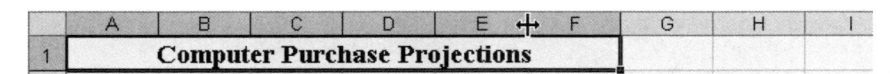

You could drag left or right to change width. This way is better.

Double-click while pointer has above shape.

Width automatically adjusts to widest entry in column E.

Repeat above steps to adjust columns A and F.

2 Change column width (method 2)

Highlight any block of cells in columns B, C, and D.

On **Format** menu, choose **Column**; on submenu, choose **Width**.

Type **10** and click **OK**.

Width of all cells in all three columns is changed.

3 Change row height (method 1)

Carefully put pointer on bottom border of header for row 7 (blank row).

When pointer changes to ⬍, you can change height of row above it.

Notice height in box near pointer as you press mouse button.

Press and drag up to adjust height to **7.50** (points).

Height indicator in text box shows change as you make it.

If you drag too far, drag back down again.

4 Change row height (method 2)

Highlight any block of cells in rows 2 through 6.

On **Format** menu, choose **Row**; on submenu, choose **Height**.

Type **15** and click **OK**.

5 Save changed workbook file

By the way

Another way to make a long label fit in a column is to make its text "wrap" inside its cell. The width of the column stays the same, and the height of the row expands to allow room for the wrapped text. To wrap text, use the Format Cells dialog box (see figure on page 141, and notice Wrap Text *check box in Text control area).*

> Computers *workbook file must be open.*

Insert & delete cells

You can insert blocks of new cells, including whole rows and columns. You can also delete existing cells.

1 **Insert whole row**

Click any cell in row 6.

On **Insert** menu, choose **Rows**.

Row 6 moves down to make room for new row of empty cells.

2 **View insert options**

To right of selected cell, click ![icon] (insert options).

New cells can have formats of cells above (by default) or below or can have any special formatting cleared. You won't change anything now.

Click new cell A6. Type `format test` and click ![check].

Text is bold, italic, and aligned left, just as in cell above.

3 **Insert multiple rows**

Press and drag through headers to highlight rows 2 and 3.

On **Insert** menu, choose **Rows**.

Two new rows of empty cells (with formats from row 1) are inserted.

4 **Delete all cells in row**

Click in header to highlight row 2. On **Edit** menu, choose **Delete**.

5 **Insert whole column of new cells**

Click any cell (except merged cell in row 1) in column B.

On **Insert** menu, choose **Columns**.

New column of empty cells is inserted. Formats are from column A.

6 **Insert rectangular block of new cells**

Highlight cells in range B3:C5.

On **Insert** menu, choose **Cells**. (Wait for full menu if necessary.)

Dialog box asks how to shift existing cells to make room for block.

> **By the way**
> You can also highlight and delete any block of cells. After choosing Delete on the Edit menu, you're asked how to move existing cells into the empty space after the block is removed. Notice this difference between deleting a cell and deleting the data in a cell. If you delete only the data (by choosing Clear on the Edit menu), other cells don't shift.

Click **Shift cells down**. Click **OK** to see effect.

7 **Close workbook file without saving changes**

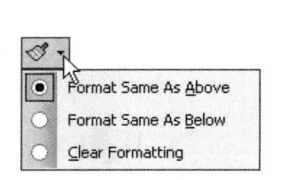

> **STOP** Computers file as saved on page 133 must be on disk.

144 / Spreadsheets with Excel

Format cell borders

You can hide the gray gridlines and add custom borders to cells and ranges. The Borders palette makes it easy to add borders.

---

1 Open Computers workbook file

2 Follow directions in this activity and next to duplicate figure below

	A	B	C	D	E	F
1		Computer Purchase Projections				
2		January	February	March	Totals by Computer	Percent of Total
3	IBM	11-Jan-00	14	9	34	21%
4	Dell	10	9	12	31	19%
5	Apple	17	12	16	45	28%
6	Sony	15	20	14	49	31%
8	Total	53	55	51	159	
9	Average	13.25	13.75	12.75	39.75	
10	Maximum	17	20	16	49	
11	Minimum	10	9	9	31	

By the way
If you have not done all the activities after page 133, data may be missing from column F and from rows below 7, and text formats and alignments may be different from what you see in this figure.

3 Hide gridlines

On **Tools** menu, choose **Options**. Click **View** tab.

Under **Window Options**, click to remove mark from **Gridlines** check box.

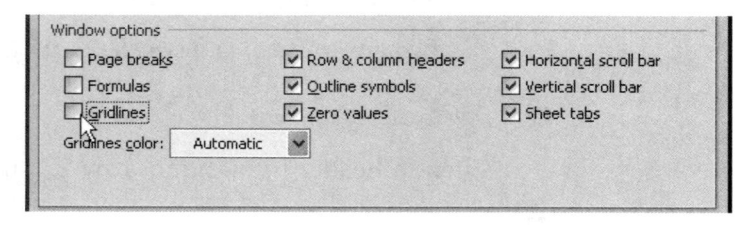

Tip
Suppressing the display of the default gridlines makes it easier to see borders you add. Default gridlines can be printed with a worksheet, but you get all or none of them. Adding borders gives you more control.

Click **OK**.

Standard gridlines no longer appear. You can add your own borders.

4 Tear Borders palette off toolbar

On formatting toolbar, click arrow on ▦▾ (borders).

Put pointer on dotted bar at top of drop-down list. With mouse button held down, drag down until **Borders** palette appears. Release mouse button.

By the way
A few other toolbar items have "tear-off" palettes like this. A palette is simply a window that always stays in front of other windows, ready for use.

By the way
Each icon on the palette shows where a border line will be added to selected cells and what type of border (thin or thick) will appear.

5 Add outline border to whole data area

Highlight range A2:F11.

On **Borders** palette, click thick-box border tool (lower-right corner).

Click any cell to deselect range and see thick borders around data area.

Border at left doesn't show up on screen but will be printed.

Format cell borders *continued*

Tip
You can also draw borders. Click Draw Borders *at the bottom of the* Borders *palette. Use the pencil tool to draw borders wherever you want them. You can use the eraser tool to remove borders.*

6 Add bottom border (method 1)

Highlight range A6:F6.

On **Borders** palette, click bottom border tool (first row, second column).

7 Add bottom border (method 2)

Highlight range B8:E8.

On **Format** menu, choose **Cells**; then click **Border** tab.

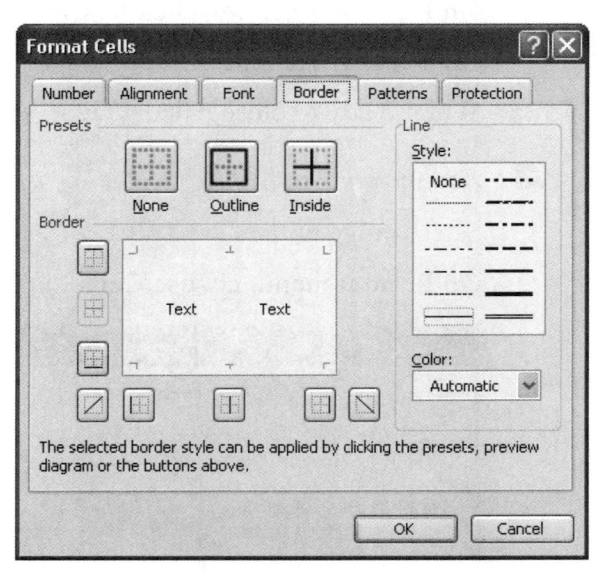

In **Style** area, click double line (last style in second column).

In **Border** area, click ▦ (bottom border). Click **OK**.

8 Add borders between cells

Highlight range A2:F11 (whole table).

On **Format** menu, choose **Cells**. If necessary, click **Border** tab.

In **Style** area, click single medium line (last style in first column).

Click ▦ to add borders between cells in selection. Click **OK**.

9 Remove and reapply borders

Make sure range A2:F11 is still selected.

On **Borders** palette, click ▦ (no border) in first row and column.

On **Edit** menu, choose **Undo Borders** to restore borders.

10 Close Borders palette

At right of **Borders** title bar, click ✕.

11 Save changed workbook file

Complete previous activity before going on.

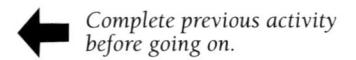

Add cell shading

You can also add a background color, pattern, or shade of gray to call attention to chosen cells.

1 **Add shading (method 1)**

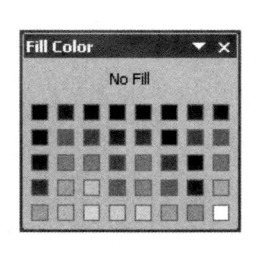

On formatting toolbar, click down arrow on [icon] (fill color).

Put pointer on dotted bar at top of drop-down menu.

Drag **Fill Color** palette down. Release mouse button.

Palette is torn off and remains in front of worksheet, ready for use.

Select cells in range B2:F2 (column headings).

On **Fill Color** palette, click to select any light color or shade of gray.

Click anywhere on worksheet to deselect cells.

When ready to close palette, click [x] at right of **Fill Color** title bar.

2 **Add shading (method 2)**

Select range B8:E8.

On **Format** menu, choose **Cells**; then click **Patterns** tab.

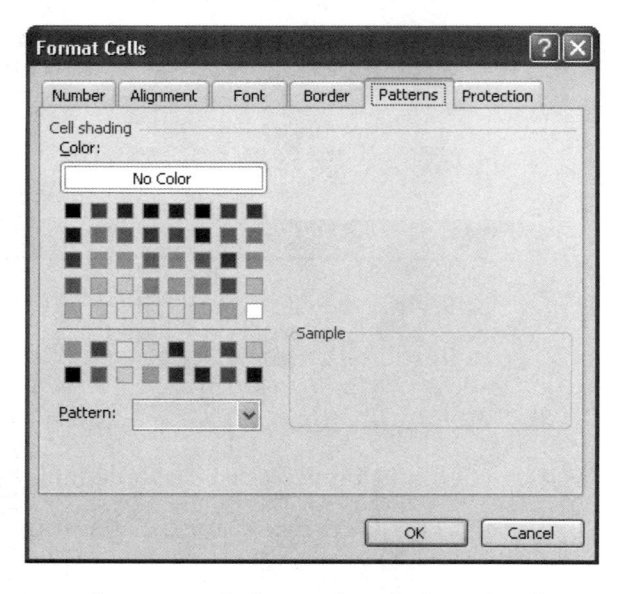

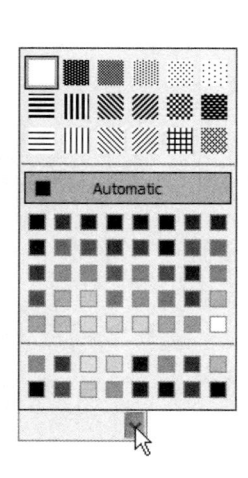

In **Color** area, click to select light color for background.

Click arrow below colors to see **Pattern** options.

At top, choose any pattern with thin diagonal stripes.

View **Pattern** options. Choose bright green for pattern foreground.

Click **OK**.

Click anywhere on worksheet to deselect cells and see result.

3 **Save and close Computers workbook file**

STOP *Numprac file as saved on page 128 must be on disk.*

Format numbers

Numbers on a worksheet can be formatted to display dollar signs, commas, and fixed decimal points.

XLS/ 147

1 **Open Numprac workbook file**

2 **On formatting toolbar, locate number tools**

$ % , .0 .00
     .00 .0

3 **Apply number format (method 1)**

Highlight range A3:D5.

On formatting toolbar, click $ (currency style).

Microsoft Excel automatically increases column widths to accommodate new number format.

4 **Compare applied format with original data**

Click anywhere to deselect block.

	A	B	C	D
3	$ 123.00	$ 321.00	$ 741.00	$ 1,417.00
4	$ 456.00	$ 654.00	$ 852.00	$ 2,582.00
5	$ 789.00	$ 987.00	$ 963.00	$ 3,693.00

Formatted numbers have dollar signs, comma separators, and two decimal places.

Click any cell with number in new format. Look at formula bar.

Number remains as you entered it. Only format on worksheet has changed.

5 **Apply percent format**

Select same range of cells.

On formatting toolbar, click % (percent style). Deselect block.

	A	B	C	D
3	12300%	32100%	74100%	141700%
4	45600%	65400%	85200%	258200%
5	78900%	98700%	96300%	369300%

Numbers have percent signs, no comma separators, and no decimal places

6 **Apply comma format**

Select same range of cells.

On formatting toolbar, click , (comma style).

Formatted numbers have comma separators, two decimal places, and no dollar signs.

	A	B	C	D
3	123.00	321.00	741.00	1,417.00
4	456.00	654.00	852.00	2,582.00
5	789.00	987.00	963.00	3,693.00

Format numbers *continued*

7 *Increase decimal places*

If not highlighted, select data range A3:D5 again.

On formatting toolbar, click ![icon] (increase decimal).

Numbers display three decimal places.

Click ![icon] again to add another decimal place.

Microsoft Excel adjusts column widths to accommodate long numbers.

8 *Decrease decimal places*

On formatting toolbar, click ![icon] (decrease decimal) twice.

Numbers have two decimal places. Columns stay wide.

Click ![icon] twice more.

Numbers have no decimal places.

9 *Apply number format (method 2)*

If not highlighted, select data range A3:D5 again.

On **Format** menu, choose **Cells**. Click **Number** tab, then click **Number** on **Category** list.

Current number format appears. Zero indicates fixed place; # indicates variable place; semicolon separates formats of positive and negative numbers.

On **Category** list, choose **General**.

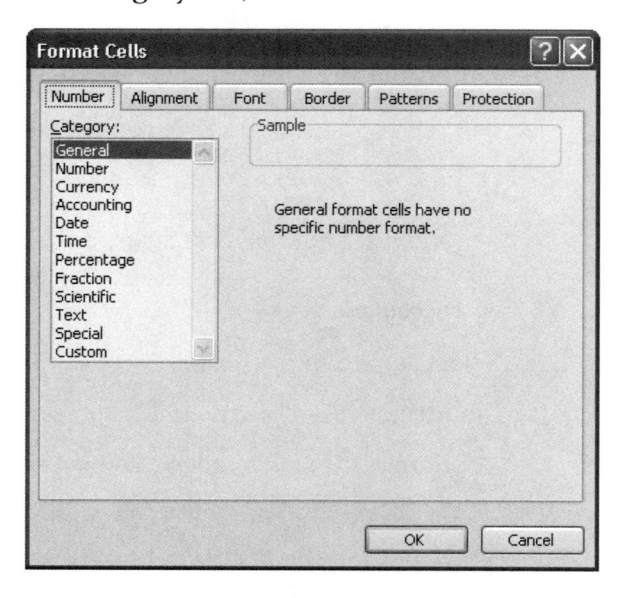

Click **OK**.

All special number formats are removed from selected cells.

10 *Close workbook file without saving changes*

Enter & format dates

Dates can be formatted in many styles. They're treated as numbers so that you can perform calculations with them.

1 Open new workbook file

Click ☐ (new) on standard toolbar.

If task pane is visible, you can also click Blank Workbook *in* New *area.*

2 Enter date

Click cell B2.

Enter today's date in month/day/year format (example: 7/11/04).

Click ✓. Check formula bar.

Excel recognizes entry as date and changes year to Windows default format.

Check worksheet cell.

Date appears on worksheet in same format.

> **By the way**
> The years 1930–2029 can normally be entered in two-digit form. If you need to enter other years, you must type all four digits.

3 View current date format, and change it

On **Format** menu, choose **Cells**. If necessary, click **Number** tab.

On Category *list,* Date *is highlighted, showing that cell A2 contains date entry. Current format is highlighted on* Type *list.*

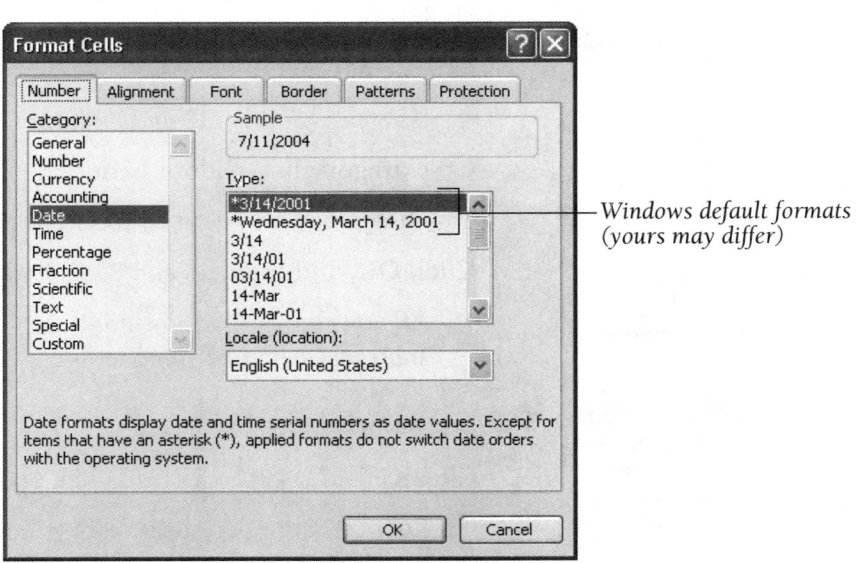

> **By the way**
> The first two formats (with asterisks before them) adapt to whatever default date format (short or long) is in effect on the computer on which the file is opened.

— Windows default formats (yours may differ)

On **Type** list, click **14-Mar-01**. Notice **Sample** area. Click **OK**.

Format changes on worksheet, but entry (shown in formula bar) is same.

4 Create new date format

On **Format** menu, choose **Cells**. On **Category** list on **Number** tab, click **Custom**.

Tap [TAB] until **Type** text box at top is highlighted.

Watch **Sample** area as you type `dddd, mmmm d`. Click OK.

Date appears with custom format; column automatically expands.

Enter & format dates *continued*

By the way
When you type a two-digit year, Microsoft Excel assumes you mean years 2000–2029 if the numbers are from 00 to 29. Numbers 30–99 are assumed to mean 1930–1999.

5 Enter another date

Click cell B3. Type date of your next birthday in m/d/yy format. Click ✓ to accept entry.

6 Apply new date format you created

With cell B3 selected, choose **Cells** on **Format** menu.

On **Category** list, click **Custom**. Scroll to bottom of **Type** list.

   Your format (dddd, mmmm d) is now listed.

Click your new format. Click **OK**.

7 Calculate how many days until your birthday

Click cell B5. Enter formula **=B3-B2** and click ✓.

On **Format** menu, choose **Cells**. On **Category** list, click **General**. Click **OK**.

   Difference between any two dates equals number of days between them.

By the way
Times work almost the same way as dates. You can subtract one time from another and get the time difference. However, the difference is formatted as a time, not a number. That way you can read the difference directly in hours, minutes, and seconds.

8 Change date formats to numbers and see what's happening

Highlight cells B2 and B3.

On **Format** menu, choose **Cells**. Look at **Category** list.

   As expected, cells B2 and B3 have Custom format. You'll now change it.

On **Category** list, choose **Number**.

Tap TAB until box next to **Decimal places** is highlighted. Type **0**.

Click **OK**, and look at cells B2, B3, and B5.

   All you changed was format. Dates really are numbers. That's why you can subtract one date from another.

Tip
If you're changing a worksheet and suddenly your dates disappear and strange five-digit numbers show up, it usually means your dates have lost their formats. Just highlight the numbers and reapply the date format you prefer. Your dates will reappear.

9 Find out what day 1 is

Click cell B7. Type **1** and click ✓.

On **Format** menu, choose **Cells**. Click **Number** tab if necessary.

On **Category** list, choose **Date**. Choose first date format.

Click **OK**.

   Day 1 is January 1, 1900. Dates are measured from then.

10 Delete custom format

On **Format** menu, choose **Cells**. If necessary, click **Number** tab.

Choose **Custom**. Scroll down and select **dddd, mmmm d**.

Click **Delete**. Click **OK**.

11 Close workbook file without saving changes

STOP Computers file as saved on page 133 must be on disk.

Sort data

You can rearrange the order of rows of cells in a spreadsheet. You can use the sort tool on the toolbar or the menus.

1 **Open Computers workbook file**

2 **Select cells to be sorted**

Highlight A2:D6. Notice A2 is active cell.

If you did not do all previous activities, formatting may be different, and data in column F may be missing.

	A	B	C	D	E	F
1		\multicolumn{5}{c	}{Computer Purchase Projections}
2		January	February	March	Totals by Computer	Percent of Total
3	IBM	11	14	9	34	21%
4	Dell	10	9	12	31	19%
5	Apple	17	12	16	45	28%
6	Sony	15	20	14	49	31%

3 **Sort data (method 1)**

Tap [TAB] until **February** cell is active.

On standard toolbar, click (sort ascending).

Highlighted rows with numbers are sorted based on column with active cell. (Formulas in columns E and F work on new data at their left.)

> **By the way**
> Notice that the cells in row 2 did not move. Excel assumes that the first row in the selection is a "header" because it contains only text labels. Only rows below the header are sorted.

4 **Sort data (method 2)**

Make sure range A2:D6 is highlighted.

On **Data** menu, choose **Sort**. View drop-down list at top.

Dialog box lets you choose column to sort on. You'll use column A.

On drop-down list, choose (**Column A**).

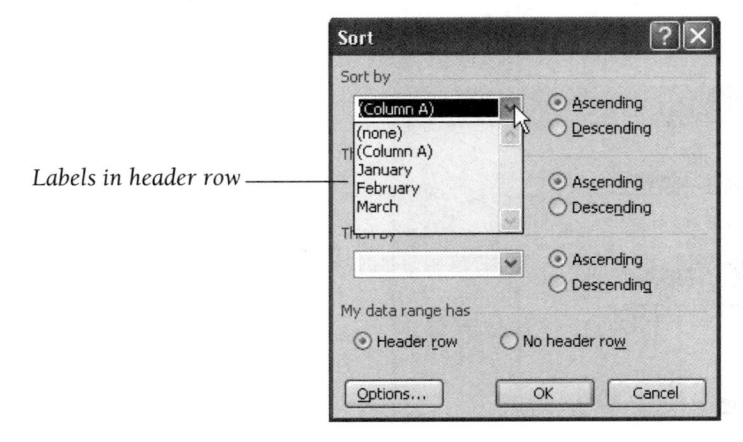

Labels in header row —

Notice that **Header row** option is already chosen.

If you wanted top row of selection to be included in sort, you would click No header row.

Click **OK**.

Deselect highlighted block.

5 Use toolbar button to sort data so highest total is first

Highlight A2:E6.

Tap TAB until cell E2 is active.

	A	B	C	D	E	F
1		Computer Purchase Projections				
2		January	February	March	Totals by Computer	Percent of Total
3	Apple	17	12	16	45	28%
4	Dell	10	9	12	31	19%
5	IBM	11	14	9	34	21%
6	Sony	15	20	14	49	31%

On standard toolbar, click (sort descending).

Top total (for Sony) is now in top row.

6 Change sort to ascending by number

On standard toolbar, click (sort ascending).

Computer with lowest total (Dell) is now in top row.

7 Sort table without selecting column labels

Highlight range A3:D6.

Row 2, with labels, is no longer in selection.

On **Data** menu, choose **Sort**. Notice selection changes to A4:D6.

Notice **Header row** is selected near bottom of dialog box.

Click **No header row**. Notice row 3 is back in selection.

Look at **Sort by** drop-down list.

On **Sort by** list, choose **(Column D)**.

Without headers, you sort by columns

Tip

Think of the **Then by** *areas of the* **Sort** *dialog box as "tie-breakers." If two rows of the selection have the same* **Sort by** *data, the rows are sorted according to the data in the* **Then by** *columns.*

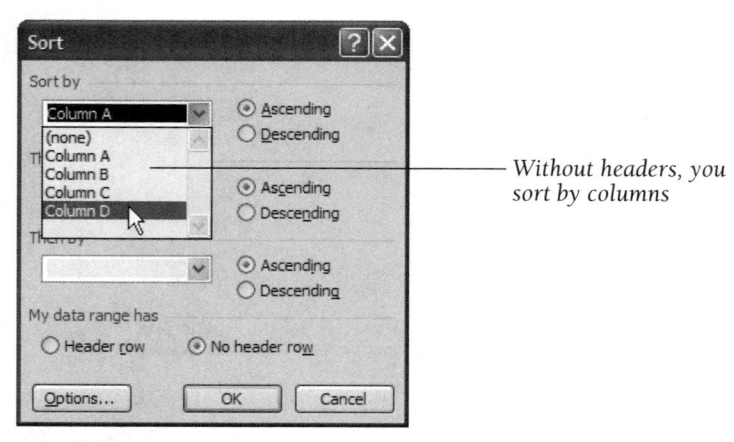

Click **Descending** radio button at top. Click **OK**.

Rows in selection are now sorted in descending order of March projections.

8 Close workbook without saving changes

> **STOP** Computers file as saved on page 133 must be on disk.

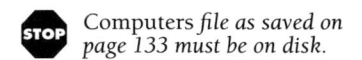

Divide window into panes

When a worksheet is large, it's handy to divide the window into panes that keep important parts in view.

XLS/ 153

---

1 *Open Computers workbook file*

2 *Split window into upper and lower panes*

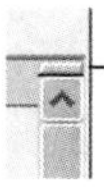

Press and drag split bar tool (see figure at left) down just below row 6.

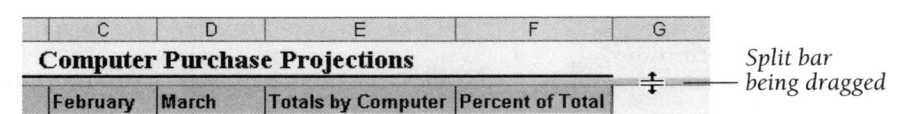

Split bar tool (left margin)

Split bar being dragged

Notice that there are now two vertical scroll bars on right of window.

Use both scroll arrows in top pane to see whole worksheet.

Use both scroll arrows in bottom pane to see whole worksheet.

Each pane has separate view of same worksheet.

3 *Lock labels in place in top pane*

In top pane, scroll so rows 1 and 2 (table and column labels) are at top.

Press and drag split bar just under row 2 in top pane.

On **Window** menu, choose **Freeze Panes**.

Split bar is now single line. Only one vertical scroll bar appears.

Use both scroll arrows to see what rows are available in lower pane.

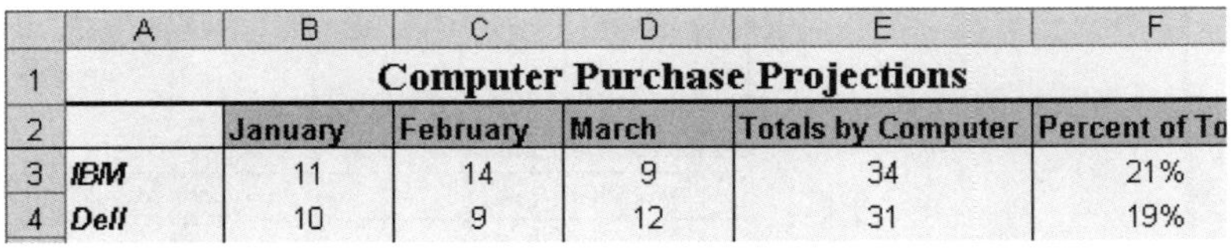

Frozen rows in top pane
Split bar
Scrolling rows in bottom pane

Rows 1 and 2 are locked in top pane. Rest of worksheet scrolls in lower pane. Arrangement would be useful for table with many rows.

4 *Unlock labels and remove split bar*

On **Window** menu, choose **Unfreeze Panes**.

Split bar reappears.

On **Window** menu, choose **Remove Split** (or double-click split bar).

5 *Split window into left and right panes*

Locate split bar tool at lower right, just right of horizontal scroll bar. Press and drag it just right of column A.

On **Window** menu, choose **Freeze Panes**. Scroll right pane to right.

Labels stay in place at left.

Unfreeze panes. Remove split.

6 *Close workbook without saving changes*

Split bar tool (lower left margin)

> **STOP** Computers file as saved on page 133 must be on disk.

Lock cells & protect worksheet

You can protect data in cells from accidental changes. Enter all data and add all formatting before locking cells.

1 **Open Computers workbook file**

2 **Unlock cells where you want changes to be made**

Highlight data cells in range B3:D6.

These cells will be unlocked for possible changes in sales numbers.

On **Format** menu, choose **Cells**; then click **Protection** tab.

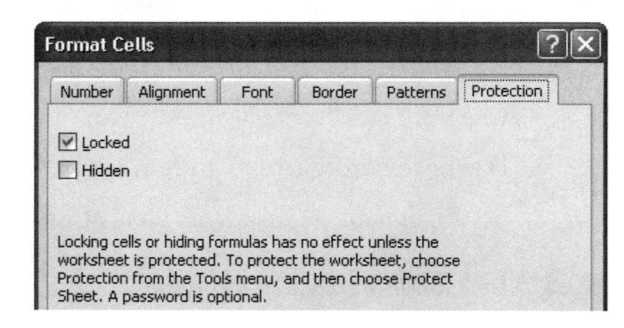

> *By the way*
> By default, all cells are locked; however, the feature is not activated until protection of the worksheet is switched on.

Click to remove mark from **Locked** check box. Click **OK**.

3 **Activate worksheet protection**

On **Tools** menu, choose **Protection**, then **Protect Sheet**.

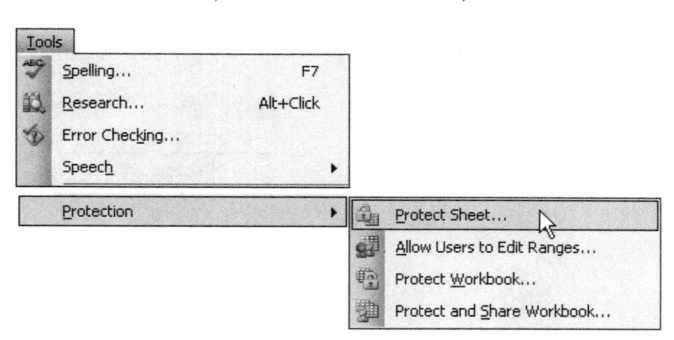

Protect Sheet *dialog box appears.*

> *By the way*
> The Protect Sheet dialog box lets you enter a password so only you can turn protection off. You won't use this feature now.

Click **OK**.

Lock cells & protect worksheet *continued*

4 **Enter data in unlocked cell with protection turned on**

Click cell B5. Type **100** and tap ENTER.

New data is entered and formulas recalculated.

5 **Try to enter data in locked cell with protection turned on**

Click cell E5, and try to type **100**.

Protected cells message appears.

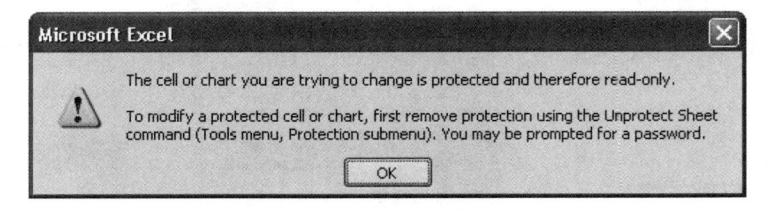

> **Microsoft Excel**
>
> The cell or chart you are trying to change is protected and therefore read-only.
>
> To modify a protected cell or chart, first remove protection using the Unprotect Sheet command (Tools menu, Protection submenu). You may be prompted for a password.
>
> OK

Click **OK**.

6 **Try to enter data in blank cell**

Click cell G3, and try to type **100**.

In protected cells message box, click **OK**.

> *By the way*
>
> *Protection is used mainly by people who design spreadsheets for other people to use. The designer wants the user to enter certain data but not to change formulas, labels, or even formats.*

7 **Try to change format of unlocked cell**

Click cell B5 (unlocked).

Notice **B** (bold) on formatting toolbar.

Tool is dimmed, telling you that no such change is allowed.

8 **Remove protection**

On **Tools** menu, choose **Protection**, then **Unprotect Sheet**.

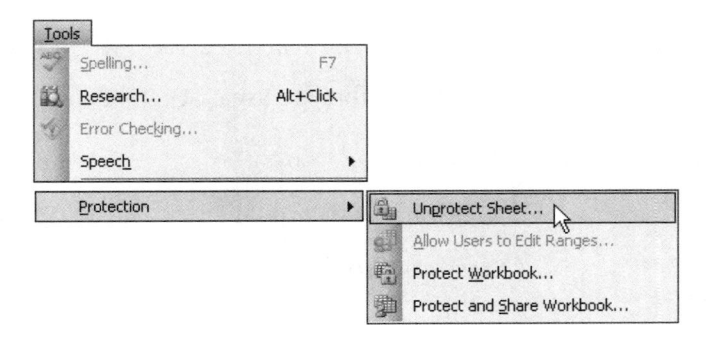

> **Tools**
> Spelling... F7
> Research... Alt+Click
> Error Checking...
> Speech ▶
> Protection ▶ Unprotect Sheet...
>   Allow Users to Edit Ranges...
>   Protect Workbook...
>   Protect and Share Workbook...

9 **Try to enter data in locked cell with protection turned off**

Click cell E5, type **100** and tap ENTER.

Number is entered, replacing formula there.

10 **Close workbook without saving changes**

> Computers *file as saved on page 133 must be on disk.*

Create pie chart

After you create a worksheet with a table of numbers, you can quickly create a chart of the same data.

1 **Open Computers workbook file**

2 **Select data to be charted**

Highlight range B2:D2 (names of months).

With CTRL held down, highlight range B8:D8 (totals for months).

Both ranges should be highlighted.

3 **Begin to create chart**

On **Insert** menu, choose **Chart** (or click on standard toolbar).

Step 1 of Chart Wizard *dialog box appears.*

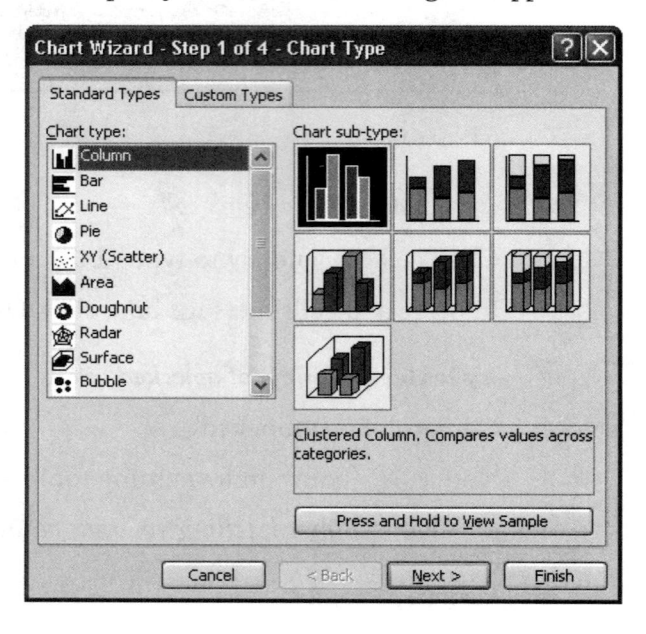

Tip
If Office Assistant *(paper clip with eyes) appears, click it. Click* Options *button. Click* Use the Office Assistant *check box to remove mark. Click* OK.

4 **Choose chart type**

On **Chart type** list, click Pie.

In **Chart sub-type** area, accept default at upper left.

5 **Preview chart**

Position pointer over **Press and Hold to View Sample** button.

Press and hold mouse button down.

Preview of chart appears.

Release mouse button.

6 **Click Next button to move to step 2**

Notice that Back *button becomes active. You can always go back through steps and make changes.* Cancel *closes the* Chart Wizard *without making chart.* Finish *ends charting process using default settings.*

Create pie chart continued

7 Verify data to be charted

Make sure **Data range** text box contains
=Sheet1!$B$2:$D$2,Sheet1!$B$8:$D$8.

These are rows you highlighted in step 2. Sheet name and dollar signs mean these cell references are absolute.

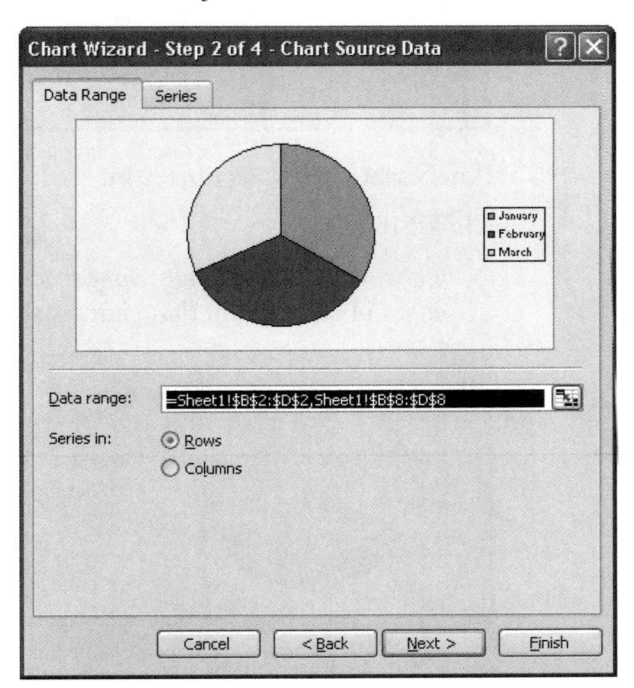

Click **Next** to move to step 3.

8 Add chart options

Click tabs to review options.

You will make no changes here.

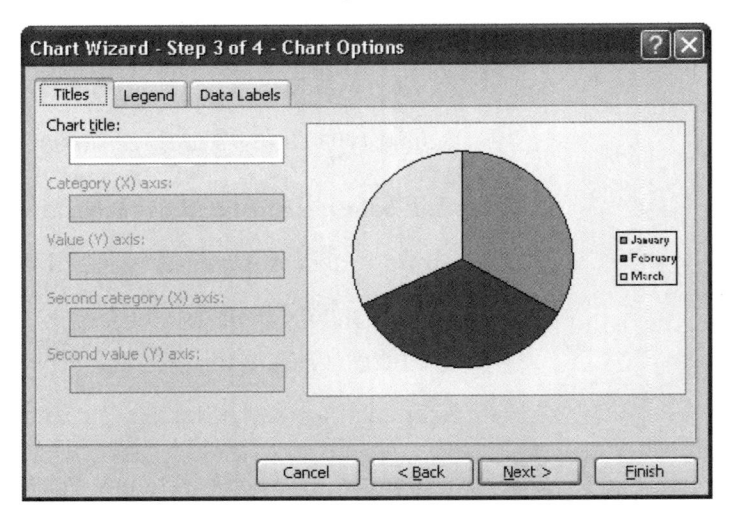

Click **Next** to move to step 4.

Tip

It is usually neither necessary nor desirable to add legends or titles to a simple chart on the worksheet.

158 / Spreadsheets with Excel   **Create pie chart**   *continued*

9 *Choose chart placement; see result*

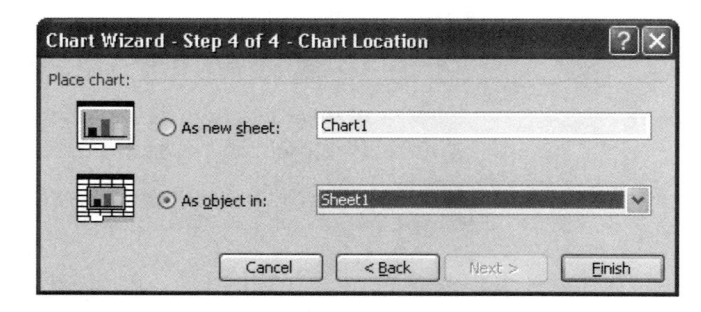

If necessary, click **As object in**.

Click **Finish**.

Chart and Chart palette appear on worksheet. Small black "handles" on edges of chart mean that chart is selected.

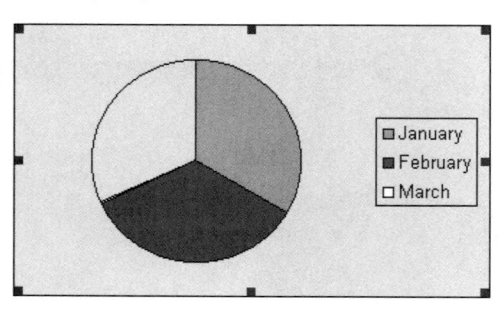

Chart palette can be used to change chart type and add legend or gridlines.

10 *Adjust chart location*

Place pointer inside chart area (but outside pie). Press and drag down below row 12 of worksheet.

11 *Change chart type*

On **Chart** palette, click down arrow at right of ▨▾ (chart type).

Click ▨ (3-D pie chart) as in figure at left.

Chart type changes to three-dimensional pie chart.

12 *See link between chart and worksheet data*

Scroll up if necessary, and click cell D6 (March Sony projections).

You may have to move chart.

Type **1 0 0**. Watch **March** slice grow as you tap [ENTER].

On standard toolbar, click ▨ to undo editing change.

13 *Save changed workbook with new chart on worksheet*

Tip

If the Chart *palette is not present, click the chart area to select it. The toolbar appears only when the chart is selected. If it's still absent, choose* Toolbars *on the* View *menu and click* Chart.

Complete previous activity before going on.

Create column chart

You'll make a chart on a separate sheet in the workbook. The chart and the data are still linked and will reflect changes.

1 **Select data to chart**

Highlight range A2:D6 (monthly projections with row and column labels).

2 **Create chart on separate sheet**

On standard toolbar, click ▦ (chart wizard).

Step 1. **Column** should be selected as **Chart type**. In **Chart sub-type** area, click 3-D column option (first column, second row). Click **Next**.

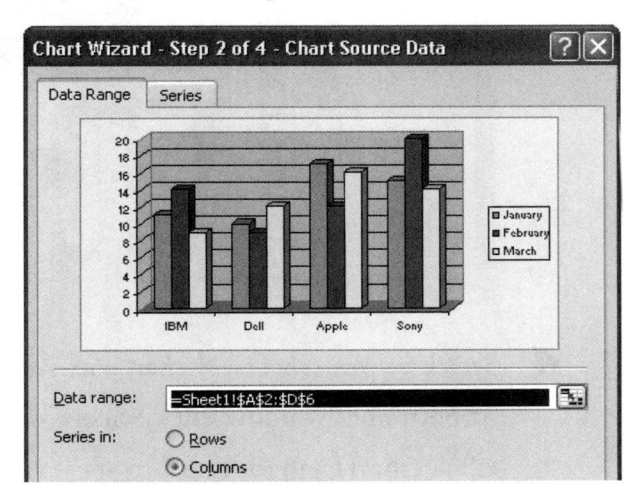

Step 2. Verify data to be charted is **Sheet1!$A$2:$D$6**. Click **Next**.

Step 3. Click **Titles** tab. Enter text for titles as in figure.

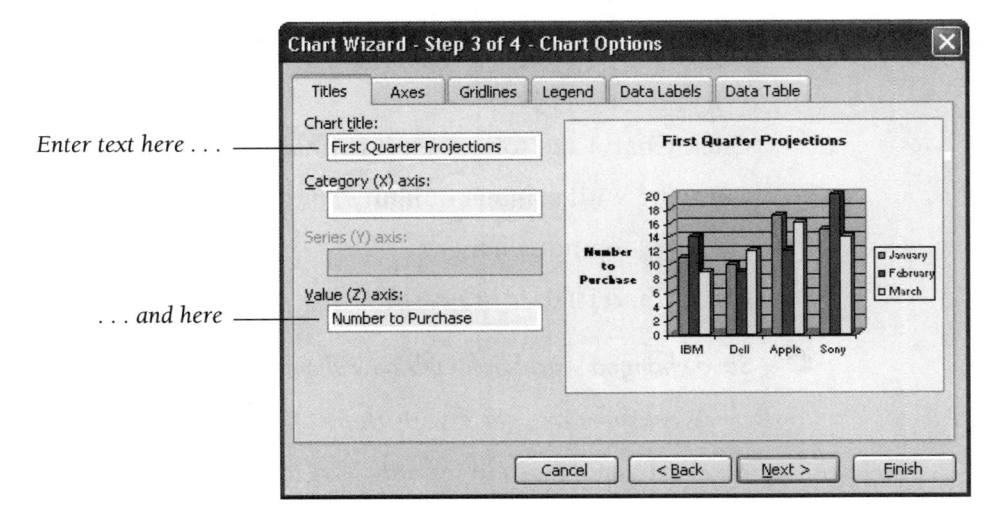

Enter text here . . .

. . . and here

Review other options.

Later you will make additional formatting changes directly on chart.

Check preview. If necessary, go back to earlier steps and make changes.

Click **Next**.

Step 4. Click **As new sheet**.

Create column chart *continued*

3 View finished chart

Click **Finish**.

Chart is inserted as separate sheet (Chart1) in same workbook file. Chart palette is always present (unless you close it).

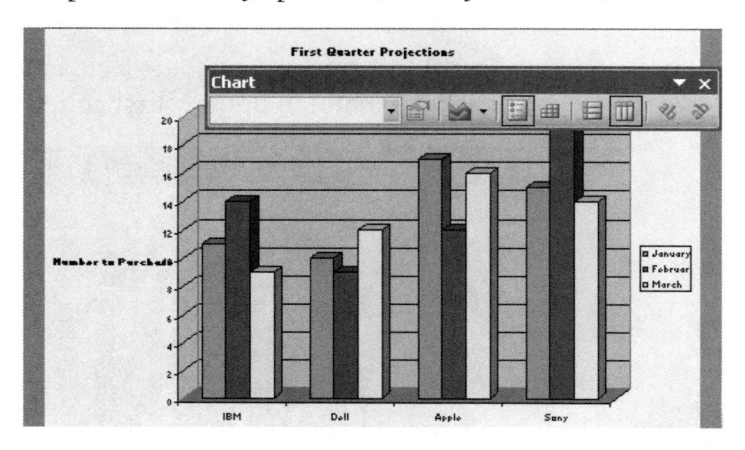

4 Switch between sheet with chart and worksheet

At bottom of window, click **Sheet1** tab to see worksheet.

Click **Chart1** tab to return to sheet with chart.

5 Go to worksheet, and make change in data

Click **Sheet1** tab.

Click cell D3 (March projections for IBM), and type **100**.

Tap ENTER.

Click **Chart1** tab to see result in chart.

Compare with original in figure above.

Click to undo change.

Click **Chart1** tab to see result.

6 Save changed workbook with new sheet

Worksheet and sheet with chart are saved together in same file.

Next you'll learn to format chart text and objects.

Complete previous activity before going on.

Format chart text

You can format any text on a chart. You can modify the font, font size, and/or font style.

1 **Format chart title**

Click title on chart.

When selected, chart title displays border with small black selection handles.

On formatting toolbar, choose **24** on font size list.

2 **Format legend**

Click legend.

On formatting toolbar, choose **12** on font size list.

3 **Format and change orientation of value axis label**

Click axis label, **Number to Purchase**. Carefully double-click border that appears.

In dialog box, click **Font** tab.

Choose **12** on **Size** list.

Click **Alignment** tab.

In **Orientation** area, drag red diamond to top.

Verify that **Degrees** number is **90**.

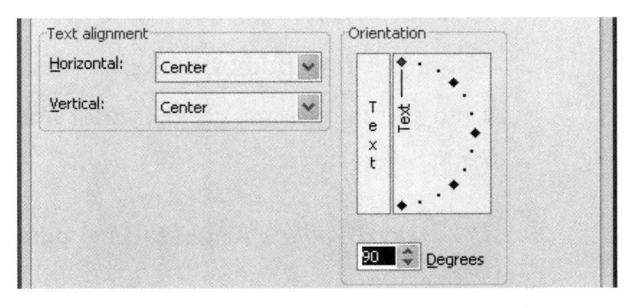

Click **OK**.

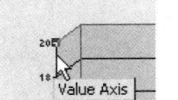

4 **Format value axis labels**

Click value (vertical) axis. Notice text label and handles at ends.

Click **B**.

5 **Format category axis labels**

Click category (horizontal) axis.

On formatting toolbar, choose **12** on size list; then click **B**.

6 **Save workbook**

On **File** menu, choose **Save**.

Format chart objects

You can format chart objects. You can change their color, location, axis scale, and other attributes.

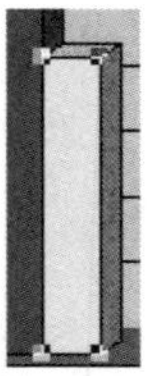

1 Format data series

Click any column (data series) on chart.

When selected, data series has small handles on each column.

On **Format** menu, choose **Selected Data Series**.

If necessary, click **Patterns** tab.

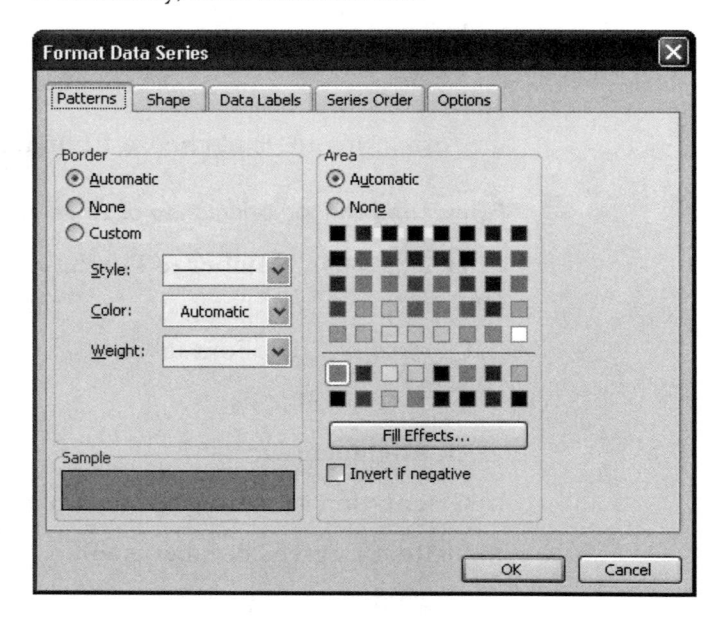

Tip
Double-click the object to be formatted as a shortcut to opening the Format dialog box for that object.

By the way
Other tabs in this dialog box allow you to make changes to the series itself, its order, and its values and to add value, name, or percent labels to a data series.

Using **Border** options, make any changes to borders of bars.

Using **Area** options, choose color and fill effect for inside of bars.

Click **OK**.

2 Using step 1, make changes to other data series columns if you like

3 Change legend placement

Click border of legend, now to right of chart.

On **Format** menu, choose **Selected Legend**.

Click **Placement** tab.

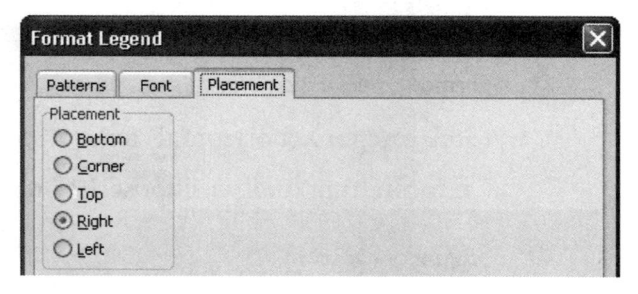

In **Placement** area, click **Bottom**. Click **OK**.

Legend moves to bottom of chart.

← *Complete previous activity before going on.*

Format chart objects *continued*

4 *Change scale of vertical (value) axis*

Click to select value axis.

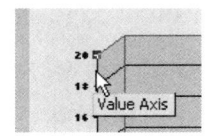

On **Format** menu, choose **Selected Axis**. If necessary, click **Patterns** tab.

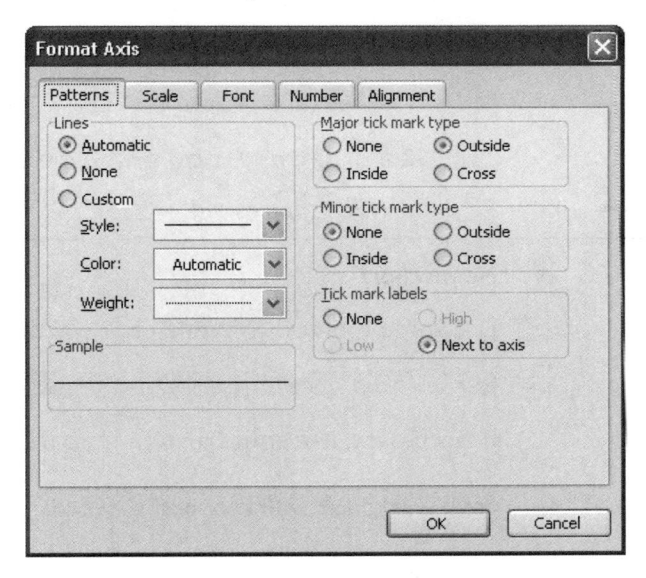

In **Major tick mark type** area, click **None**.

Click **Scale** tab.

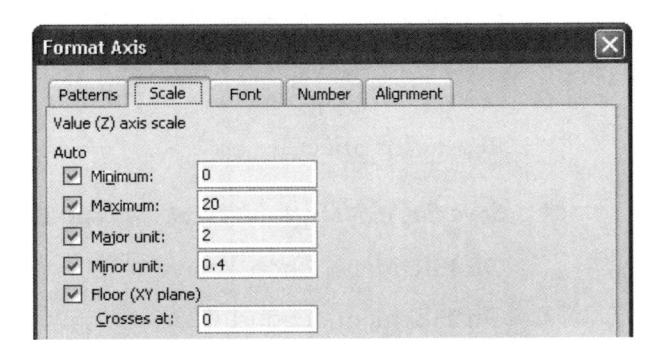

Change **Major unit** to 5.

Click **OK**.

5 *View chart with modifications*

6 *Make additional changes to chart if you like*

7 *Save workbook with modified chart*

Complete previous activity before going on.

164 / Spreadsheets with Excel

Reorganize sheets

You can change the order in which sheets appear in a workbook, and you can assign a name to a worksheet.

1 **Move sheet tab**

Point to **Chart1** tab at bottom of window.

Press and drag to move small page icon between **Sheet1** and **Sheet2** tabs.

Click **Sheet1** tab to activate worksheet.

It is now first sheet in workbook.

2 **Name sheet**

Double-click **Sheet1** tab.

Type `1st Qtr Projections` and tap ENTER.

New title replaces old.

3 **Name chart**

Use same method to name chart `Chart of Projections`.

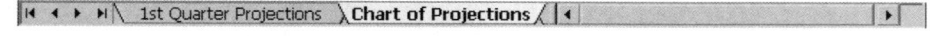

If necessary, use split bar to adjust tab area.

4 **Save workbook with changed sheet names and changed order of sheets**

5 **Delete other sheets**

Click **Sheet2** tab.

On **Edit** menu, choose **Delete Sheet**.

If sheet 2 had data on it, you'd be warned deletion is permanent. You can't undo Delete Sheet command!

Repeat for **Sheet3**.

6 **Save file, exit Microsoft Excel, and end session at computer**

On **File** menu, choose **Save**.

On **File** menu, choose **Exit**.

If you're using floppy disk, eject it and take it with you.

Shut down Windows, and switch off computer (see page 2, step 3).

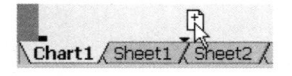

By the way
You can use up to 31 characters for a sheet name.

Tip
If the Delete Sheet *command is not on the menu, wait a few seconds, or click the arrow at the bottom to see the full menu.*